Managing Successful Programmes

London: TSO

Published by TSO (The Stationery Office) and available from:

Online
www.tsoshop.co.uk

Mail, Telephone, Fax & E-mail
TSO
PO Box 29, Norwich NR3 1GN
Telephone orders/General enquiries: 0870 6005522
Fax orders: 0870 600 5533
E-mail: customer.services@tso.co.uk
Textphone: 0870 240 3701

TSO Shops
16 Arthur Street, Belfast BT1 4GD
028 9023 8451 Fax 028 9023 5401
71 Lothian Road, Edinburgh EH3 9AZ
0870 606 5566 Fax 0870 606 5588

TSO@Blackwell and other Accredited Agents

First edition Crown Copyright 1999
Second edition Crown Copyright 2003
Third edition Crown Copyright 2007

First published 2007

ISBN 978 0 11 331040 1

Printed in the United Kingdom for The Stationery Office
N5570298 c40 09/07

Contents

PART 3 THE TRANSFORMATIONAL FLOW

13 Transformational Flow overview

14 Identifying a Programme

15 Defining a Programme

16 Managing the Tranches

Appendix C: Programme Office

Appendix D: Health checks

List of figures

List of tables

Foreword

Good programme management is essential to delivering high quality public services; to delivering value for money; and to delivering change, to meet new requirements and the increasingly high standards the public expects.

Standards are playing an increasingly key role in effective programme and project management, and in driving the transformation of procurement, which is closely integrated with effective programme management.

The Office of Government Commerce's own portfolio of policy and standards sets out what 'good' looks like for those involved both in procurement and in programme and project management. The portfolio draws on the knowledge and experience of others, which ensures consistency and quality throughout.

The origins of *Managing Successful Programmes* (MSP) can be traced back to the practices of the best policy makers in Government. Even though they may not have realised it at the time, they were using many of the tools that are now associated with good programme management to successfully transform policy into desired outcomes and, essentially, benefits.

Realisation of benefits is, of course, the ultimate goal and this latest version of MSP explores this in greater detail. It includes guidance on managing benefits throughout the programme. There is also a comprehensive view on governance that looks at organisation, control, leadership and roles. Through its partnerships, OGC is able to provide a comprehensive accredited training programme, which helps individuals to understand and apply MSP.

I am confident that this publication, along with the training that supports it, will help current and aspiring Programme Managers and their support teams successfully deliver transformational change for their organisations.

S. Collier

Sally Collier

Executive Director

Office of Government Commerce

Acknowledgements

Lead author

Rod Sowden   Aspire Europe

Authoring team

Geof Leigh   Goaldart Ltd

Patrick Mayfield   pearcemayfield

Chris Venning   Henley Change Management Ltd

Mentors

Gerald Bradley and Andrew Schuster

Further contributions

In order to maintain *Managing Successful Programmes'* reflection of current best practice and to produce guidance with lasting value, OGC consulted widely with key stakeholders at every stage in the process. OGC would like to thank the following individuals and their organisations for their contributions to refreshing the MSP guidance:

The MSP reference group (alpha list)

Pippa Bass	OGC
Graham Bird	GCHQ
Mark Fensome	DfES
Nick Meadham	National School for Government
Siobhan O'Connell	OGC
David Partington	Cranfield School of Management
Andrew Richards	Holos Consulting
Andrew Schuster	Department of Health
Andy Taylor	APMG Chief Examiner for MSP
Martin Wickes	KPMG

Reviewers (alpha list)

John Bartlett	Great Stave
Denise Blunn	OGC
John Brinkworth	Serco Consulting
Terry Dailey	Deliverables Management Consultants
Alan Ferguson	AFA
Charles Fox	Core IS
Melanie Franklin	Maven Training
Peter Glynne	Northern Ireland Department of Finance and Personnel
Alan Harpham	APM Group
Bert Hedeman	Insights International B.V.
David Hillson	Risk Doctor & Partners
Peter Johnson	OGC
Hosam Mostafa	Olympic Programme Support Unit
Ruth Murray-Webster	Lucidus Consulting
Nita Patel	NHS
Geoff Reiss	Geoff Reiss Limited
Michelle Rowland	A&J Project Management Ltd
Magnus Schoeman	Xansa
Graham Tanfield	Department for Children, Schools and Families
Sue Vowler	Project Angels
Nick Walker	National Policing Improvement Agency
Peter Weaver	The PSO

Additional support

A number of people generously contributed their time and expertise to ensuring the quality of this publication. Anne-Marie Byrne, as OGC Project Executive, is grateful for the additional support to the authoring team provided by Graham Williams and Ian Stanbury.

Pieter deWet, Colin Bartle-Tubbs, Anne Middleton and Dez West provided additional quality assurance as members of the Change Control Panel.

Part 1 Introduction and programme management principles

1

Introduction

1 Introduction

1.1 PURPOSE OF THIS GUIDE

Today's organisations exist in a climate of constant and increasing change. The many, dynamic and contradictory drivers for change include innovations in technology, working practices (including outsourcing and partnerships), mergers, increased demands from regulation and, for the public sector, delivery of policy driven by changing political parties and/or ministers. Whatever the organisation, wherever it is located, however it is structured, the rate of change is increasing.

Organisations that have learned how to transform themselves through effective leadership and strategic control are more likely to survive and prosper. Programme management is increasingly being recognised as a key tool to enable organisations to manage that transformation.

Managing Successful Programmes (MSP) represents proven programme management good practice in successfully delivering transformational change, drawn from the experiences of both public and private sector organisations.

This guide provides:

- An adaptable route map for programme management, bringing together key principles, Governance Themes and a set of interrelated processes to facilitate the flow of business transformation
- Advice on how these programme management principles, themes and flow can be embedded, reviewed and applied, to gain measurable benefits from business change.

The MSP framework is based on three core concepts as shown in Figure 1.1.

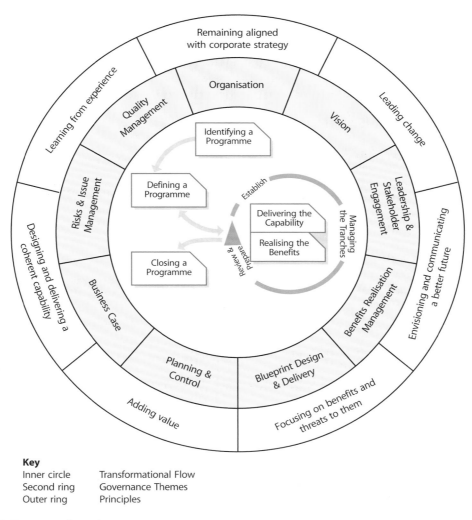

Key

Inner circle	Transformational Flow
Second ring	Governance Themes
Outer ring	Principles

Figure 1.1   MSP Framework and concepts

- **MSP principles**. Derived from lessons learned in programmes that had both positive and negative results. They represent common factors that underpin the likelihood of success of any programme of transformational change.
- **MSP Governance Themes**. An organisation's approach to programme management needs to be defined, measured and controlled. The Governance Themes allow organisations to put in place the right leadership, delivery team, robust organisation structures, controls and control information (e.g. Blueprint, Business Case, Quality Management Strategy), giving the best chance of delivering the planned outcomes and realising the desired benefits.
- **MSP Transformational Flow**. The flow provides a route through the lifecycle of a programme from its conception through delivering the new capability, outcomes and benefits, on through the transition to the realised future state, and finally on to the close of the programme.

This guide is intended primarily for those who are involved in the direction, management, support and delivery of programmes. It is presented as a reference manual for Programme Managers, Change Managers and Programme Office staff. It also provides guidance for owners and sponsors of programmes of change.

1.2 WHAT IS A PROGRAMME?

In MSP, a programme is defined as a temporary, flexible organisation created to coordinate, direct and oversee the implementation of a set of related projects and activities in order to deliver outcomes and benefits related to the organisation's strategic objectives. A programme is likely to have a life that spans several years.

A project is also a temporary organisation, usually existing for a much shorter duration, which will deliver one or more outputs in accordance with a specific business case. A particular project may or may not be part of a programme.

Programmes deal with outcomes; projects deal with outputs. Programme management and project management are complementary approaches. During a programme lifecycle, projects are initiated, executed, and closed. Programmes provide an umbrella under which these projects can be coordinated. The programme integrates the projects so that it can deliver an outcome greater than the sum of its parts.

Programme management does not replace the need for competent project direction and management.

Programmes must be underpinned by a controlled project environment of effective direction, management, delivery and reporting disciplines that are common to all projects within a programme.

1.3 WHAT IS PROGRAMME MANAGEMENT?

MSP defines programme management as the action of carrying out the coordinated organisation, direction and implementation of a dossier of projects and transformation activities (i.e. the programme) to achieve outcomes and realise benefits of strategic importance to the business.

Programme management aligns three critical organisational elements:

- Corporate strategy
- Delivery mechanisms for change, and
- Business-as-usual environment.

It manages the natural tension that exists between these elements to deliver transformational change that meets the needs of the organisation and its stakeholders.

It manages the transition of the solutions developed and delivered by projects into the business operations, whilst maintaining performance and effectiveness. It does this by breaking things into manageable chunks (tranches) with review points for monitoring progress and assessing performance.

Programme management provides a framework that integrates and reconciles competing demands for resources, providing a context and control framework for the projects of the programme.

Programme management often involves changes to the culture, style and character of organisations. The people aspects of change must be recognised and accommodated if the programme is to succeed.

1.4 WHY USE PROGRAMME MANAGEMENT?

Where there is major change there will be complexity, risk, many interdependencies to manage, and conflicting priorities to resolve. Experience shows that organisations are likely to fail to deliver change successfully where:

- There is insufficient board-level support
- Leadership is weak
- There are unrealistic expectations of the organisational capacity and capability
- There is insufficient focus on benefits
- There is no real picture (blueprint) of the future capability

- There is a poorly defined or poorly communicated vision
- The organisation fails to change its culture
- There is insufficient engagement of stakeholders.

Adopting a programme management approach such as MSP provides a structured framework that can help organisations avoid these pitfalls and achieve their goals.

Organisations make choices in how they will manage their activities and need to decide on the most appropriate approach to successfully deliver their business goals:

- Is this is a portfolio of change programmes and projects that needs to be coordinated corporately?
- Is this a single programme of business change implemented through the coordination of several projects and business activities?

Understanding the nature and scale of the proposed change activities and also the context of the organisation(s) owning the benefits will be essential for making this decision.

For example, building a new school may be a simple project for the construction company carrying out the work, with the output being the completed building. However, for the education authority, the building is merely one of several different interdependent deliverables, which together will ensure that the longer-term benefits of providing an additional school in a particular community are realised.

In this example, the corporate portfolio would be held by the government department responsible for education, and would be aimed at delivering a strategic objective to raise standards of education nationally.

Appendix B looks at the key differences between corporate portfolios, programmes and projects in more detail.

1.5 THE PROGRAMME MANAGEMENT ENVIRONMENT

A programme is a major undertaking for most organisations, meaning significant funding and substantial change for the organisations and individuals involved. Figure 1.2 shows a typical environment for programme management.

Figure 1.2   Programme management environment

The organisation's corporate strategies, initiatives and policies are influenced and shaped from both the internal and the external environment. Programmes are then defined, scoped and prioritised to implement and deliver the outcomes required. Programmes in turn initiate, monitor and align the projects and related activities that are needed to create new products or service capabilities or to effect changes in business operations. The projects will deliver and implement the required outputs into operations, until finally, the full benefits of the programme can be realised.

Even as programmes are in the process of implementing changes and improvements to the target operations, they may need to respond to changes in corporate strategies or accommodate new initiatives or policies. A continual process of realignment is required to ensure that the programme remains linked to strategic objectives.

Figure 1.3 shows some of the drivers for change and the areas that may be affected by change, and Appendix B looks in more detail at the drivers for change that are likely to contribute to the initiation of a transformational change programme.

1.6 TYPES OF PROGRAMME

The need for a programme-driven approach to manage change can arise in a number of ways, as set out below.

1.6.1 Vision-led programme

■ Has come into existence to deliver a clearly defined vision that has been created and is owned by the top of the organisation

■ Tends to be top down in approach, with cross-functional implications for the organisation's operations

■ Likely to focus on innovation or strategic opportunity offered by the business environment

■ In the public sector, this could be the translation of political priorities into a programme which will refine and deliver the desired changes.

1.6.2 Emergent programme

■ Evolves from concurrent, uncoordinated projects that have grown within an organisation. There is now recognition that coordination of the projects is necessary to deliver the changes and the desired benefits.

■ Is transitory, as it becomes a planned programme when its vision, context and direction have been defined and established.

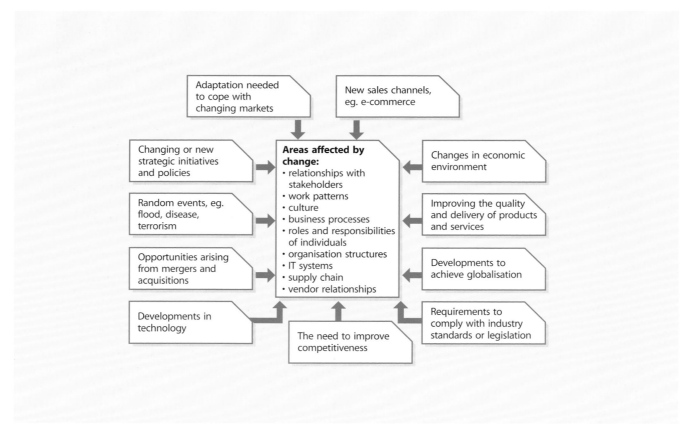

Figure 1.3   Drivers for change

1.6.3 Compliance programme

- May also be referred to as a 'must do' programme.
- The organisation has no choice but to change as a result of an external event, such as legislative change.
- Outcomes may be expressed in terms of compliance, achievement and avoidance of negative implications rather than measurable improvements in performance.

1.7 WHEN TO USE MSP

Programmes may be set up to deliver change in parts of an organisation, across the entire organisation, across more than one organisation, or in the environment in which the organisation operates. In deciding on the best approach to managing a programme it is useful to assess its likely impact on the organisation, and this can be done by looking at the nature of the change a programme is expected to deliver.

A programme may be used to deliver a range of different types of change. The impact matrix in Figure 1.4 shows how different types of change give a different focus for the programme, together with some of the tools and techniques applicable in each case.

Some programmes will be highly complex in nature, but have a reasonably well-defined expectation, i.e. there will be high levels of predictability in terms of outcome even though the journey may be costly and complex. On the other hand, change to societal behaviours over a long period, driven by policy and legislation, will have low levels of predictability due to the long timescales, and the cause and effects may not be fully anticipated as other societal trends develop. The programme impact matrix can be used to decide whether an MSP approach is required and, if not, which programme management techniques could be useful in those circumstances.

1.7.1 Specification-led programmes

Where the change being delivered is based on the making and delivering of new facilities, the programme will tend to be led by the specification of the outputs required, for example a major capital construction programme. There will be relatively low levels of ambiguity about what the programme is to deliver but there may be high levels of complexity and risk in the delivery. The scope will be reasonably well defined and adjusted according to circumstances. MSP's approach can be used in this type of programme but may need to be scaled down as some of its elements may not be required.

Focus of the change	Predictability of Outcome		
	High	**Medium**	**Low**
Technology, engineering infrastructure	Specification led Complex product based on known design Technically complex to deliver	Globalisation of services Adoption of technology that is new to the organisation	Pioneering production techniques Unproven technology Scale of the implementation
Business transformation	Adoption of approaches used in similar organisation Adoption of Best Practice Process change	Changes to organisational capability and behaviour Challenges to historical working practices Value chain changes, e.g outsourcing of services	Volatility of the marketplace Internal, external and customer behaviour Diverse or new products and services
Community & society	Change to current legislation or policies Increase or decrease to investment programmes Predictable or clear stakeholder base	New legislation reacting to societal trends Legislative change to affect economic behaviour Medium-term effect	Changes to societal values and behaviour Incentive-driven change to lifestyles and economic behaviour Long-term societal effects

Figure 1.4   Sample programme impact matrix

1.7.2 Business transformation programmes

Where the change is more focused on transforming the way the business functions – for example, implementing a new service partnership or moving into a new market – the programme will tend to be vision led with desired outcomes and associated benefits. There is likely to be ambiguity about the overall implication of the changes; for instance it may not be known how some parts of the organisation will react. The greater the impact on customers and the markets, then the greater the levels of ambiguity and risk. MSP is designed to provide structure for such programmes.

1.7.3 Political and societal change programmes

Where the change is focused on improvements in society the level of predictability will be reduced, as there will be many uncontrollable external factors also at play. For example a change that aims to improve the early education of pre-school-age children in order to increase their likelihood of achieving a more meaningful contribution to society when they leave full-time education will not only take time to design and introduce but the implications for the students and the economy will not necessarily be controllable or predictable in the long term. The scope may need to be adjusted as ambiguities are clarified and the changes are delivered in steps (tranches) over a number of years.

MSP is highly suitable for the latter two types of programme, being an approach designed to accommodate high levels of complexity, ambiguity and risk. Adopting a programme approach is not necessary where something new is delivered within the existing business model. Improvements to an existing product or service would not normally warrant a programme approach. Nor is a programme relevant in organising all the projects within an enterprise solely for prioritising and allocating resources. Organisations have successfully used MSP, or elements of it, in such situations; however, the programme management framework of MSP is primarily designed to cater for leading and managing transformational change.

Programme management principles may be applied to any change whatever the level of its focus or the nature of its outcomes, and can provide structure and process to support all types of change. However, it is important to remember that using programme management requires significant resourcing (including the provision of appropriately skilled and experienced individuals) with relatively high levels of funding. Therefore it is less likely such an approach will be needed in full for the specification-led programmes.

A programme is always planned and managed with an end in mind. Programmes are designed as temporary management environments that are expected to end. Changes to the drivers of the programme may mean the programme having to change its boundaries (e.g. re-plan an end date farther into the future). This could happen several times during the life of a programme but it will always be managed as if it will end one day.

However, if a programme drifts into becoming never-ending, then it is no longer a true programme but becomes another expression of operational management, part of business-as-usual. In this case, although elements of programme management may be employed, much of this programme management framework in MSP becomes less appropriate.

1.8 OGC BEST PRACTICE GUIDANCE

Managing Successful Programmes is part of a suite of guidance developed by the Office of Government Commerce (OGC), aimed at helping organisations and individuals manage their projects, programmes and services. Where appropriate, this guidance is supported by a qualification scheme and accredited training and consultancy services.

1.8.1 Management of Risk: Guidance for Practitioners

Programmes exist in a fundamentally uncertain world and as such effective management of risk is crucial to managing the delivery of the outcomes and benefits identified by the programme. Risk management is a key Governance Theme of MSP, and *Management of Risk* (M_o_R®) puts the management of programme risk into the context of the wider business environment.

1.8.2 Managing Successful Projects with PRINCE2™

PRINCE2™ is a structured method to help effective project management. Adopting a structured project approach is necessary in successfully implementing MSP. Using PRINCE2 to manage the projects within a programme can greatly assist in ensuring the project outputs are delivered as required throughout the programme.

1.8.3 OGC Gateway™ Review Process

OGC Gateway™ is a well established project and programme assurance review process which is mandated for all UK Government high-risk programmes and projects.

OGC Gateway delivers a peer review, in which independent practitioners from outside the individual programme/project use their experience and expertise to examine progress and assess the likelihood of successful delivery of the programme or project. It is used to provide a valuable additional perspective on the issues facing the internal team, and an external challenge to the robustness of plans and processes. This service is based on good practice and there are many similar examples across all business sectors of this type of peer review designed to provide assurance to the owner of the programme or project.

Programme reviews are carried out under the OGC Gateway Review 0: Strategic assessment. A programme will generally undergo three or more OGC Gateway Review 0s:

1 An early Review
2 One or more reviews at key decision points during the course of the programme and
3 A final Review at the conclusion of the programme.

Any Gateway Review of a project must take into account the programme context within which the project is located and possible interdependencies with other projects in the programme. The Gateway Review will also indicate how far procurement aspects of programmes are in alignment with strategic and policy objectives. Full details of the OGC Gateway Review Process are available from the OGC website.

1.8.4 IT Infrastructure Library – service management

A well-managed transition of the outcomes into business-as-usual is a crucial part of MSP's approach, and where organisations have adopted the IT Infrastructure Library (ITIL) for their IT service management practices, there will be a useful read across both for managing this transition and for the future realisation of the benefits in the long term via ongoing service management.

1.9 SOME MSP TERMINOLOGY

The Glossary provides explanations of all the terms commonly used in this guide that have a specific meaning in a programme context. However, throughout MSP, there are three key terms used that have a hierarchical relationship that it is important to understand from the start.

Corporate Strategy defines the organisation's approach to achieving its corporate objectives in any given area of its business. Corporate strategy or strategies give rise to the formulation of a **policy** or policies (such as the Risk

Management Policy described in M_o_R) that lay out the rules for all parts of the organisation to follow when implementing that particular aspect of management. In MSP, the programme will itself design individual strategies to ensure that the resources being applied are used as effectively as possible for that particular aspect of the programme. These strategies will be aimed at achieving or contributing towards a particular programme goal, and will be delivered by a series of **plans**. The MSP plans provide the detail of how the relevant programme objective will be achieved – what, where and when action will be taken, and by whom.

1.10 HOW TO USE THIS GUIDE

This manual is not intended to be read from cover to cover. It is a reference guide designed to help those involved in programmes to understand how business transformation should be delivered and their roles in this.

In addition to this introduction it is recommended that all readers familiarise themselves as a minimum with Chapter 2 'Programme management principles', Chapter 3 'Governance Themes overview' and Chapter 13 'Transformational Flow' to gain a good overview of MSP. These chapters provide an insight into the key principles that underpin all successful change programmes, explain how Governance within a programme works, and describe the lifecycle of a programme and how it passes through the various stages of development and delivery to achieve the outcomes and benefits desired.

For people who have a role within a programme or who have responsibility for programme delivery, together with anyone wishing to gain a deeper understanding of programme management, the guide is navigated as follows:

- **Part 2** provides useful reading on the Governance Themes (the management controls that keep the programme on track). They are relevant throughout the lifecycle of the programme and should be adhered to throughout to maximise the likelihood of the successful achievement of the programme objectives.
- **Part 3** – The Transformational Flow – describes the iterations through which the programme passes on its journey. There are distinct states that it travels through and may require different skills and approaches depending on its state of evolution.
- **Part 4** – The Appendices – provide more in-depth coverage of topics relevant to MSP that will be of interest to practitioners and people with management responsibilities within a programme environment:

- Appendix A: 'Programme information' – to be read by Programme Managers and Programme Office staff
- Appendix B: 'Adopting MSP' – to be read by those with responsibility for organisational standards, senior managers and Programme Managers
- Appendix C: 'Programme Office' – to be read by Programme Managers and Programme Office staff
- Appendix D: 'Health checks' – outlines the areas that should be regularly reviewed to ensure that the programme is being well run. To be read in conjunction with Appendix B: 'Adopting MSP'
- Further information – useful reading references that can supplement knowledge of MSP and provide practitioners with further research sources
- Glossary – contains a list and explanation of the terms used in this guide.

Programme management principles

2

2 Programme management principles

2.1 INTRODUCTION

It is possible to provide a common framework of understanding for all programmes. *Managing Successful Programmes* is such a framework, because it is principles-based. These principles are:

- Universal in that they apply to every programme
- Self-validating in that they have been proven in practice
- Empowering because they give practitioners of this framework some added ability or power to influence and shape transformational change towards success.

2.2 THE PRINCIPLES

If the following principles are observed when applying the rest of this guide (the Governance Themes and the Transformational Flow), the programme will be more likely to achieve its objectives. These principles are:

- Remaining aligned with corporate strategy
- Leading change
- Envisioning and communicating a better future
- Focusing on the benefits and threats to them
- Adding value
- Designing and delivering a coherent capability
- Learning from experience.

2.2.1 Remaining aligned with corporate strategy

A programme is a typically large investment that should make a significant contribution towards achieving corporate performance targets. A well-managed programme maintains good links with a sometimes-volatile corporate strategy.

Programmes often have to prove or disprove strategic ideas. There needs to be effective feedback from programmes to the strategists, so they can refine future strategies based upon the feedback evidence from the programmes. As external drivers may cause frequent changes of direction, the programme must be durable yet adaptable enough to keep pace with strategy.

The programme must also ensure the strategic drivers are extended downwards into the governance of its projects and business change activities. The programme must not allow projects to become detached from, or misaligned with, corporate strategy.

Thus a programme needs to create a working environment that is both robust and flexible enough to be able to cope with frequent, and sometimes radical, changes of boundary.

The programme's business case must also be robust, considering options, and once approved, be regularly reviewed to ensure ongoing strategic alignment. The programme must have a porous boundary and be able to cope with frequent changes to what is included within the programme and what is not. This is not so with its projects, where a flexible, dynamic scope usually spells disaster. This is a major reason why effective programme management can never be codified into a rigid set of rules and procedures: it is necessarily agile and adaptive.

A global food manufacturer was implementing a programme to improve its supply chain processes when it merged with a competitor. The programme was robust enough to identify new benefits and to persist into the new organisation, providing a new common capability for both parts of the company. Shortly after, the company responded to the approaching threat of the 'millennium bug' by accelerating parts of the programme's timetable so that legacy systems could be replaced rather than being amended.

So, although this programme had to cope with two major boundary changes, it was able to remain aligned to the company's strategy.

2.2.2 Leading change

Seeing through change in a programme is a leadership challenge. In addition to the need to manage a large number of complex tasks, people need to be led. It is impossible to move to a better future without clear leadership. The kind of leadership that is required in programme management:

- Gives clear direction (see paragraph 2.2.3 'Envisioning and communicating a better future' below)
- Engenders trust with consistent and transparent behaviours
- Actively engages stakeholders
- Appoints the right people at the right time
- Can live with a measure of uncertainty
- Solves problems and create novel solutions
- Supports the transition until new ways are established and embedded.

Good leaders engender trust through leading with consistency and transparency. Programme management is most effective when issues are debated freely and risks evaluated openly. This requires personal courage and openness to challenge. Conversely, where there is lack of trust, stakeholder engagement and teamworking are so much harder. It is a sign of weak leadership to dismiss risks, issues and concerns by members of the team without appropriate examination and consideration.

> A government agency had to relocate 200 miles away. Anticipating how tough this decision would be for all the staff in the agency, the senior management team decided that they would move first and forego senior management perks, but committing to the same relocation package as everyone else. Moving plans of the senior team became part of the regular communications within the programme, as well as intelligence about housing, schools and other facilities in the new locality. The senior team also agreed to be very open as individuals about how they felt about the move, so in personal presentations they appropriately referenced their own sadness at leaving their old neighbourhoods, their discomfort, struggles and surprises. This made a huge difference in influencing enough people to move with the agency.

Leading change means actively engaging stakeholders. In achieving transformational changes, programmes will change the working practices, culture and style of organisations. The people aspects of change must be recognised and addressed if the programme is to succeed. A good programme actively engages stakeholders and takes seriously their perceptions of value and benefit. Programme management needs to be much more actively people-oriented than might be the case in a project.

> A programme handled the merger of two large organisations. However, when the merger was complete, management realised that there remained two very different and sometime conflicting cultures. Senior management saw that this new state was insufficient to realise their stated vision. Transition to the desired culture would take a long time, but this need should have been recognised and included as part of the programme.

Leading change also means assembling the right people first. Recent research suggests that organisations that have succeeded in making breakthrough change have assembled the right team at the start of the change. Assembling this team early and with the right focus was a critical success factor. Some of the most successful strategic changes began with assembling key stakeholders as an early part of a visioning process (i.e. to build,

establish and communicate a clear vision for the programme).

Well-led change focuses on people, using their strengths and abilities, and bringing these people and their skills into play at the right times in a programme. This can make a clear difference to the programme's progress and ultimate success. The people leading the change should look to early appointments of people with the experience and knowledge to design and implement the programme's frameworks and approaches.

Certain people may be more right at different times in the programme. For example, some may be more suited to initial conceptual exploratory leadership rather than in later periods of the programme, where attention to logistics and the integrity of completed outcomes may be more vital.

> An insurance company had to comply with new pension legislation through the products it offered to its customers. Very early in the programme, the managers realised that they needed to appoint 'change champions' in the six regional offices affected. These change champions would need to continue in their operational roles but also take on significant change management duties within their own offices. By appointing the change champions early, people in the offices knew to whom they could put questions. Also the change champions fed back early intelligence to the Programme Office. Regular video conferences were organised that helped identify where some individuals could develop their skills and understanding of their roles, and where others had advice to give. Although the operational changes were up to two years off in some cases, it proved vital that these people were appointed and involved early on.

Good change leaders can live with the uncertainty that inevitably comes with managing programmes. Uncertainties can be made worse if:

- The path to achieving the vision is not clear at the start
- It has to deviate during the course of the programme
- The vision itself needs refining as work progresses.

Such leaders need to cope with complexity and ambiguity, particularly in the early parts of a programme. The early work of a programme may be more exploratory and uncertain about the detail of the eventual outcomes (and also about the route to get there) than is the case later on. This is often the nature of engaging with transformational change, where the programme does not have examples or lifecycle templates to follow.

Change leaders are able to solve problems and create novel solutions, to see the big picture as well as identify and grasp critical detail. Competent programme management has a much more inclusive and adaptive view of its role and of its context than is the case with, say, a project management role. A programme role frequently requires a mental agility that thinks less in black and white terms. Some programmes are created to meet a single objective, some to meet multiple objectives. Sometimes, two or more of these objectives can appear contradictory; sometimes stakeholders have competing and mixed agendas. These are some of the normal challenges of leading change in programmes, to which there is no routine correct solution.

Leading change also means supporting the change through the transition from the old to the new until the new ways of working are fully embedded. This area is often neglected or underestimated. It can result in excellent project outputs and the capability they offer not being exploited. The programme may then be branded a failure, when in fact it was a failure of change leadership, not the programme or any of its projects. Leading this way involves planning changes, preparing for their implementation, resourcing and then implementing them. The transition process should ensure business stability is maintained. Managing the transition involves leading people through change into an unfamiliar and probably uncomfortable new way of doing things.

All these aspects of change leadership can be provided by different individuals in a variety of roles throughout the programme's life and into transition. The important factor is that this leadership role is always visible and accounted for in the programme.

2.2.3 Envisioning and communicating a better future

A programme is relevant where there is a need to achieve transformational change, where there is some marked step change or break with the present required in the future capability. In order to achieve such a beneficial, future state, the leaders of a programme must first describe a clear vision of that future.

A vision should be developed and refined in the early part of the programme. This should exist throughout the life of the programme and be one of the main tools for ensuring the ongoing strategic alignment of the programme. For example, if the Vision Statement is changed significantly it could indicate that the programme itself has changed significantly and needs to be reassessed against its original objectives.

Whilst creating a clear vision is necessary, it is insufficient without the clear and consistent communication of it towards gaining commitment and buy-in from a range of stakeholders. If the goal of a programme is a beneficial, transformational change then a clear picture or vision of what the future outcomes will look like is vital. Effectively communicating this message to stakeholders is part of the ongoing leadership task of engagement. A programme that continues without a clear vision will risk leaving stakeholders confused about the future intent, thereby reducing the likelihood of the programme's success.

A faith community leader had a goal of setting up a day care centre for single mothers and other vulnerable groups within a city centre. This centre was such a departure from what his community had seen or experienced that the leader found it very difficult to explain to them in a way that generated enthusiasm and essential commitment.

When he began to express the vision of the centre in terms of a story, for example 'a day in the life of Jane, a single mother', he found that this made the vision real, and people rallied to him. He also found he needed to create a short form of the vision story and repeat it regularly to the same stakeholders. He found that initially some did not quite get the picture, while others remained sceptical that this was nothing more than a fad. By repeating the same vision regularly he was able both to demonstrate his commitment to realising this vision as well as to mobilise and sustain support from others.

2.2.4 Focusing on the benefits and threats to them

Best practice programme management aligns everything towards satisfying strategic objectives by realising the end benefits. Thus the programme's boundary, including the projects and activities that become part of the programme, are determined to enable the realisation of these end benefits.

The ultimate success of a programme is judged by its ability to realise these benefits and the continuing relevance of these benefits to the strategic context. If the benefits are of strategic value, then effective risk management is crucial. (See in particular Chapter 11, 'Risk Management and Issue Resolution'.)

A medical organisation embarked on several major changes to its service, integrated into one major programme. As part of this, it found that doctors, nurses and administrators all appreciated clear Benefits Maps, which showed them the big picture as well as their individual contributions to the overall programme. 'In terms of getting engagement, the [Benefits Mapping] exercise helped when people saw the benefits coming out,' said a member of the programme management team. The organisation also found that the Benefits Maps also helped de-clutter the overall change, by showing which projects did not help towards any of the benefits and so could be removed.

2.2.5 Adding value

A programme only remains valid if it adds value to the sum of its constituent projects and major activities. If it is found to add nothing then it is better to close the programme and allow the projects to proceed independently, coordinated by corporate portfolio management.

One confirmation of this synergy is the existence of programme benefits over and above individual project benefits – that is, benefits the projects themselves are able to identify and claim. Related and dependent business change is often best managed at programme level so that these additional benefits can be identified and realised. For example, avoiding the double-counting of benefits by projects can be seen as a major value-adding activity from a programme.

2.2.6 Designing and delivering a coherent capability

The programme will deliver a business architecture or final capability. This should have such internal coherence that all quality requirements are optimised, being released into operational use according to a schedule delivering maximum incremental capability with minimal adverse operational impact.

Project scope and outputs need careful delineation; there should be rigorous identification and management of inter-project dependencies, and a clear understanding of programme versus project responsibilities. The programme needs to focus on realising the bigger picture and should not take over the responsibilities of project management. However, clear direction should be given to the projects and regular reviews held to verify continual alignment to the programme objectives and plans. This ensures that everything that can be done is done to facilitate a smooth transition of the project outputs into the operational part of the business.

2.2.7 Learning from experience

A programme is a learning organisation in that it reflects upon and improves its own performance during its life. Good governance requires approaches to managing the different Themes that are regularly adjusted and adapted on the basis of experience and results so far. For example, part of good Benefits Realisation Management means that stakeholders are identifying new opportunities to realise benefits as their awareness and experience increases.

Programmes perform better where members of the management all assume the attitude of being learners. Such a reflective stance may require certain adjustments to be built into the programme, typically at major review points, so that the management team and the individuals within it can formally assimilate and express this learning as the programme progresses further.

Part 2
The
Governance
Themes

Governance Themes overview

3

3 Governance Themes overview

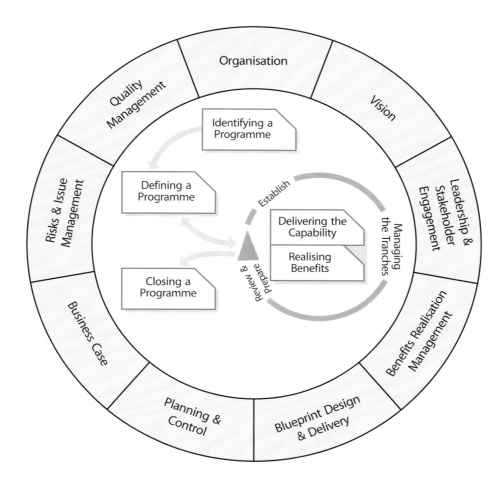

Governance is the control framework through which programmes deliver their change objectives and remain within corporate visibility and control. A programme needs clear and open governance if it is to be successful. It will need to negotiate the resource it wants, manage the resources made available to it, and adjust to changing organisational contexts whilst delivering its agreed outcomes and benefits. The focus of this section is the core elements of an effective governance framework.

The need for governance over change is manifested in two ways:

- Control and ownership of the transformation programme (in itself, and in relation to other change within the organisation)
- The control and ownership/stewardship of the organisation as a corporate entity.

The programme will need to integrate its control framework with the control framework of the organisation. Given that MSP concentrates on programmes delivering transformational change, the programme will need to

integrate with the corporate governance framework. Where they exist, the programme should ideally look to use the organisations' existing governance and control frameworks as these should provide the necessary structures and visibility.

This alignment should extend to (in terms of expression, unit of value, nature of analysis and minimum frequency of reporting) the corporate controls used in, for example:

- Finance and accounting
- Human resource management
- Risk and issue management
- Quality systems
- Operations and performance
- Information technology
- Customer and stakeholder satisfaction
- Sourcing and procurement
- Contract management
- Legislative compliance
- Information management.

To a greater or lesser extent, each of the Governance Themes provides guidance and tools to the Transformational Flow activities. More than one Governance Theme is likely to influence more than one of the Transformational Flow activities.

Governance Themes are like a constant pattern in a fabric, and like a pattern should be woven into the programme; they are not one-off or occasional activities. For example, risk management should be central to every decision at each step and level in the programme; it is not a case of updating a log from time to time.

Part 2, The Governance Themes, details the consistent controls needed to manage the programme whilst Part 3, The Transformational Flow, explains the activities and work of the programme lifecycle.

3.1 GOVERNANCE THEMES

Each of the chapters in this Part contains information to help you manage a particular aspect of the programme. There will be a full description of:

- Why the Theme is important to the successful delivery of the programme
- Which programme management strategies, approaches and plans will need to be developed to ensure the control framework and governance arrangements around the Theme are in place and rigorous
- The tools and techniques that can be used in the day-to-day management of the Theme
- MSP documentation that is developed as part of the Theme, bringing out context and/or providing control for the programme
- The generic process or cycle of activities that should be regularly undertaken to ensure that the Theme is being applied to the programme
- The roles and responsibilities for application of the Theme.

3.2 INTEGRATING PROGRAMME MANAGEMENT INTO THE ORGANISATION CONTROL FRAMEWORK

Any programme delivery framework that is to be adopted or used by the organisation will initially be seen as an add-on to the business-as-usual activities of the organisation. Whilst communications activities may raise the profile of the programmes, there is still a risk that the programmes are not fully accounted for by the organisation. This means that the resources to be demanded and consumed, the changes to be introduced by, and the possible impact of, the programmes may not be fully visible to the organisation. In such a situation the organisation cannot be said to understand or own the programmes of change.

The keywords in achieving this understanding and ownership are visibility and control. To achieve these, organisations must understand the programme in terms of its business-as-usual controls, giving the visibility of the programme not only in terms of itself, but also in terms of its impacts on and constraints within the organisation's policies, strategies, resources, assets, plans and activities.

Programmes that try to operate as an independent entity are unlikely to gain the organisational buy-in required to succeed. The programme management strategies and plans (see section 3.3) provide a vehicle for ensuring this integration.

For more information on integration with corporate frameworks, see Appendix B: 'Adopting MSP'.

3.3 PROGRAMME MANAGEMENT STRATEGIES AND PLANS

As it is established, the programme will define a number of strategies and plans. These have a dual function:

- The strategies set out the approach the programmes will take to achieve its end (and intermediate) goals, including the process, content and ownership around that particular Governance Theme. The programme strategies and controls are derived from, consistent with, and aligned to the organisation's policies for managing that Governance Theme. This consistency should extend to ownership, lexicon, units of measure and control, reporting etc.
- The plans explain what activities will take place to deliver that element of governance, as well as where, when and by whom.

The appropriate sign-off and endorsement of these strategies and plans validates them as both:

- Addressing the organisation's need for visibility and control
- Ensuring the programme has the right level of ownership, visibility, control and detail for that Governance Theme.

Table 3.1 sets out the relationship between programme management strategies and their delivery mechanisms.

Table 3.1   Relationship between the programme management strategies and the delivery mechanisms

Programme management strategy	Comments	Primarily delivered by
1.Resource Management	Covers resource to be consumed by the programme. Finances, people, systems, accommodation, facilities and specialisms will all be covered by this strategy	Resource Management Plan
2. Monitoring and Control	Sets out how the programme will monitor progress in terms of expected and actual delivery of outputs, outcomes and key milestones	Programme Plan
3. Information Management	How programme information will be catalogued, filed, stored and retrieved, and how the programme creates and manages information	Information Management Plan
4. Quality Management	How the delivery of quality activities will be incorporated into the management and delivery of the programme	Quality Management Plan
5. Risk Management	How the programme will establish the context in which risks will be identified and assessed, and responses planned and implemented	Risk Register
6. Issue Resolution	How issues will consistently be managed across the programme and change control managed	Issue Log
7. Stakeholder Engagement	Describes who the stakeholders are, what their interests and influences are likely to be, and sets out how the programme will engage with them	Stakeholder Profiles and Programme Communications Plan
8. Benefits management	Sets out the delivery framework for achieving the programme's objectives (as defined in the Vision Statement).	Benefits Realisation Plan

3.4   ILLUSTRATION OF THE RELATIONSHIP BETWEEN THE GOVERNANCE THEMES AND THE TRANSFORMATIONAL FLOW

If the Transformational Flow is the programme's time-based to-do list, then the Governance Themes can be seen as the reference manual. If the Flow requires action, then the Themes should provide guidance on how it should be done.

The analysis in Table 3.2 for the 'Identifying a Programme' process will help to illustrate this.

Table 3.2   Interaction between Governance Themes and Transformational Flows – Identifying a Programme

Flow Activity	Governance Theme
Sponsoring the Programme	**Leadership and Stakeholder Engagement** provides guidance on how to identify the critical stakeholders that need to be engaged.
	Organisation explains the roles, responsibilities and purpose of the Sponsoring Group.
Confirm Programme Mandate	The **Business Case** explains the purpose of the importance of the Mandate, and of the sources of the information that is used to provide the Mandate to the programme. Though not a Theme, Programme Information advises what content to include. **Benefits Realisation Management** and **Risk Management** also provide guidance on what to consider when preparing the document justifying the programme.
Appoint the SRO and Programme Board	**Organisation** provides a description of the role of the SRO, the characteristics needed to fulfil the role, and who should be on the Programme Board.
Develop the Programme Brief	Nearly all the Themes are relevant when writing this document. Whilst the Themes may be more relevant to the detailed work later in the Flow (e.g. in Defining a Programme), in creating a robust Brief it is necessary to anticipate work that happens later in the programme.
	Vision Statement describes the purpose and types of content for the Outline Vision Statement section.
	Risk Management describes managing the risks and issues the programme will face.
	The **Business Case** defines the costs and options to consider.
	Planning and Control develops timescales and estimates, showing how the programme will be controlled.
	Benefits Realisation Management guides the describing and detailing of expected benefits.
	Blueprint Design and Delivery develops the Vision Statement and defines the end goal. (Appendix A: 'Programme information' provides guidance on content.)
Develop the Programme Preparation Plan	**Organisation** explains the roles and responsibilities of individuals during Defining a Programme; these should be reflected in the Plan.
	The **Governance Themes** overall provide input into what the plan should cover to enable effective control during programme definition. (Appendix A 'Programme information' provides guidance on content.)
Review of Programme Brief and Programme Preparation Plan	**Quality Management** provides guidance on effective process and decision making; this Review meets that criteria.
	Organisation explains how Audit and Assurance should be conducted
Approval to Proceed	**Organisation** and **Leadership and Stakeholder Engagement** provide guidance on who should be involved in this approval process, and how they should be engaged to gain support.

The same interaction between the Governance Themes and Transformational Flows happen in each of the processes. If you have responsibility for implementing MSP into an organisation, these interactions should be built into your process models wherever possible.

3.5 ROLES AND RESPONSIBILITIES

Table 3.3 shows the roles and responsibilities involved in Governance.

Table 3.3 Governance: roles and responsibilities

Role	Responsibilities
Senior Responsible Owner (SRO)	Overall accountability and responsibility for the design and approval of, and compliance of the programme with: ■ Corporate controls ■ Governance strategies ■ Initiations of assurance reviews.
Programme Manager	Design and implementation of the programme governance strategies Consultation with corporate governance Stakeholder consultation Supporting the SRO in implementation and control.
Business Change Manager	Review and contribution to governance development Implementation of governance arrangements where they impact on operations Input to programme assurance reviews Initiating assurance reviews of business operational areas Specific focus on benefits and stakeholder governance.
Programme Office	Maintenance of records Supporting governance assurance reviews Application of governance arrangements on behalf of the Programme Manager as appropriate Monitoring actions from assurance and audit reviews Providing expertise to support assurance reviews on other programmes.

4

Organisation

4 Organisation

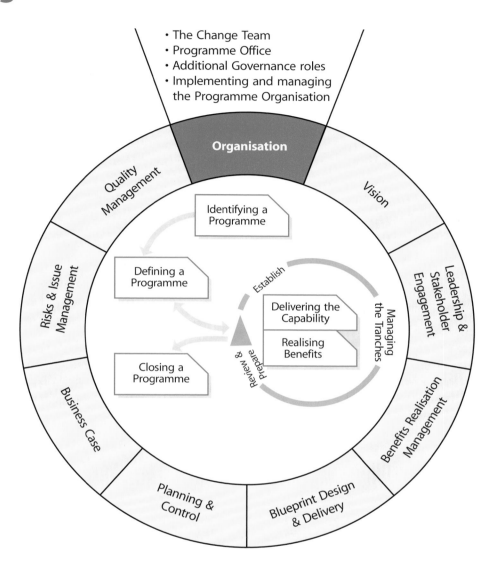

- The Change Team
- Programme Office
- Additional Governance roles
- Implementing and managing the Programme Organisation

4.1 INTRODUCTION

Establishing a clear and effective organisation is critical to programme success. Ensuring that the Programme Organisation meets the needs of the programme in its context is an initial and ongoing task that cannot be ducked, dealt with lightly or done once and then forgotten.

Effective Programme Organisation means the combination of:

- Defined roles
- Clear responsibilities of each of these roles
- Management structures and reporting arrangements that are needed to deliver the programme's desired outcomes.

The roles, responsibilities and structures discussed below provide the basis for effective programme management. They will need to be tailored to suit individual programmes.

4.2 PROGRAMME ORGANISATION

However competent the personnel and however effective the procedures are, some things will go wrong. The unexpected will arise, and major unplanned changes may be called for. Effective leadership of a programme can only be achieved through informed decision-making and a flexible management regime. Selecting a team with a good blend of personalities and skills and a structure that lets them carry out their roles effectively will support decision-making and management. Continuity and stability of the Programme Organisation structure is also important to ensure that commitment to the programme is maintained.

Programme management is most effective when issues are debated freely and risks evaluated openly. This requires a leadership style and culture that encourages the flow of information between projects and the programme. Every opportunity to advance the programme towards its goals should be welcomed and converted into constructive progress.

4.3 PROGRAMME LEADERSHIP

Programmes take and combine strategic objectives by translating them into concrete targets for individual projects. Leading and directing a programme provides the bridge between strategic objectives and projects.

The key principles for effective leadership of a programme (which fall primarily to the members of the Programme Board including the Senior Responsible Owner (SRO), Programme Manager and Business Change Manager) are:

- Vision-creating, showing an ability to envision a beneficial future and to communicate this future in compelling ways to all kinds of stakeholders
- Empowered decision-making, giving individuals the autonomy to fulfil their roles effectively. Motivation, reward and appraisal systems are vital for fostering the attitudes and energy to drive the programme

- Visible commitment and authority, with enough seniority to:
  - Ensure the correct resources are available to the programme
  - Influence and engage with stakeholders
  - Balance the programme's priorities with those of the ongoing business operations
  - Focus on realisation of the business benefits
- Relevant skills and experience to provide active management of:
  - The cultural and people issues involved in change
  - The programme's finances and the inevitable conflicting demands on resources
  - The coordination of the projects within the programme to see through the transition to new operational services, while maintaining business operations
  - Risk identification, evaluation and management.

4.4 PROGRAMME STRUCTURE

Figure 4.1 shows the core programme executive groups and how they relate to each other. The following sections describe the generic responsibilities for each, together with the specific roles and the skills that the individuals fulfilling them will need.

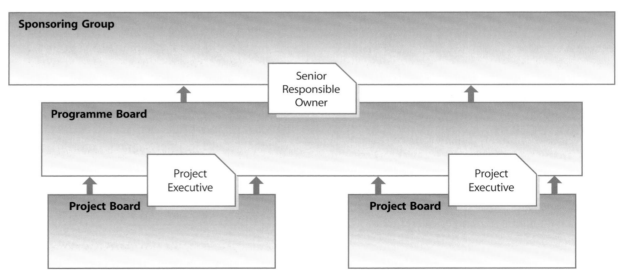

Figure 4.1   Layering of Programme Organisation, control and reporting

4.5 SPONSORING GROUP

The Sponsoring Group represents those senior managers who are responsible for:

- The investment decision
- Defining the direction of the business
- Ensuring the ongoing overall alignment of the programme to the strategic direction of the organisation.

The Sponsoring Group will appoint the SRO who, as part of the Sponsoring Group, is likely to be a peer of the other members of the Sponsoring Group. The role of the Sponsoring Group may well be performed by an existing executive committee or board of the organisation. The Programme Mandate, as owned and taken forward by the SRO, will be agreed by the Sponsoring Group.

4.5.1 Sponsoring Group and multiple programmes

In a multi-programme environment (where the organisation or a part of it is running more than one transformation programme at a time), there is a need to coordinate across programmes to ensure cohesive strategic alignment and prioritisation. Here, sponsorship means making the investment decision and providing top-level endorsement of the rationale and objectives for the programme in relation to other programmes and possible investments.

Championing the implementation of the new capabilities delivered by the programme must be balanced to ensure that expected benefits are realised and the desired outcomes achieved across the range of programmes, without undue or unbalanced focus on the delivery of the outcomes of one programme at the expense of another, i.e. ensuring the alignment of business priorities.

In a multiple programme environment the role of the Sponsoring Group may be performed by a standing 'Corporate Portfolio Board'. This board would have the responsibility of ensuring ongoing strategic alignment and prioritisation across all the programmes of the business portfolio. The *OGC Guidance on Portfolio Management* can offer further information on this topic.

4.5.2 Responsibilities of the Sponsoring Group

- Establishing the organisational context for the programme
- Authorising the Programme Mandate
- Approving funding for the programme

- Resolve strategic and directional issues between programmes, that need the input and agreement of senior stakeholders to ensure the progress of the change
- Confirming the organisation's strategic direction, against which the programme is to deliver
- Approving the progress of the programme against the strategic objectives
- Leading by example the values implied by the transformational change
- Providing continued commitment and endorsement in support of the programme objectives at executive and communications events
- Advising and supporting the SRO
- Championing the programme
- Confirming successful delivery and sign-off at the closure of the programme.

4.5.3 Sponsoring Group formality

Due to the nature of the Sponsoring Group, it may meet either on a formal and regular or ad-hoc basis. The greater the degree of transformational change predicated by the programme, the greater will be the need to have formal, visible control over the aggregate change. As a minimum, a Sponsoring Group will normally meet to give formal approval for the programme at the end of Identifying and Defining a Programme, the end of each tranche, and to approve Closure.

Members of the Sponsoring Group must take the lead in establishing a style of leadership appropriate to the organisation and the nature of the change. In most change situations there will need to be increased emphasis on motivation of staff, promotion of teamworking, empowerment at all levels, encouragement of initiatives, and recognition of appropriate risk-taking.

4.6 SENIOR RESPONSIBLE OWNER

The SRO is ultimately accountable for the programme, ensuring that it meets its objectives and realises the expected benefits. The individual who fulfils this role should be able to lead the Programme Board with energy and drive, and must be empowered to direct the programme and take decisions. They must have enough seniority and authority to provide leadership to the programme team and take on accountability for delivery.

4.6.1 Responsibilities of the Senior Responsible Owner

The SRO is accountable for the success of the programme and is responsible for enabling the organisation to exploit the new environment resulting from the programme, meeting the new business needs and delivering new levels of performance, benefit, service delivery, value or market share. The SRO:

- Owns the vision for the programme (as defined and ratified by the Sponsoring Group)
- Leads the programme, providing clear leadership and direction throughout its life
- Secures the investment required to set up and run the programme, and fund the transition activities so that the desired benefits are realised
- Provides overall direction and leadership for the delivery and implementation of the programme
- Has personal accountability for its outcome (this should be an important measure of their individual performance)
- Is accountable for the programme's governance arrangements
- Owns the Business Case
- Manages the interface with key senior stakeholders, keeping them engaged and informed
- Manages the key strategic risks facing the programme
- Maintains the alignment of the programme to the organisation's strategic direction.
- Chairs the Programme Board.

4.6.2 Key attributes of a Senior Responsible Owner

- Have the seniority for the responsibilities and accountabilities the role involves
- Be proactive and visible as the driving force behind the programme
- Possess strong leadership and decision-making skills
- Have the experience, character and personality that are right for the programme

- Combine realism with openness and the clarity of expression to communicate the programme's vision effectively
- Able to give purpose and direction to the programme and take strategic decisions
- Focus on delivery of the benefits and realising the end goal
- Build productive relationships across the programme team
- Have access to and credibility with key stakeholders.

Given the high level of personal responsibility that the SRO takes for the programme, this person will want to ensure that those selected to be on the Programme Board are able to contribute and support the programme with comparable levels of authority, commitment and ability.

4.7 PROGRAMME BOARD

Established by the SRO (and often coming into existence out of the approval of the Programme Mandate, or possibly the Programme Brief), the prime purpose of the Programme Board will be to drive the programme forward and deliver the outcomes and benefits. Members will provide resource and specific commitment to support the SRO who is accountable for the successful delivery of the programme.

The Programme Board reports to the SRO (Figure 4.2). Whilst the SRO may delegate responsibilities and action to members of the Programme Board, its existence does not dilute the SRO's accountabilities and decision-making authority.

Programme Board members must take the lead in supporting the authority and control of the SRO over the programme as a whole, including ensuring the appropriate coordination across the projects that comprise the programme.

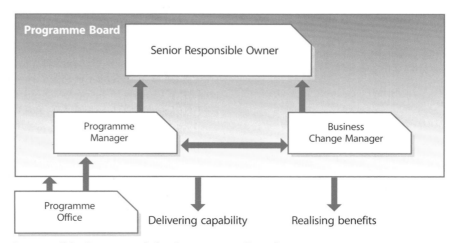

Figure 4.2   Senior Responsible Owner and the Programme Board

4.7.1 Responsibilities of the Programme Board

Members of the Programme Board are individually accountable to the SRO for their areas of responsibility and delivery within the programme as follows:

- Defining the acceptable risk profile and risk thresholds for the programme and its constituent projects
- Ensuring the programme delivers within its agreed parameters (e.g. cost, organisational impact and rate/scale adoption, expected/actual benefits realisation, etc.)
- Resolving strategic and directional issues between projects, which need the input and agreement of senior stakeholders to ensure the progress of the programmes
- Ensuring the integrity of benefit profiles and realisation plan and ensuring that there is no double-counting of benefits
- Providing assurance for operational stability and effectiveness through the programme delivery cycle.

Each member of the Programme Board will provide and commit to the SRO for some or all of the following as appropriate for the area they represent:

- Understanding and managing the impact of change
- Benefits estimates and achievement
- Owning the resolution of risks and issues that the programme faces
- Resolving dependencies with other pieces of work, whether change or business operations
- Representing local strategy as expressed in, for example, medium-term plans and operational blueprints
- Supporting the application of and compliance with operating standards, etc.
- Making resource availability for planning and delivery purposes.

4.7.2 Membership of the Programme Board

The following should be considered as standing members of the Programme Board:

- Programme SRO
- Programme Manager
- Business Change Manager
- Project executives of the projects in the programme (where the executive is not the Programme Manager)
- Representatives of corporate functions (e.g. finance, risk, etc.) as necessary

- Lead supplier (if there are different senior suppliers across the projects of the programme, it may be advisable to appoint a lead supplier to work with and through at the programme level).

4.8 PROGRAMME MANAGER

The Programme Manager is responsible for leading and managing the setting up of the programme through to delivery of the new capabilities and realisation of benefits. The Programme Manager has primary responsibility for successful delivery of the new capabilities and establishing governance. The Business Change Manager is responsible for benefits realisation via the organisational adoption and usage of the capability and transition to the desired outcome.

The Programme Manager will normally be appointed as part of forming the team for 'Defining a Programme', though it is important that someone with a Programme Manager perspective is in place when the Programme Brief and plans for programme definition are being developed in 'Identifying a Programme'.

4.8.1 Responsibilities of the Programme Manager

The Programme Manager is responsible for:

- Day-to-day management of the programme, including taking the programme forward from appointment (usually in 'Identifying a Programme' or 'Defining a Programme'), supervising and closing the programme
- Being the day-to-day agent on behalf of the SRO, for successful delivery of the new capability
- Planning and designing the programme and proactively monitoring its overall progress, resolving issues and initiating corrective action as appropriate
- Defining the programme's governance framework
- Effective coordination of the projects and their interdependencies
- Managing and resolving any risks and other issues that may arise
- Maintaining overall integrity and coherence of the programme, and developing and maintaining the programme environment to support each individual project within it
- Managing the programme's budget, monitoring the expenditures and costs against benefits that are realised as the programme progresses
- Facilitating the appointment of individuals to the project delivery teams

- Ensuring architectural coherence within the programme via design authority alignment (and possible creation)
- Ensuring that the delivery of new products or services from the projects meets programme requirements and is to the appropriate quality, on time and within budget
- Ensuring maximum efficiency in the allocation of resources and skills within the projects dossier
- Managing third-party contributions to the programme
- Managing the communications with stakeholders
- Initiating extra activities and other management interventions wherever gaps in the programme are identified or issues arise
- Reporting progress of the programme at regular intervals to the SRO.

4.8.2 Key attributes of the Programme Manager

- Ability to work positively with the full range of individuals and groups involved in the programme
- Ability to develop and maintain effective working relationships with other members of the programme management team, senior managers, the project teams and third-party service providers
- Necessary seniority to be able to take on the responsibilities required of the role
- Strong leadership and management skills
- Understanding of the wider objectives of the programme
- Credibility within the programme environment and ability to influence others
- Good knowledge of techniques for planning, monitoring and controlling programmes, including risk management
- Good knowledge of project management approaches such as PRINCE2
- Good knowledge of budgeting and resource allocation procedures
- Ability to find innovative ways of solving or pre-empting problems.

4.8.3 Business Change Manager

There is a fundamental difference between the delivery of a new capability and actually realising measurable benefits as a result of using that capability. This difference is reflected in the complementary roles of Programme Manager and Business Change Manager. The Programme Manager is responsible for delivering the capability; the Business Change Manager is responsible for realising the resultant benefits by embedding that capability into business operations. The individuals appointed to each

role must be able to work in close partnership to ensure that the right capabilities are delivered and that they are put to best use.

It is likely that the programme Business Change Manager will be supported by a team to ensure business understanding, commitment, ownership and adoption. The Business Change Manager's team will need to ensure operational engagement and ownership of benefits at the project and possibly workstream level. This, possibly matrix, structure must bridge between the formal organisation of the programme and projects, and that of the organisation's operations. Hence the Business Change Management activities will have impacts both within the programme and project organisation, and within the business operations.

Each separate business organisation that is affected by the programme should have its own Business Change Management representation in the programme. This may be via the Business Change Manager, the Business Change Manager's team, or possibly even multiple Business Change Managers on the programme.

Exactly how many people will be required to ensure business benefits understanding, commitment, ownership and realisation will depend on the number of business areas targeted for benefits realisation, the scale and complexity of the changes proposed, and the level of visibility of the benefits hierarchy and benefits ownership that the programme requires.

The appointment of the Business Change Manager should be coordinated by the SRO with the business operations and should be confirmed by the business operations.

4.8.4 Role of the Business Change Manager

The delivery of change will not happen on its own. The outputs required from projects need to be defined and targeted, based on the contribution they will make to realising benefits and achieving outcomes.

The Business Change Manager will normally be appointed as part of forming the team for 'Defining a Programme', though it is important that someone with a Business Change Manager perspective is in place when the Programme Brief and plans for programme definition are being developed in 'Identifying a Programme'.

The Business Change Manager has responsibility for benefits definition and management throughout the programme. The Business Change Manager is key to providing the bridge between the programme and the business operations since the individual(s) will be an integral part of the business operations. To realise benefits, the programme must be closely integrated with mainstream business activities. It is only when changes become business operations (business-as-usual) that the benefits will be realised.

Where substantial change in business operations is required, the individual appointed to the role of Business Change Manager will be responsible for creating the new business structures, operations and working practices. The Business Change Manager should have appropriate responsibility and authority within the business areas within which change will take effect and benefits realised.

4.8.5 Responsibilities of the Business Change Manager

The role of Business Change Manager is primarily benefits-focused. The Business Change Manager is responsible, on behalf of the business operations and the SRO, for:

- Defining the benefits
- Assessing progress towards realisation
- Achieving measured improvements
- Monitoring performance.

This need to define and realise benefits in terms of measured improvements in business performance means that the Business Change Manager must be 'business-side', in order to provide a bridge between the programme and business operations.

The Business Change Manager responsibilities will include the following:

- Maintaining the focus on realising beneficial change
- Ensuring development and business ownership of Benefit Profiles and Benefits Realisation Plan
- Confirming delivery of expected benefits
- Defining the performance metrics that will be monitored to assess the operational 'health' of the organisation
- Monitoring business stability and ongoing capability to cope with the level of change, this will include acceptable levels of performance variation (deterioration) whilst the change is embedded
- Assuring the Programme Board of the delivery of new capability and realisation of benefits
- Advising the Programme Manager whether the work of the programme and each project covers the necessary aspects required to deliver the products/outputs and services/outcomes that will lead to operational benefits
- Confirming the projects that will contribute to realising benefits and achieving outcomes
- Identifying, defining and tracking the benefits and outcomes required of the programme

- Managing the realisation of benefits, and ensuring that continued accrual of benefits can be achieved and measured after the programme has been completed by identifying and implementing the expected improvements in business operations as projects deliver their products or services into operational use
- Implementing the mechanisms by which benefits can be realised and measured
- Advising the Programme Manager at key points to allow decisions on progress, ensuring that business stability is maintained during the transition and the changes are effectively integrated into the business
- Preparing the affected business areas for the transition to new ways of working; potentially implementing new business processes
- Initiating business assurance reviews to ensure capabilities are being embedded and established
- Optimising the timing of the release of project deliverables into business operations.

As the programme progresses, the Business Change Manager is responsible for monitoring outcomes against what was predicted.

4.8.6 Key attributes of the Business Change Manager

The individual appointed as Business Change Manager, including any individuals appointed to the Business Change Manager's team, should:

- Be drawn from the relevant business areas in order to demonstrate detailed knowledge of the business environment and direct business experience
- Have ongoing operational responsibilities within their business areas. Their participation in the programme may be an integral part of their normal responsibilities, to enable changes resulting from the programme to be firmly embedded in the organisation
- Understand the management structures, politics and culture of the organisation(s) involved in the programme
- Have management skills to coordinate personnel from different disciplines and with differing viewpoints
- Have change management skills and enough experience to be able to bring order to complex situations and maintain focus on the programme's objectives
- Have negotiating skills, interpersonal fluency, comfort with ambiguity, dynamic prioritisation
- Have access to specific skills including process analysis, benefits identification, modelling and analysis, and business continuity management.

In a UK government agency, there was a growing recognition of the adverse impact of current projects and programmes on the business. Concerns about the need to balance appetite and capacity for change had been raised, as had the overall lack of adoption (and benefits realisation) across the organisation.

A change management function and structure was put into place. This established a Business Change Authority role at a directorate/business unit level. Three senior managers were appointed to share/fulfil the remit of the role with 20% of their time dedicated to enabling change in their respective parts of the directorate. Below, they were supported by a Business Change Manager who took on the coordination activities and managed a team of Change Managers to work at the projects level (sitting on the project boards), ensuring transition and maintaining business stability whilst enabling the change. Between 20% and 100% of their time was dedicated to this. Each of the Change Managers had a proven operational track record and had the respect of the business management.

This approach proved successful in ensuring benefits were identified, owned and delivered by the organisation.

4.8.7   Change Team

A Business Change Manager cannot deliver change alone. A Change Team can be formed to help one or more of the Business Change Managers take their stakeholders in their operational areas through such a change cycle. Such a team considers the interests of those parts of the organisation to be changed, and will ensure those parts are thoroughly prepared for the transition. Its focus is on helping the operational unit transition as smoothly as possible. It is a support function for when operational people need the most support.

Reporting to the relevant Business Change Manager for that part of the organisation, such a team requires Business Change Management skills, operational knowledge and experience, as well as the influence and authority of appropriate senior managers. Each tranche might make changes to different parts of the organisation. For these reasons, the Change Team needs to be reviewed at the beginning of each tranche.

Where there are a number of divisions of an organisation involved in the change then each should consider appointing a Business Change Manager to look after their specific interests. It may be necessary for the programme to appoint someone to act as the senior voice of the business within the programme; this role should assume a

title that fits with their status and the organisation hierarchy, for example 'Business Change Authority'.

4.8.8   Programme Office

Programmes are major undertakings, often affecting large numbers of people and organisations and generating a substantial volume of information. The nerve centre and information hub of a programme is the Programme Office. All information, communication, monitoring and control activities for the programme are coordinated through the Programme Office.

The larger the organisation and/or scale of change, the more likely it is that the Programme Office will be supporting multiple programmes. In organisations where the programmes are part of a portfolio, then Programme Office activities may be provided by a Corporate Portfolio Office, Programme Management Office or Centre of Excellence.

It is important to distinguish between two distinct roles of the Programme Office. One is providing support for the programmes. The other is providing assurance and governance across the programmes. In this second role the Programme Office must be independent of the programmes, as it is the home for governance and control, including standards, approvals, financial monitoring, assurance, provision of health checks, etc. Appendix C expands on the roles of the Programme Office.

4.8.9   Programme assurance

Assurance is a value-added function for the Programme Board involving the assessment of specific aspects to generate confidence that the programme is being managed effectively, and is on track to realise the expected benefits and achieve the desired outcomes. Assurance, like audit, should be carried out independently of the programme management team. Assurance may be focused on any number of aspects, for example:

- **Risk management assurance** – assessing the implementation and performance of the programme according to the Risk Management Strategy
- **Business assurance** – assessing the management of the Business Case and the continued viability of the programme against it
- **Stakeholder assurance** – assessing the mechanisms and performance of the Stakeholder Engagement Strategy.

All programme management roles include a responsibility for making sure assurance is carried out for that role's particular areas of interest, regardless of whether the programme will be subject to more formal audit scrutiny. For example, the SRO will require assurance that the programme's Business Case is being managed appropriately and that it remains aligned with strategic objectives.

More formal assurance/peer reviews may be carried out by individuals or groups from elsewhere in the organisation, by specifically contracted personnel or by the Programme Office. There should be a clear brief for each assurance review. Assurance reviews may be carried out at any time during the programme, may be aligned with gateway reviews and should be repeated in areas where problems were identified and recommendations made for improvements.

4.8.10 Additional governance roles

The following additional programme roles should be considered, though they may be part time or temporary during the different parts of the programme's life:

- **Risk Manager** provides expertise and management support for risk and issue management.
- **Programme Accountant** supports and ensures compliance to corporate accounting procedures, also provides useful support in Business Case development.
- **Design Authority** provides expert advice or owns some corporate function, service, standard or strategy that will be affected, or a major programme outcome or change that needs to be controlled. This could be an IT or property infrastructure design, or a major service contract; it could also be a business process model or the programme or corporate blueprint. The Design Authority provides expertise and guidance on a specific area to ensure there is appropriate alignment and control when changes are being planned and implemented.
- **Benefits Realisation Manager** provides assurance and overview of the Benefits Realisation Plan. A key element of this role is to ensure that there is no overlap between individually owned profiles. This should sit at the corporate level, to give visibility across the whole portfolio of change, and ensure both do-ability and no duplication across the portfolio. This role would provide assurance against the role of the Business Change Manager.
- **Procurement expertise** should be involved early to ensure compliance to corporate strategies and alliances and provide advice. Most programmes will involve some aspect of procurement.

4.9 IMPLEMENTING AND MANAGING THE PROGRAMME ORGANISATION

There is no single Programme Organisation that will fit every type of programme. Each programme should be

directed and managed with the appropriate level of management resources to facilitate clear direction setting and effective management of ongoing progress, but without incurring excessive management overheads.

The Programme Organisation will have to meet needs that include:

- The level of integration and overlap required with project organisations
- The need to split the responsibilities of the core programme roles across more than one individual to cope with large-scale programmes
- The requirement for building cross-organisation structures.

The Programme Organisation is defined in the Organisation Structure in Appendix A. It is critical that the Programme Organisation is in empathy with the organisation culture, and careful consideration is given to how it interfaces and merges with other corporate groups and initiatives so that boundaries are clear.

4.9.1 Programme evolution

There is an argument that the evolution of a programme and its different tranches implies a possibility of different leaders and managers for the different phases. If such a decision is taken, there would be a need to balance the appropriateness of the leadership and management styles in the different tranches with the risk of a lack of continuity of leadership, management and in-depth understanding across the whole life of the programme.

Programmes evolve and change over their life, having both linear and cyclical characteristics. This is not just in terms of the progression from a state of ambiguity, through 'Identifying a Programme', 'Defining a Programme' into the programme delivery of 'Managing Tranches' and on into 'Closing a Programme'. In moving through these tranches, the programme will draw on different skills from the organisation and may benefit from different styles of leadership and management complemented by different skills, competence and knowledge, reflected in the make-up of the Programme Board and focus of individual responsibilities. An example of how the leadership and management styles may be varied across the tranches of the programme is shown below.

Identifying a Programme

The research/analysis-intensive nature of this tranche means the team is often composed of subject matter experts. Such an environment can best lead by facilitating, providing guidance and suggestions as there will still be considerable ambiguity at this stage. An instructing management style would be both inhibitive and counter to the inherently exploratory nature of this phase. The leadership style must be suitably receptive and open.

Defining a Programme

Here the principle of design is paramount, and this must be supported by coordination across the different design groups and Themes. Here the management style must drive the coordination, whilst ensuring the primacy of the right and best elements emerging from across the design agenda. The leader must support the definers in this essentially egalitarian process.

Managing the Tranches

As their names suggest, these areas of a programme concentrate on outcome and delivery, so the activities and tasks to achieve this must be driven with a suitably focused style of leadership and management. What is expected or contracted to be delivered must be delivered. This more didactic style must ensure task completion with minimal disruption.

Closing a Programme

Both ensuring benefits and closure of the programme require a management focus on ensuring that works are finished off, adoptions are made, procedures are followed and changes are made. The management style required here has more completer-finisher characteristics, combined with the ability to analyse results and deal with the people issues arising from acceptance of the changes.

4.9.2 Integrating programme and project structures

Designing the appropriate levels of engagement between the projects and the programme is a key part of establishing an effective Programme Organisation. Project-level organisation structures need to have clear leadership, direction-setting, decision-making and management, whether they are operating within a programme or independently. There are different forms of project organisations and different ways of integrating project organisations into a Programme Organisation; Figure 4.3 shows some examples.

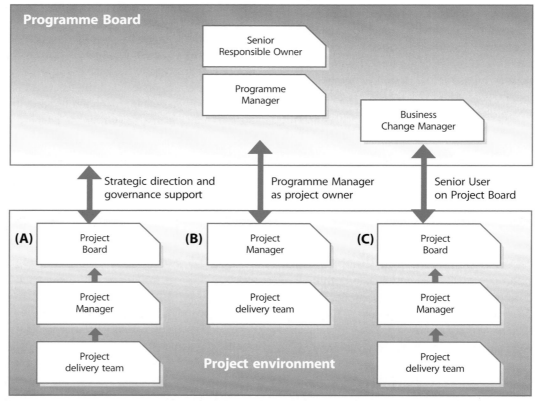

Figure 4.3   Integrating project organisations

- **Scenario (A).** Some projects will benefit from a dedicated Project Board to provide the required level of management direction and decision-making. The Project Board should have a clear set of responsibilities, agreed at the programme level, for directing the project and defining how the project should interface with the programme. The chair of the Project Board will be the Project Executive. This scenario may be well suited to larger projects within the programme.

- **Scenario (B).** Projects that are central to the programme may work well with the Programme Manager fulfilling the project executive role and maintaining a very tight, direct link between the project and the programme.

- **Scenario (C).** The Business Change Manager may provide valuable user-side input and assurance to projects within the programme. In this scenario, the Business Change Manager may fulfil the senior user or project executive role on the Project Board.

It is important to consider how the Business Change Manager responsibilities are cascaded down into the Project Board and project teams. There is a link with the PRINCE2 Senior User role, which could have an extended brief to include transitional stability and benefits achievement. Alternatively a separate Business Change Manager can be included within the Project Board structure, with a specific focus on transition, stability and benefit realisation; this role could have a number of other possible titles, which include 'Business Assurance', 'Business Champion' or 'Voice of the Business'.

4.9.3   Cross-organisational programmes

When two or more organisations come together to work on a programme, managing and directing their respective contributions can be complex. One example of cross-organisational working might be where one organisation is providing the majority of the funding and purchasing capital assets such as a new building and the other providing the staffing, infrastructure and systems for a new service facility. Both organisations require a return on their respective investments and so need to collaborate effectively to make the partnership deliver the required outcome. Each participating organisation should have a clearly defined role that is agreed and understood by all the participating organisations.

One approach to designing an appropriate programme structure is to establish a separate entity for the purposes of coordinating and leading the programme. This separates the business of making the partnership work from the internal priorities of each participating organisation. Figure 4.4 shows an example of a structure bringing together three organisations. The structure may be a specifically created legal entity, or it may be based on formal terms of reference or contractual agreements.

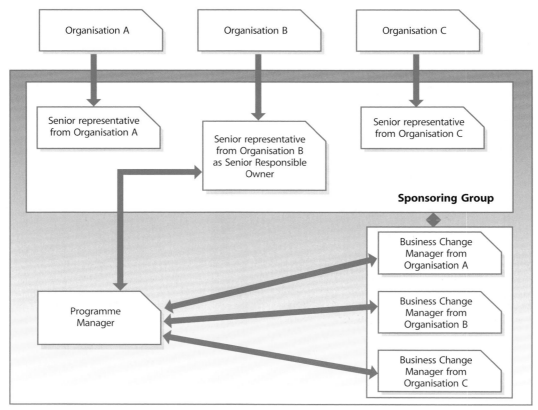

Figure 4.4   Cross-organisational programmes

The terms of reference and/or contractual arrangements will need to address such Themes as board representation and responsibilities, appointment to and resignation from the board, etc. The challenges facing cross-organisational programmes are generally the same as for all major programmes. However, increased complexity can mean that different types of issue, with greater impact, can arise. Chapter 2 'Programme management principles' gives greater detail of aspects that present challenges and will need to be managed.

4.10 ROLES AND RESPONSIBILITIES

Table 4.1 is a summary of the key responsibilities for the delivery of an effective Programme Organisation.

Table 4.1   Effective Programme Organisation: roles and responsibilities

Role	Responsibilities
Senior Responsible Owner	Ensuring that the Programme Organisation has the necessary skills and experience required to deliver the change
	Sponsoring Group members have a clear understanding of their roles
	Appointment of the Programme Manager
	Approval of the Business Change Manager appointment.
Programme Manager	Design of the programme team
	Appointment of the Programme Office
	Appointment of project teams
	Ensuring all roles have clearly defined responsibilities
	Ensuring that the organisation design is implemented through the programme lifecycle.
	Efficiency of resources
Business Change Manager	Design of the Change Team
	Appointment of individuals to the Change Team.
Programme Office	Maintenance of information
	Advice and guidance on roles and responsibilities
	Support in recruitment and appointments.

Vision 5

5 Vision

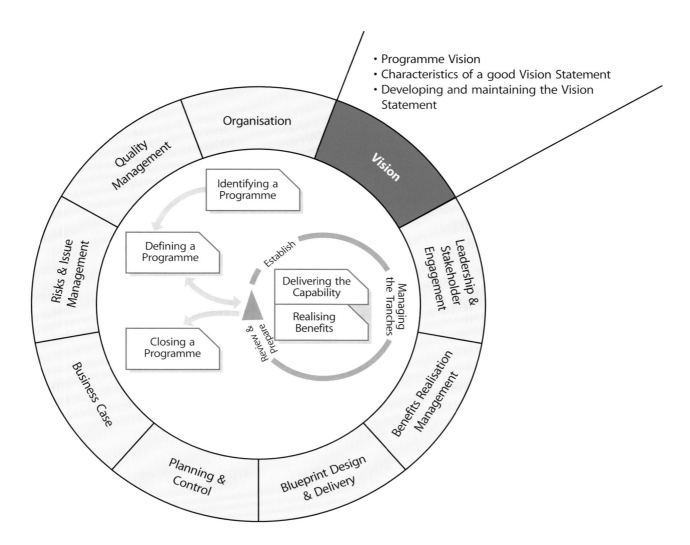

- Programme Vision
- Characteristics of a good Vision Statement
- Developing and maintaining the Vision Statement

5.1 VISION, VISION STATEMENT AND BLUEPRINT

A vision is a picture of a better future. In MSP it is the basis for the outcomes and delivered benefits of the programme. As such it is a vital focus and enabler for the buy-in, motivation and activity-alignment of the large community of people involved in any programme. See the principle in paragraph 2.2.3 'Envisioning and communicating a better future'.

The Vision Statement is used to communicate the end goal of the programme, being a summary impression of the desired future state. In contrast, the Blueprint, which is derived from the Vision Statement, is primarily a design document, being a description (in meticulous, process-level detail) of both the current organisation and the changed organisation. The two should be aligned and fully consistent with each other. The Vision Statement is the outward-facing description of the future state following programme delivery (supported by the detail of the to-be elements of the Blueprint). The Vision Statement will describe the new services, improved service levels, or innovative ways of working with customers, or any combination and should be used to engage and gain commitment from as many stakeholders as possible.

When any organisation goes through transformational change, different stakeholders will not necessarily understand the big picture without such a Vision Statement.

5.2 CHARACTERISTICS OF A GOOD VISION STATEMENT

A good Vision Statement:

- Is written as a future state. It is not to be confused with an objective, strategy, intention or mission, all of which could begin with the word 'To'. Instead it is a snapshot of the organisation in the future.
- Can be easily understood by a wide variety of stakeholders; it is easy to communicate. This means it does not use jargon understood by only one group. It is clear in the Vision Statement how this better future is different from the present.
- Is written with the broadest groupings of stakeholders as the target audience.
- Describes a compelling future that engages the heart as well as the head. This does not mean it is emotional, but nor is it dry and factual.
- Matches the degree of transformation change with the boldness of the vision conveyed. Vision Statements should motivate everyone and need to do justice to the challenge of transformational change.
- Avoids target dates unless the vision is truly time-dependent. For example, the vision of a new international sports complex may be legitimately dependent on delivering the capability in time for hosting a major international event. However, in many other programmes the vision is not so time-dependent; the Vision Statement still remains valid even if timescales slip.
- Describes a desirable future, in terms of the interests of key stakeholders. Key benefits are implicit.
- Describes a vision that is verifiable but without too many detailed performance targets. A Vision Statement that contains an aspirational future that is not verifiable can breed scepticism among stakeholders. It should be clear when the organisation has arrived at the future state. However, a primary purpose is consistent communication of the better future to a wide variety of stakeholders. Too many statistics and numeric targets will be a turn-off for some stakeholders and make the Vision Statement less memorable to many others. Such detail is more appropriate in the Blueprint and its target performance levels.

- Is sufficiently flexible to remain relevant over the life of the programme. It does not contain too many constraints.
- Is short and memorable. Some of the best Vision Statements are no more than a paragraph. The vision is repeatedly communicated at all kinds of events and ideally stakeholders can recall it from memory almost word for word.

For further details on the Vision Statement see Appendix A, 'Programme information'.

5.3 DEVELOPING AND MAINTAINING THE VISION STATEMENT

It takes time and the involvement of a number of people to draft a clear, compelling and inclusive Vision Statement. In Transformational Flow, work on the Vision Statement should begin soon after the Programme Mandate has been agreed and the Senior Responsible Owner (SRO) has been appointed (see Chapter 14, 'Identifying a Programme'). The SRO would assemble a representative group of interested senior management and affected stakeholders and begin building outline Vision Statement options based on the information in the Programme Mandate (see the 'Leading change' principle in paragraph 2.2.2, and in particular 'Assembling the right people first'). Once agreed, the outline Vision Statement is included in the Programme Brief.

The Vision Statement is regularly reviewed during 'Defining a programme' to maintain strategic alignment of the programme. The Vision Statement underpins the programme design and development. (see the principle of 'Remaining aligned with corporate strategy', paragraph 2.2.1).

The Vision Statement should be regarded as a constant and stable foundation for the programme. Improvements to its wording or, for example, embracing newly emerged business drivers, may be allowed. However, if the Vision Statement does require major changes, it:

- Risks confusing stakeholders, possibly even undermining the credibility of the programme
- Could indicate that the current programme is no longer strategically aligned, and that a possibly different programme is now required.

5.4 ROLES AND RESPONSIBILITIES

Table 5.1 shows the main roles and responsibilities involved in Vision.

Table 5.1 Vision: roles and responsibilities

Role	Responsibilities
Sponsoring Group	Contribute to the development of the document
	Approve the content
	Commit to supporting the aspirations and transformation described.
Senior Responsible Owner	Develop the document
	Gain Sponsoring Group and senior support
	Ensure that the organisation is capable of achieving the transformation described
	Lead the delivery and maintaining focus on of the Vision Statement by the programme
	Authorise any changes.
Business Change Manager	Support the SRO in the development of the content relating to the business areas to be changed
	Communicate the Vision Statement
	Deliver the operational changes needed to achieve the desired end state.
Programme Manager	Develop programme documentation aligned to the Vision Statement
	Ensure the Vision Statement underpins the Programme Communications Plan
	Coordinate the development of the Blueprint based on the Vision Statement
	Process any changes or updates that will be required.

Leadership and stakeholder engagement

6

6 Leadership and stakeholder engagement

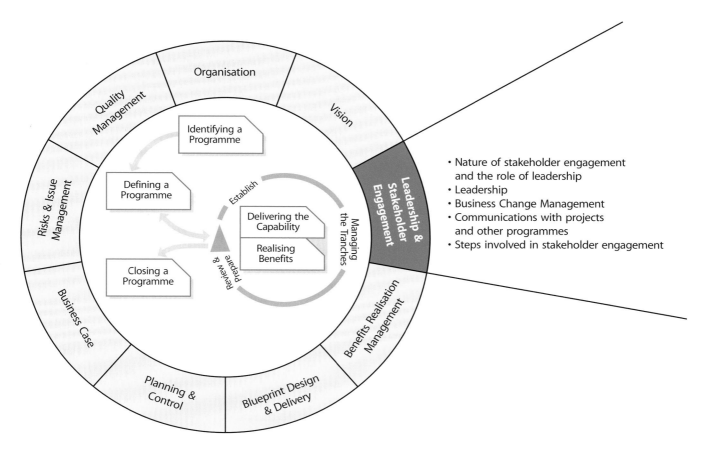

- Nature of stakeholder engagement and the role of leadership
- Leadership
- Business Change Management
- Communications with projects and other programmes
- Steps involved in stakeholder engagement

6.1 INTRODUCTION

A stakeholder is an individual or group that has an interest in the programme, its outcomes or benefits/dis-benefits. One key aspect of the 'Leading change' programme management Principle (paragraph 2.2.2) is that it actively engages stakeholders:

- Leaders use the programme Vision Statement to influence and persuade stakeholders to commit to the beneficial future
- Business Change Managers engage their operational stakeholders, leading them through the uncertainty of transition to the new ways of working
- A focus on benefits (see paragraph 2.2.4) recognises that a 'benefit' is only such when it is perceived to be advantageous by one or more stakeholders. In a community of different interests and attitudes the leader must engage stakeholders so that benefits are identified, clearly communicated and understood, owned, and realised, as well reducing the threats to realising them (see Figure 7.10)

- Some stakeholders will be identified as resources within the delivery of the new capability, some with unique or scarce skills and competencies.

How a programme engages its stakeholders is crucial to its success.

There are many illustrations of programmes that fail adequately to engage certain stakeholders, and risk overall failure. This underlines the importance of this Governance Theme. For example, a multi-agency programme that was restructuring a significant part of public service was, in most respects, well led and well managed. However, the leaders of the programme failed to engage a key group of stakeholders in one organisation; consequently these stakeholders failed to own the realisation of a stream of benefits for that part of the organisation. The result was that the programme significantly underperformed, realising fewer benefits than if these stakeholders had been committed to the programme and its vision.

6.2 NATURE OF STAKEHOLDER ENGAGEMENT AND THE ROLE OF LEADERSHIP

Managers sometimes forget the obvious: stakeholders are people with feelings, perceptions, desires and influence. In any transformational change, there will be those who:

- Support or oppose it
- End up gaining or losing when benefits are realised (see Figure 7.10, 'Benefits distribution matrix of stakeholders')
- See only a threat, perhaps convinced that they will lose despite all evidence to the contrary
- Are inherently indifferent to the change. They may become helpful or unhelpful, depending on how they themselves are managed and influenced
- May become either supporters or blockers to the realisation of these benefits depending on how and to what level they are engaged.

Leadership is part of how stakeholders are engaged. Programme managers need to think of Stakeholder Engagement not just as a system of tasks and managing **things**, but also as a way of achieving influence and positive outcomes through effective management of relationships.

Strong leaders understand that people need to be engaged as more than resources to be used or obstacles to be removed. This will include considering matters of internal politics, and individual emotions and motivations.

Good leaders take seriously the attitudes and agendas of individuals. They need to understand the challenges transformational change bring for people. Such leaders are likely to be more successful in influencing people around them, and in turning stakeholders from blockers into advocates.

One mechanism some programme leaders employ to influence key stakeholders is to conduct early 'visioning' workshops to help draft the programme Vision Statement (see Chapter 5, 'Governance Theme: Vision'). Such a workshop is an opportunity:

- To engage the right stakeholders early (the 'Leading change' Principle), even including clients and suppliers
- For leadership to explore and define what might be called the 'do-nothing vision'.

The do-nothing vision allows the leaders to create and foster the belief in the need for change: 'We can't stay where we are because this is what will come about ...'. This is also sometimes known as the 'burning platform' or 'burning bridge', on the premise that you can't stay on either and you have to jump from the platform or cross over the bridge. Skilful leaders, effectively using communications, stories, visions and metaphors, manage perceptions of the:

- Current reality
- Beneficial future
- Tension between the two

to build and maintain the organisational impetus and commitment to change. The do-nothing vision is often a useful way of showing potential blockers the possible negative impact of their actions, and bring them round to support the change.

6.3 LEADERSHIP

Understanding the essential nature of Leadership is helped by contrasting it with that of management, as shown in Table 6.1.

This distinction does not mean that managers cannot be leaders. People occupying roles in the programme's

Table 6.1 Leadership and management

Leadership is ...	Management is ...
Particularly required in a context of change. It clarifies the 'as is', the vision of the future, and thrives in the tension between the two	Always required, particularly in business-as-usual contexts, and focuses more on evolutionary or continual improvement
Inclined to clarify the 'what' and the 'why'	Focuses on the 'how' and the 'when'
More concerned with direction, effectiveness and purpose	Concerned with speed, efficiency and quality
Most effective when influencing people by communicating in face-to-face situations	Most effective when controlling tasks against specifications or plans
Focused on meaning, purpose and realised value	Focused on tasks, delivery and process

management team need to display both sets of competencies and outlooks. Nor does it mean that leadership is exclusive to the Senior Responsible Owner (SRO) and the Sponsoring Group. A best practice programme evidences dispersed leadership: at some time or other, all roles in the management team must display leadership qualities. However, the SRO, the Sponsoring Group and Programme Board roles generally need to display leadership on a more continual basis.

Research carried out at the Cranfield School of Management using a sample of 15 strategic programmes across seven industry sectors revealed multiple attributes of programme management work each conceived by individual Programme Managers at one of four different levels, or 'mindsets'. The research showed that the levels were cumulative: managers with a higher-level mindset could also conceive their work in terms of the lower levels, enabling them to move between levels as appropriate to a given situation. Managers with a lower-level mindset could only see that lower level.

Table 6.2 lists the 17 key behavioural attributes of programme management work identified in the Cranfield research, with a summary description of the conception for each attribute found at either end of the scale (Levels 1 and 4). It is clear that the conceptual agility of managers with a Level 4 conception was linked to higher leadership traits than lower levels. However, an individual's level of conception did not always correlate with their level of seniority within programme governance. For example, a Programme Manager might be alert to wider stakeholder issues, but their SRO might not, thus inhibiting the effectiveness of that Programme Manager. Overall the Principle of 'Leading change' (paragraph 2.2.2), in particular the ability to live with uncertainty, was found to be a key characteristic of managers able to operate at the higher levels.

6.4 BUSINESS CHANGE MANAGEMENT

Business Change Management considers how change happens in its broadest sense, within individuals, within teams and within the organisation, and how people can be led through such change.

A programme is always commissioned in a wider context of change. At this macro level of viewing change a programme may be seen as a part of a larger strategic change initiative or part of a corporate portfolio of change.

At a micro level each individual is affected by the programme and goes through their own cycle of change as they transition from the old way of doing things to the new.

Change is ubiquitous and iterative: it is often best represented as a circular process rather than linear. There are several well-established change management models, each one with merit. Figure 6.1 shows one such model,

Table 6.2 Conceptions of programme management

Attributes	Cumulative conceptions of programme management	
	Level 1	**Level 4**
Relationship between self and work		
Granularity of focus	Plans in detail	Selects detail with external & future focus
Emotional attachment	Emotionally detached, factual	Committed to outcomes
Disposition for action	Procedural trouble-shooter	Intuitively reconfigures & makes the rules
Approach to role plurality	Focused, single role	Adopts multiple viewpoints
Relationship between self and others		
Relationship with team	Supportive & responsive	Confidence-inspiring leader, able to influence behaviour
Approach to conflict & divergence	By seeking procedures	Facilitates towards creative solutions
Education & support	Assists with problem solving	Coaches to enable influence
Use of questions	Own clarification	To challenge, encourage creative thinking and reframe purpose
Expectations of others	Contracted effort	Exploits and extends individuals' talents
Relationship with programme environment		
Adaptive intent	Does what worked in the past	Adapts self and environment to suit purpose
Awareness of organisational capabilities	Assumes departments can deliver	Awareness of the shortcomings; prepared to go outside
Approach to risk	Procedural. Manage out internal risks	Ready for the consequences of failure
Approach to face-to-face communications	Reports facts in consistent style	Sells vision with cultural sensitivity
Approach to governance	Reports in hierarchy	Embeds programme structure within business
Attitude to Boundary	Follows change control	Shapes to meet emerging and changing needs
Attitude to time	Schedule driven; reschedule when necessary	Conscious of issues of timeliness and maturity
Attitude to funding	Budget driven	Aware of budget uncertainties: creates budget from achievement

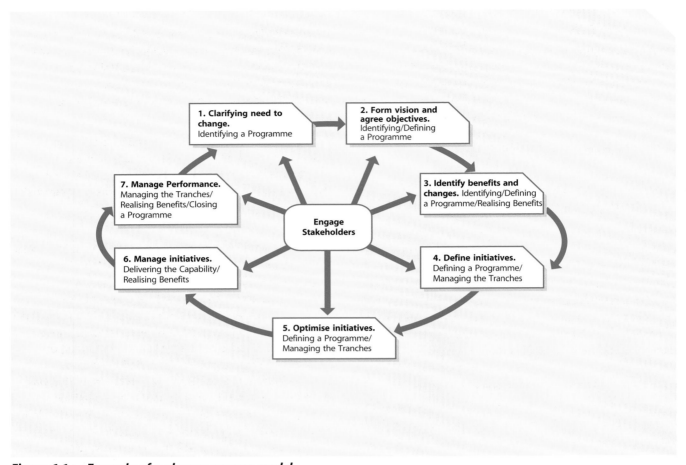

1. Clarifying need to change. Identifying a Programme

2. Form vision and agree objectives. Identifying/Defining a Programme

7. Manage Performance. Managing the Tranches/ Realising Benefits/Closing a Programme

Engage Stakeholders

3. Identify benefits and changes. Identifying/Defining a Programme/Realising Benefits

6. Manage initiatives. Delivering the Capability/ Realising Benefits

4. Define initiatives. Defining a Programme/ Managing the Tranches

5. Optimise initiatives. Defining a Programme/ Managing the Tranches

Figure 6.1   Example of a change process model

with parts of the Transformational Flow mapped onto each step.

Business Change Management and ensuring organisational commitment to change should be a dominant programme concern and focus of action for the management team. In response to this, a Business Change Manager must be effective in leading an operational team through a transition cycle (paragraph 7.11) that embeds new working practices.

6.5   COMMUNICATIONS WITH THE PROJECTS AND OTHER PROGRAMMES

Whilst projects within the programme will need to communicate with their own stakeholders, the programme will need to control this to ensure that the communications are consistent, clear, timely and accurate.

A good place to start is with some general stance or policy within the Stakeholder Engagement Strategy (Figure 6.2, Step 3). Some typical example solutions are:

■ A general guideline, briefed to the projects through the Programme Office and the Programme Manager, that planned, routine communications are first reviewed by the Programme Office
■ Certain identified stakeholders are always referred to the SRO or to the Programme Manager, or to the person in the programme specifically responsible for maintaining the relationships with these stakeholders
■ Certain stakeholders may have nominated 'custodians' through which all communications are channelled
■ Certain topic areas identified that are sensitive enough always to be referred up to the programme for communication, e.g. industrial relations
■ Regular communications briefings to constituent projects so that they stay on message (e.g. the provision of presentation packs).

Whatever the approaches taken, care should be taken to allow the projects to manage their own communications, whenever this is reasonable. Too much control of communications by the programme can easily disempower the projects as well as generating new sources of discontent from stakeholders within the projects themselves.

Keeping communications consistent across other programmes is a necessity in a corporate portfolio environment, and also in multi-agency programmes driven by external factors (e.g. educational, health, environmental, transport and other services driven by legislative reform). Failure to achieve coherence risks confusion and a lack of stakeholder confidence and buy-in.

6.6 STEPS INVOLVED IN STAKEHOLDER ENGAGEMENT

Programmes that stress the **management** of stakeholders can lapse into relying on planned communications that are little more than a task list with a bias toward outbound information. This does not sufficiently engage stakeholders, who generally do not appreciate being **managed**. In such an approach, the management is more of perceptions, objections, messages and communications rather than of the stakeholders themselves. As stakeholders are people, attempting to manage them from a purely mechanistic mindset is unlikely to work.

Figure 6.2 illustrates the Stakeholder Engagement Process that underpins the MSP Stakeholder Engagement Strategy. Each step in this process is described in the following six sub-sections.

6.6.1 Identifying stakeholders

Stakeholder Engagement begins with identifying all the stakeholders involved in or affected by the programme and its outcomes. As the programme's Vision Statement and Blueprint are developed, these documents provide the basis for identifying further stakeholders and what outcomes they want.

During the life of the programme, stakeholders will change. Some stakeholders will participate in the programme in advisory or assurance roles; others will be important in assessing the realisation of the programme's benefits; others will have an audit or assurance perspective.

Programmes are likely to have large numbers of individual stakeholders. It can therefore be useful to organise the programme's stakeholders by category, such as: users/beneficiaries; governance (management boards, steering groups, audit); influencers (e.g. trade unions, the media); providers (suppliers, business partners). These high-level categories can be broken down further, or alternative groupings can be identified in order to organise communication by shared interests. In this way, key messages can be targeted at and consultations undertaken with the relevant people. Groupings should be practically identifiable rather than abstract; for example, 'employees based in the Dublin office' is a readily identifiable group, whereas 'members of the public who

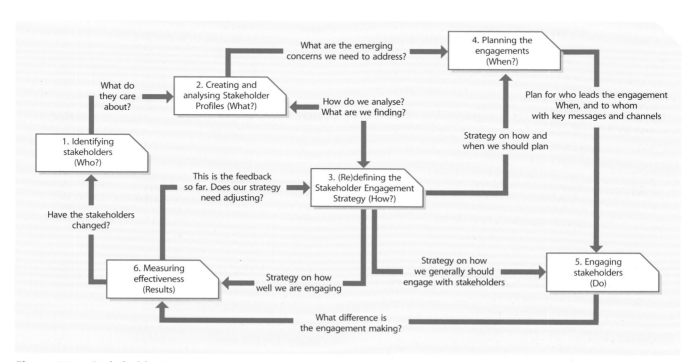

Figure 6.2   Stakeholder Engagement Process

support human rights' is not. This exercise may identify the same individuals in different categories and groupings, but it is often a useful way of differentiating between stakeholders with multiple interests.

6.6.2 Creating and analysing Stakeholder Profiles

Identifying stakeholders is only the first step. Analysis means gaining an understanding of the:

- Influences, interests and attitudes of the stakeholders towards the programme's outcomes
- Importance and power of each stakeholder.

Gathering this information together into a single source can reveal important insights about a programme's stakeholders.

Stakeholder Map

Such a document will contain a list and analyses of stakeholders. This will show the different interest areas in the programme. For example, some stakeholders will be concerned with how the programme will affect their working environment while others will be concerned about how the programme will change the way customers are handled. The Stakeholder Map in Figure 6.3 compares the various stakeholders against their interests in a programme dealing with urban regeneration following the construction of an international sports complex.

Because of the evolving and potentially volatile nature of a programme, the Stakeholder Map should be regularly revisited and checked to see whether other stakeholders have now appeared, new interests have emerged and whether earlier assessments of stakeholders should now be changed. As with all documents in MSP, the objective is not creating the map, but using it to inform decisions, so revising it throughout the programme is key to ensuring its maximum contribution.

Further analysis

Stakeholders' influence and interests, whether rational and justifiable or emotional and unfounded, must all be taken into account. They will affect the business change process and hence the programme. Fears may be unfounded or perceptions mistaken, but must be addressed.

It is useful to analyse the significance and potential influence of each stakeholder against their areas of interest. This analysis will also help:

- Prioritise stakeholder engagement
- Focus programme resources to contribute the most towards successful outcomes
- Ensure communication channels are well exploited
- Align message content, media, frequency of engagement and level of detail to meet the relevant needs of the stakeholders.

Interest Areas: / Stakeholders	Sports Facilities	Transport Infrastructure	Public Transport Service	City Image/ Prestige	Local Economy	Housing	Hotel Accommodation	Local Environment	City Taxes
Planning Department		U			U	U		U	
City Mayor	U	U	U	U	U	U		U	U
City Government	U	U	U	U	U	U	U	U	U
Transport Department		U	U		U				
Sports Minister	U	U	U	U			U	U	
National Government	U	U	U	U	U	U	U	U	U
Local Residents	U	U	U		U	U		U	U
National Sports Council	U						U	U	
Tourists	U	U	U	U			U	U	
Athletes	U			U			U		
Rail Company		U	U		U				
Local Businesses	U	U	U	U	U	U		U	U

Figure 6.3   *Example Stakeholder Map of a sports-complex programme*

The communications channels may need to be worked to engage stakeholders who cannot be engaged directly by the programme. In such cases working through partners, industry groups, volunteer organisations etc. may be required.

One of several techniques for analysing stakeholders is to consider each stakeholder in terms of their influence on the programme and their potential interest in the programme outcomes and plot these on a matrix. The level of their importance to the programme and its impact on them will determine the level and type of Stakeholder Engagement the programme should undertake with them. For example, in the programme to exploit an international sports complex illustrated in Figure 6.4, the sports minister will have **high** importance to the programme, and also **high** influence upon it and so is a **key player** and should be treated accordingly, whereas the local residents, despite having a similarly high interest in the legacy of the sports complex, don't have so much direct influence on the programme or its outcomes; hence the primary mode of engagement is active consultation.

As stakeholders may move on the matrix as the programme progresses and capabilities are delivered, it is important to rework the stakeholder analysis regularly. For example in Figure 6.4 the importance of engaging the tourists towards the latter stages will become more crucial to the success of the main event being staged in the complex and they should therefore be moved towards **maintain interest** (or higher) in the matrix.

Another kind of analysis examines stakeholder attitude. The attitude of a stakeholder towards the programme might be negative. The aim of the targeted elements of the Programme Communications Plan (Step 4) might well be to influence that stakeholder to an at least neutral position.

The Stakeholder Map can be enriched and developed further such that power, strength of interest and attitude values from the analysis can be included in each cell, or against each stakeholder row.

Collectively, all the identification and analysis information, in the form of a Stakeholder Map, an influence/interest matrix or any kind of similar analysis, is gathered together into the Stakeholder Profiles document.

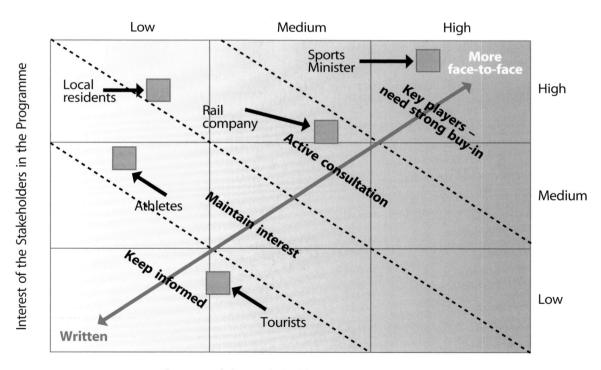

Figure 6.4   Influence/interest matrix of a sports-complex programme

6.6.3 (Re-)Defining the Stakeholder Engagement Strategy (How?)

The key question a Stakeholder Engagement Strategy answers is: 'How will the programme effectively engage with the stakeholders?' The programme management team must specify:

- The key messages
- Who takes on particular roles
- How stakeholders will be identified, categorised and grouped
- Who is responsible for particular stakeholders or groups of stakeholders
- How the interfaces between the programme and its projects' stakeholders will be managed
- How feedback and dialogue will be managed

so that the engagements always support consistent and cohesive communications. See Appendix A, 'Programme information', for details on the content of the Stakeholder Engagement Strategy.

Programme management teams not being physically co-located increases the risk of uncoordinated and inconsistent engagement with particular stakeholders. Some stakeholders are likely to exploit any apparent inconsistencies to support their own agendas. Geographically dispersed teams will find that they acquire greater control and influence through employing a rigorous Stakeholder Engagement Strategy.

Implementing the Stakeholder Engagement Strategy means considering a range of factors including:

- The scale of cultural, organisational or societal change
- Managing expectations over an extended period
- Adequate resource and energy to ensure:
  - Business ownership of the overall programme
  - Stakeholder buy-in and involvement
  - PR, marketing and communications expertise to support the programme
  - Clarity and consistency of messages and benefits
- Maintaining documents such as the Programme Communications Plan and Stakeholder Profiles as valid tools for engaging stakeholders.

For further information about the contents, see Appendix A, 'Programme information'.

The programme management team should actively adjust and redefine the Stakeholder Engagement Strategy. The Programme Office will often be called upon to conduct such reviews or to give a view on who is best equipped to do so. Independent PR and communications specialists can make an important contribution at such reviews.

6.6.4 Planning the engagements (When?)

Communications are best planned after defining how the programme will engage the different stakeholders as reflected in the Stakeholder Engagement Strategy.

Engagement is more active and embracing than communication. It covers including stakeholders in decision-making and implementation, as well as consulting with them and informing them. And communication is central to all of these and any change process.

The greater the change, the greater the need for clear communication about the reasons and rationale behind it, the benefits expected, the plans for its implementation and its proposed effects.

The objectives of the communications process are to:

- Keep awareness and commitment high
- Ensure that expectations do not drift out of line with what will be delivered
- Explain what changes will be made and when
- Describe the desired future end state (see the 'Envisioning and communicating a better future' principle in paragraph 2.2.3).

Successful communications will be judged on the ability to meet these objectives.

> **Tip**
>
> Successful communications are based on four core elements:
>
> - Message clarity and consistency: ensure relevance and recognition, and engender trust
> - Stakeholder identification and analysis: send the right message to the right audience
> - A system of collection: obtain feedback and assess the effectiveness of the communications process
> - A system of message delivery: get the right messages to the right stakeholders in a timely and effective way.

Messages must be consistent. Leaders undermine their own credibility and risk hesitancy among stakeholders with inconsistent messages.

Messages should be few in number, simple, brief and derived from the programme's objectives. It is useful to establish key phrases ('touchstone statements', 'sound bites' or 'word bites' are alternative terms) as the foundation for more complex communications and then to repeat these throughout the programme. This also ensures the programme and its organisation are seen to be speaking with one voice.

Many organisations have access to public relations and communications specialists. People with such skills should be used wherever possible to help shape the programme communications.

Programme Communications Plan

The Programme Communications Plan describes what will be communicated, how it will be communicated, by when, and by whom, during the programme. It should be defined and implemented as early as possible and then maintained throughout the programme.

Using information from the Stakeholder Profiles, the Programme Communications Plan should be designed to:

- Raise awareness amongst all stakeholders of the benefits and impact of the planned outcomes.
- Gain commitment from stakeholders in the target business area(s) to the changes being introduced – thus ensuring the long-term success of the improvements.
- Keep all stakeholders in the target business area(s) informed of progress before, during and after implementation or delivery of programme outcomes.
- Promote key messages from the programme.
- Demonstrate a commitment to meeting the requirements of those sponsoring the programme (the Sponsoring Group).
- Make communications truly two-way (i.e. A dialogue, not a broadcast) by actively encouraging stakeholders to provide feedback and ensuring they are informed about the use of their feedback to influence the programme. All types of feedback should be expected and responses to it carefully considered. Feedback may sometimes be negative, impractical or harshly critical.
- Ensure all those responsible for projects have an understanding of the scope, nature and outcomes of the programme.
- Promote outcomes to maximise the benefits obtained from the new business operations.

A key objective is to communicate early successes (sometimes referred to as 'quick wins') to those directly concerned with the business operation and to other key audiences, especially where rapid progress in realising benefits needs to be seen. The aim is to secure commitment and build momentum.

The Programme Communications Plan should answer the following questions:

- What are the objectives of each communication?
- What are the key messages?
- Who are the stakeholders the communications are trying to reach?
- What objections is the stakeholder likely to have?

- What are the ways we can manage these objections?
- What information will be communicated and by whom?
- When will information be disseminated and what are the relevant timings?
- How much information will be provided and to what level of detail?
- What mechanisms will be used to disseminate information?
- How will feedback be encouraged; what will be done as a result of feedback?
- How will feedback be recorded, reviewed and resolved?

The answers to these questions may be different for each stakeholder. The Stakeholder Map, developed during analysis, can also be extended to list the specific communications activities for each stakeholder group.

Since the early tranches of some programmes may be highly exploratory and speculative, and the programme may be liable to change, the Programme Communications Plan is likely to be frequently revised.

NB – the part of the Programme Communications Plan covering how to manage anticipated objections is not normally made public. For further information about the Programme Communications Plan, see Appendix A: 'Programme information'.

Communications channels

Communication channels should be established to ensure stakeholders' expectations of the programme are managed and maintained throughout the programme's life.

The channels used for communications may be a mixture of participative approaches, for example seminars or workshops, and non-participative media, for example announcements or newsletters. The effectiveness of each channel should be monitored as the programme progresses. Changes should be made to cater for the evolving requirements of the stakeholders, as their knowledge increases and demand for information grows. Some possible channel options are summarised in Table 6.3.

Table 6.3 Communication channels

Channel	Purpose and benefits
Seminars, workshops, video conferences and live webcasts	Powerful tools for engagement with specific groups of stakeholders. A key benefit is that they provide the programme management team with an opportunity for direct contact with stakeholders and for obtaining first-hand feedback on issues directly affecting them
Café conversations	These are unstructured meetings where a broad issue is aired with those stakeholders who are concerned enough to attend. Such meetings are useful means of gaining information as well as engaging stakeholders early in the process, helping to give them a sense of ownership in the change that is still emerging.
Press/media packs and briefings	The press and media are vehicles for getting messages about the programme to an external audience and for providing the programme team with confirmation that their work is significant and important.
Bulletins, briefings, announcements, press releases, blogs (electronic- or paper-based)	There are two types: (1) general information about the programme for all audiences and (2) specific information relevant to one or more stakeholder groups. General information should provide an update on the programme, addressing issues of concern to all stakeholders, such as overall progress or any changes to the programme objectives. The more specific information should provide the particular stakeholder(s) with information relating to their own issues. Such may be distributed via intranet home pages, websites or e-mail. However, it is important to make sure that stakeholders have access to e-mail or the home pages, are aware of their existence and want to visit them. In addition to electronic media, it is often useful and more convenient to distribute in paper form, such as newsletters. Frequently asked questions (FAQs), together with appropriate responses, are often included.
Site exhibitions	Static or rolling displays are useful in providing a continuing presence and awareness within the organisation about the programme.
Video, CD, DVD and podcasts	CDs are useful for presenting large amounts of information about the programme by enabling individuals to search for information relevant to their particular interests. Video films and DVDs, when targeted appropriately, are a cost-effective means of communication to large, widely dispersed audiences and can be used to provide updates on progress and for selling the key programme messages in a visually appealing and effective manner. Video, DVDs and podcasts circulated over a restricted network have the added advantage of conveying tacit aspects of the personalities and passions of leaders in the programme, in a way that purely written media rarely achieve.

6.6.5 Engaging stakeholders (Do)

The first two steps in stakeholder engagement – identifying and analysing – engage stakeholders to some degree. Identification may well involve stakeholders in early workshops. In analysis the simplest and often most effective method of analysis is to ask the stakeholder and listen: 'First seek to understand, then to be understood.'

In terms of the concepts presented in Table 6.3, able Programme Managers will always recognise the need for more subtle and informal means of communication. The programme management team will often need to influence, lobby, cajole, manipulate, co-opt, flatter and apply pressure to stakeholders in order to maintain momentum and keep the programme on track.

6.6.6 Measuring effectiveness (Results)

It is easy for the programme management team to believe its own myths, such as:

- 'Everybody who needs to know, knows'
- 'People are generally positive towards the change, and if they are not, they soon will be when they see the benefits being realised.'

Simple methods of checking perceptions include sampling stakeholder communities. One simple question early in the programme might be 'What is the programme's Vision?'.

Communications specialists agree that people do not retain information until they have heard it several times. Feedback will reveal under-communication or mis-communication.

Good Programme Managers will not wait for the end-of-tranche reviews or an external audit to find out how effective the programme's stakeholder engagement is. They make it their business to gain this evidence in person.

An independent review of stakeholder perceptions can provide a valid sense check on programme assumptions about stakeholder perceptions and commitment, and could be included as part of a Programme Health Check.

6.7 ROLES AND RESPONSIBILITIES

Table 6.4 shows the roles and responsibilities involved in leadership and stakeholder engagement.

Table 6.4 Leadership and stakeholder engagement: roles and responsibilities

Role	Responsibilities
Senior Responsible Owner	Engaging key stakeholders early and at appropriate milestones throughout the programme
	Managing relationship with key stakeholders, including the Sponsoring Group
	Showing visible leadership at key communications events
	Being accountable for the creation, execution and maintenance of the overall Stakeholder Engagement Strategy.
Sponsoring Group	Demonstrating visible commitment and support to the programme at key events
	Anticipating and resolving stakeholder issues in their own areas of business governance that might affect the programme
	Briefing the SRO on programme-wide stakeholder issues and on new or changing external business drivers.
Programme Board	Supporting the SRO and taking specific ownership for stakeholder engagement in each member's own organisation or area of the organisation
	Reviewing and approval of Stakeholder Engagement Strategy and Programme Communications Plan.
Programme Manager	Developing and implementing the Stakeholder Engagement Strategy, that is, the day-to-day execution of the whole stakeholder engagement process
	Developing and maintaining of the Stakeholder Profiles
	Controlling and aligning project communications activities
	Developing, implementing and updating of the Programme Communications Plan. Much of the proactive day-to-day stakeholder engagement will be done through the Programme Manager role.
Business Change Manager(s)	Engaging and leading those operating new working practices through the transition, generating confidence and buy-in from those involved. Active stakeholder engagement is a major part of discharging this role.
	Alerting the Programme Manager to the net winners and losers (if any) in their area of change
	Briefing and liaising with the Change Team
	Communicating with affected stakeholders to identify new benefits and improved ways of realising benefits
	Making key communications to their business operations.
Programme Office	Maintaining the information relating to the stakeholders
	Facilitating activities specified in the Programme Communications Plan:
	■ Being called upon to provide assurance, conduct reviews and measure effectiveness of the stakeholder engagement ■ Reviewing and authorising project communications.

Benefits Realisation
Management

7

7 Benefits Realisation Management

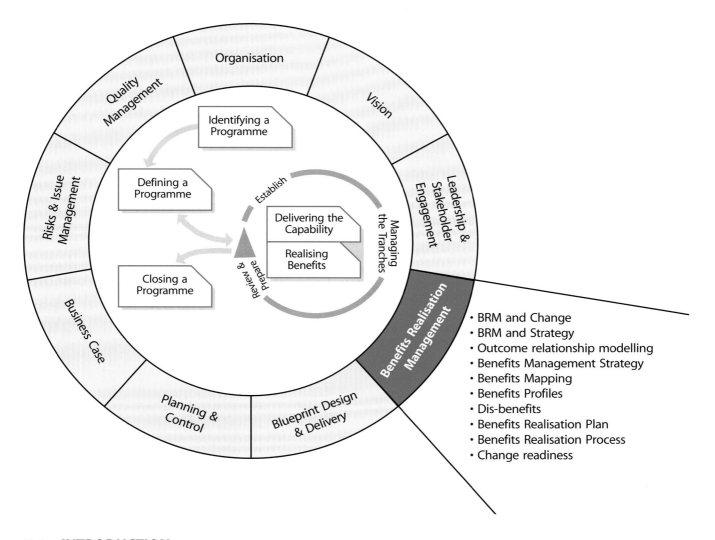

- BRM and Change
- BRM and Strategy
- Outcome relationship modelling
- Benefits Management Strategy
- Benefits Mapping
- Benefits Profiles
- Dis-benefits
- Benefits Realisation Plan
- Benefits Realisation Process
- Change readiness

7.1 INTRODUCTION

A benefit is the measurable improvement resulting from an outcome which is perceived as an advantage by a stakeholder. Benefits are anticipated when a change is conceived.

7.1.1 Objectives of Benefits Realisation Management

The objectives of Benefits Realisation Management are to:

- Ensure benefits are identified and defined clearly at the outset, and linked to strategic outcomes
- Ensure business areas are committed to realising their defined benefits with ownership and responsibility for adding value (e.g. by identifying opportunities for more or different benefits) through the realisation process

- Drive the process of realising benefits, including benefit measurement, tracking and recording benefits (and other notable achievements) as they are realised
- Use the defined, expected benefits as a roadmap for the programme, providing a focus for delivering change
- Provide alignment and clear links between the programme (its vision and desired benefits) and the strategic objectives of the organisation(s) involved.

Undertaking Benefits Realisation Management allows delivery against the programme management principle – 'Focusing on the benefits and threats to them' (paragraph 2.2.4). For this reason, Benefits Realisation Management drives the other Governance Themes and major elements in the programme as shown in Figure 7.1.

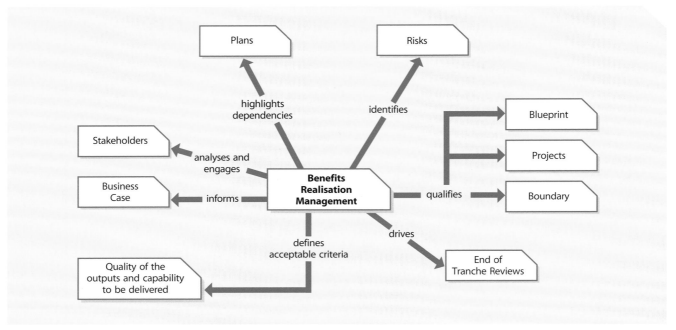

Figure 7.1   Benefits Realisation Management as the key driver

Given its centrality to the programme, it is not surprising that the scope of Benefits Realisation Management covers:

- Managing the risks and issues that may impact on realising benefits
- Confirming the alignment and integrity of the Blueprint against the projects, activities and associated business changes needed to deliver the new capabilities and benefits
- Providing a focal point at end-of-tranche reviews for adjustments to governance (and programme shape and direction) throughout the programme
- Defining what a fit-for-purpose capability and the critical quality-checking mechanisms throughout the programme would be
- Setting the aggregate of achieved benefits, expected benefits, costs-to-date and expected cost against the business case; providing a crucial test of the ongoing viability of the programme
- Being a focus for continual analysis of, and engagement with, stakeholders
- Providing the Benefits Realisation Plan, which should be one of the main foundations for planning the programme.

7.2   BENEFITS RELATIONSHIP MANAGEMENT AND CHANGE

MSP is designed for transformational change (e.g. a retailer who chooses to abandon physical outlets and to retail solely through an online presence) rather than incremental changes within an existing enterprise model (e.g. improving another similar product or service offering). (See the 'Envisioning and communicating a better future' principle in paragraph 2.2.3.)

Figure 7.2 shows a simple view of the cause and effect of the programme delivering change. The organisational changes – sometimes enabled by project outputs, sometimes initiated on their own – result in desired outcomes. A benefit is the measurable improvement from such an outcome. In turn, these benefits should contribute, directly or indirectly, towards one or more of the strategic objectives of the organisation.

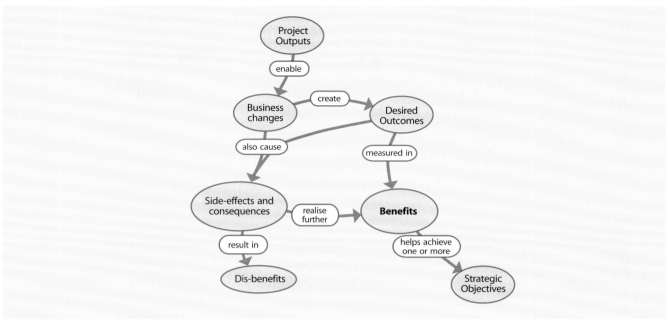

Figure 7.2 Path to benefit realisation and strategic objectives

Changes cause side-effects and consequences, often leading to dis-benefits – outcomes perceived as a disadvantage by one or more stakeholders. Side-effects and consequences may also lead to opportunities for realising additional benefits. Benefits Realisation Management covers managing all of these.

Figure 7.3 illustrates how outputs from projects together with associated organisational changes will produce outcomes, but changes alone will not produce measured improvements (benefits). Realising benefits requires active, focused management throughout the change process. Identifying, measuring, tracking and reporting on benefits are fundamental activities of successful programme management. An 'end benefit' is a benefit that directly contributes to achieving a strategic objective. See also Table 7.1.

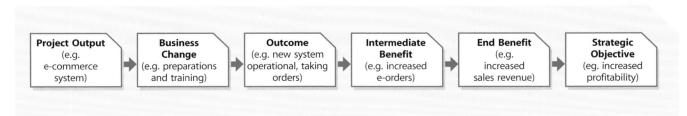

Figure 7.3 Example of a project output to strategic objective chain

Table 7.1   Differences between outputs, outcomes and benefits

Project outputs/capability →	Outcome →	Benefit
Enables a new outcome in part of the operational organisation	Is the desired operational result	Is the measurement of an outcome or a part of an outcome. An end benefit is a direct contribution to a strategic objective
Describes a feature	Describes part or new operational state	Describes an advantage accruing from the outcome
Answers at least in part the fundamental question: What new or different things will we need to realise beneficial change?	Answers the questions: What is the desired operational state of the organisation using these new things?	Answers the question of what a project delivers: Why is this required?
An example of an output: a new hospital building	An example of an outcome: an additional hospital is now fully operational and servicing regional demand for hospital care thereby reducing waiting lists	An example of a benefit from this outcome might be: reduced waiting times for hip operations to an average of three weeks from ten weeks
Another example of an output: an e-commerce system	An example of an outcome from this output: ability to process, fulfil and charge for web-based orders	An example of a benefit from this: increased sales revenues of x%

It is important to note that Benefits Realisation Management may well continue beyond the end of the programme. This is because:

- Benefits may occur after the programme has been completed
- Other benefits may have to be realised, but will need to be owned and managed to pre-agreed target levels that are yet to be achieved.

A degree of post-delivery support by the programme is often required to help business operations take full advantage of the new capability or service delivered. This could be provided by a permanent Benefits Realisation Manager, who manages the organisation's Benefits Realisation Management regime, providing scrutiny and embedded support and coordination across the programmes (see Table 7.4).

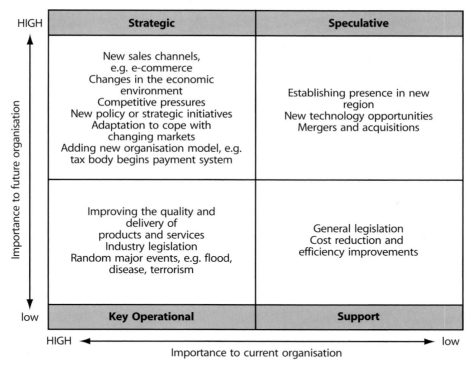

Figure 7.4   Mapping of organisational drivers and their change portfolio implications

7.3   BENEFITS REALISATION MANAGEMENT AND STRATEGY

There will be many drivers for change acting on the organisation (see Appendix B: 'Adopting MSP'). Such drivers vary in nature and urgency. There will also be drivers that resist change and encourage inertia, making progress more difficult. The need for change must be set against the needs of the current environment. Hence the organisation's strategy provides the context and balance for planning, running and completing change programme sets.

Figure 7.4 sets the scale of future importance from strategic (top) to tactical (bottom) against the level of current importance (high to the left, low to the right).

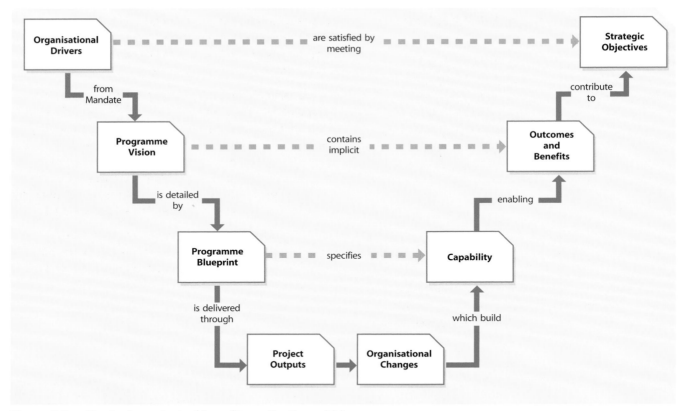

Figure 7.5 *Strategic context of benefits realisation within a programme*

Plotting current and potential change activities using such a grid can help the organisation build a portfolio of programmes and projects (often called the corporate portfolio) that meets its appetite across a range of dimensions (e.g. risk, rate of change, spend, regulation, commitment to provide to current customer and stakeholders, etc.).

The intended programme benefits should be clearly linked to the strategic objectives that satisfy the original organisational drivers (Figure 7.5). This is often done by describing strategic objectives and end benefits in terms of key performance indicators (KPIs). When using KPIs in this way note that:

■ Some KPIs may not be suitable for measuring intermediate or end benefits
■ Some KPIs may need to be changed as a result of operational changes (the programme may need to define new KPIs and provide processes and tools to support them)
■ Current KPIs may need to be supplemented by other measures to assess the benefits realised

■ Performance criteria from relevant or affected contracts, service level agreements, compliance targets etc. should be reviewed to ensure change congruence (e.g. any penalties that might be incurred because of deterioration in performance)
■ Some measures may be subject to fluctuations from normal process variation or seasonal trends. It is important this is understood and reflected in plans.

7.4 USING AN OUTCOME RELATIONSHIP MODEL

In some situations, particularly within emergent programmes, the detailed understanding of potential outcomes cannot be completed before the programme gets under way. The programme team should work with the strategy or policy teams to develop the required level of detail. One approach for doing this is to build a model of the outcomes and consider how these interrelate and affect the environment in which they will operate.

The Outcome Relationship Model is a relational mapping technique where there is no attempt at first to categorise entities (as enablers, benefits, dis-benefits, business change or strategic objectives) or to infer direct cause-and-effect relationships between the entities. These hard attributions are left until later. The technique engages the team in systems-thinking, i.e. to consider non-linear, contributory and connecting relationships. In the early stages of

business case building this can greatly help in benefit identification, and also in defining the programme's boundary with a full understanding of the contributors and enablers for benefits delivery.

For example, in Figure 7.6 we can identify several links where outcomes could reinforce and amplify each other (e.g. 'Increased attraction to tourists' leads to 'More day visitors', which in turn leads to 'Increased revenues from tourism', leading to 'Increased capital for further development', leading to 'Additional attractions', which further raises the attractiveness to tourists of this inner city area. Likewise, spirals of dis-benefit can be identified.

Some apparent benefits may be quite intangible ('Increased Attraction to Tourists') but we have identified other benefits that can measure it by proxy ('More day visitors').

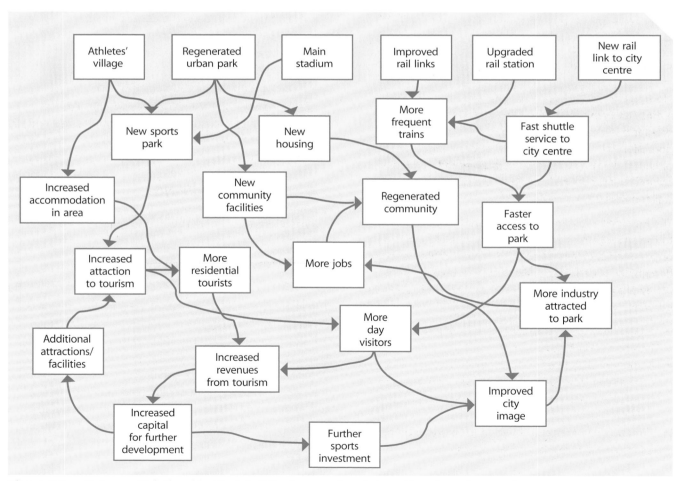

Figure 7.6   Outcome Relationship Model of the legacy of an international sports complex

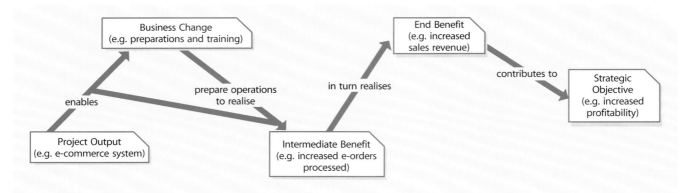

Figure 7.7   Chain of benefits from output to objective

7.5 BENEFITS MANAGEMENT STRATEGY

The Benefits Management Strategy provides the programme with a framework for realising benefits. It sets out the rules of engagement on how to identify, map, monitor and review the benefits realisation process.

The Benefits Management Strategy defines how:

- Benefits will be quantified and measured
- Linkages between benefits and outputs, and between one benefit and another, should be mapped and tracked
- Benefits realisation will be achieved.

The Benefits Management Strategy is a key component of the programme's governance. It should specify how the Benefits Map maps against the Blueprint, ensuring benefits are matched to the delivery of capabilities. For further details on the content of a Benefits Management Strategy and Benefits Map, see Appendix A: 'Programme information'.

Where the owners of programme benefits are widely spread across the organisation(s) and the **how to** of realisation is complex, a clear and robust Benefits Management Strategy is required. Without such a strategy, people may be measuring the same benefit with different measures and reporting at different frequencies.

Benefits Management Strategy checklist

When the Benefits Management Strategy has been developed, the following additional checks can be helpful to ensure it is complete:

- Has the level of granularity for the Benefits Realisation Plan been defined?
- Have the relevant stakeholders been sufficiently engaged with the development of the strategy?
- Does the organisation have the necessary capabilities and capacity to deliver the strategy?
- Have appropriate accountabilities and responsibilities been identified and allocated?
- Is the strategy integrated with the other plans and strategies related to the programme?

7.6   BENEFITS MAPPING

A Benefits Map is developed to show how the benefits relate both to each other and the projects (which deliver the outputs that allow the realisation of benefits). A Benefits Map covers the entire set of benefits and becomes a major planning document for the programme.

The Benefits Map is so important because benefits (and dis-benefits) do not typically happen in isolation. Figure 7.7 shows just one possible chain within a Benefits Map. Using the Benefit Profiles (see section 7.8 below), the Benefits Map builds a total 'picture' of the changes, shows the prerequisites for each benefit, and how they fit into this total picture. The Benefits Map should include any dependencies that are outside the boundary or control of the programme, as they may affect the realisation of benefits.

Tip

Ideally the Benefits Map would be created working from right to left, from strategic objectives, through end benefits and intermediary benefits. It should then define the enablers (project outputs) and business changes required. Where the enablers are given, for example in an emergent programme (Chapter 1), the Benefits Map can be created from both ends and join in the middle.

The Benefits Map is a key element of the Benefits Realisation Plan, showing the realisation sequence through a chain of benefits. Timescales can be developed from the Benefits Map to inform the creation of the schedule within the Benefits Realisation Plan.

The example Benefits Map shown in Figure 7.8 uses the same example programme from the Outcome Relationship Model (Figure 7.6). This has been transformed from the Outcome Relationship Model and simplified for the sake of illustration:

- There are two Strategic Objectives on the right
- Four End Benefits lead into the two Strategic Objectives; in one case ('Increased revenues from tourism') an End Benefit feeds into both Strategic Objectives
- Other Intermediate Benefits are shown with their Business Changes and Project Outputs/Enablers
- Some Business Changes are dependent on project outputs, some are not, and could be initiated by the Business Change Managers at appropriate moments.

Tip

Benefits are best titled with a change term at the beginning (such as 'increased', faster', 'lower', 'cheaper', 'bigger'); avoid 'better' or 'improved' as these terms are not specific enough for further analysis.

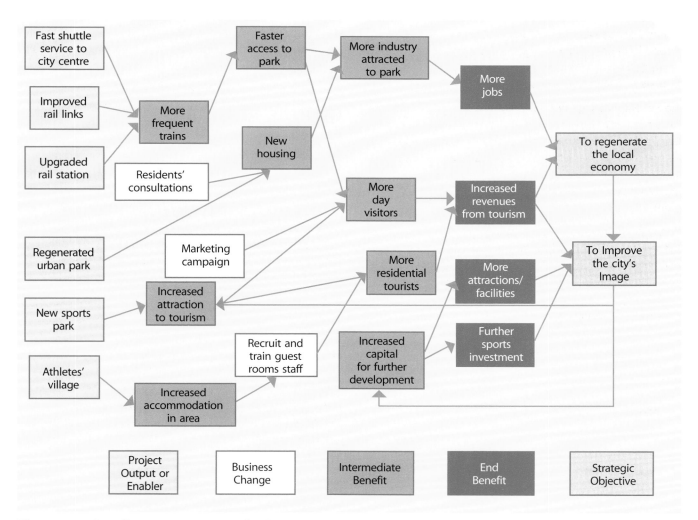

Figure 7.8   Benefits Map: sports-complex legacy example

7.7 BENEFIT OWNERSHIP

Clear ownership of benefits, collectively and individually, is a key requirement for successful Programme Benefits Realisation. Each benefit should be owned by an appropriate individual, who must be accountable for the successful delivery. It is important that benefit ownership remains with those operations affected. Dis-benefits should also be clearly allocated to appropriate owners.

The Business Change Managers will normally own the Benefit Profiles within the programme environment, but they may attribute specific responsibilities to managers across the broader organisational management structure. This should be explained in the Benefit Profile.

Ownership of the overall set of benefits remains with the Senior Responsible Owner (SRO). One way to make benefit ownership more meaningful might be to link benefits realisation to personal performance targets.

7.8 BENEFIT PROFILES

A Benefit Profile (derived from the Benefits Map) is a document describing a single benefit (or dis-benefit), including its attributes and dependencies. A good Benefit Profile will identify, describe and analyse the benefit and its interdependencies, confirming the Benefits Map, allowing the building of a detailed Benefits Realisation Plan.

The set of Benefit Profiles forms the repository of all the benefit-related information for a programme, and as such provides the means for maintaining control over the process of Benefits Realisation Management.

Typically a Benefit Profile is created with a description and an operational owner as soon as it is identified. Population of many of the other fields is generally achieved through Stakeholder Engagement. As a minimum, a Benefit Profile should be written for every End Benefit that appears in the Programme Business Case.

A benefit should pass four critical validation tests:

- **Description** – What precisely is the benefit?
- **Observation** – What verifiable differences should be noticeable between pre- and post-programme implementation?
- **Attribution** – Where will this benefit arise? Can this programme claim its realisation? Is the ownership of delivering the change clear and agreed?
- **Measurement** – How and when will the achievement of the benefit be measured?

For further details on Benefit Profiles, see Appendix A: 'Programme information'.

7.8.1 Dis-benefits

There will be some dis-benefits from negative outcomes in the programme. Dis-benefits are not risks, as they will happen because of the programme and so will need to be managed. However, management action is required to minimise their impact. Since dis-benefits reduce the total value of benefits there is always a risk that dis-benefits may grow to unacceptable levels and eventually undermine the Business Case for the programme.

A dis-benefit should be identified, measured and tracked in the same way as a benefit. The programme will seek to minimise the impact of dis-benefits on the overall improvements from the programme by exploring any business change options to minimise the dis-benefits.

Early stakeholder engagement and analysis will help identify such dis-benefits as well as possible new benefits.

7.8.2 Measuring benefits

Without measurement of benefits, the realisation of benefits cannot be managed.

Ideally, benefits should be quantified and measurable, preferably in financial terms.

Measures – and the targets set against these measures – can have a very distorting effect upon operations if they are not considered in the overall context of achieving the Vision Statement.

> A public heath service was targeted by its government to reduce waiting times in accident reception units. The target was measured in terms of the time elapsed between a patient registering at arrival and being examined by a medic. In order to meet the tough targets set, accident units met these targets by triage (initial assessment and prioritisation) by a nurse. The target did nothing to improve the speed at which the injured were actually treated. On the contrary, scarce clinical resources were diverted to perform the triage so that the target was met.

Another example might be a local government wanting to reduce the number of children 'at risk'. There may be measurable cost (a dis-benefit) associated with maintaining the 'children at risk' register, but the key measure would be the number of children actually at risk.

There is often a tendency to be over-optimistic when defining and setting target measures for the expected benefits from a programme. Over-optimistic expectations can create buy-in and commitment from stakeholders but the support will quickly evaporate at the benefit reviews (see section 7.9) when the reality is understood. However,

Table 7.2   Benefit value types

Value type		Definition	Example	
			Cashable	Non-cashable
Tangible	Definite	Value may be predicted with certainty	Reduced Costs	Fewer steps in a process
Tangible	Expected	Value may be predicted on the basis of historic trends and high levels of confidence	Increased sales	Quicker performance of tasks
Tangible	Anticipated	The benefit is anticipated but its value is not reliably predictable	Lower insurance premiums	Greater customer satisfaction
Intangible		May be anticipated but difficult to substantiate. Proxy measurement of other causally-related benefits may give evidence of realisation	Improved image (Proxy: increased number of positive testimonials)	

less optimism in setting expectations may stop the programme from even getting started – so a balance is required.

> **Tip**
>
> Consider the application of a sensitivity analysis on key benefit estimates to provide best-case, most-likely and worst-case scenarios.

7.8.3   Benefit value types

There are several different types of benefit. One established set of types is shown in Table 7.2.

Many programmes aim for outcomes such as changing the culture of the organisation, or improving the working environment. These benefits are often referred to as intangible or 'soft' benefits. Measuring these intangible benefits will require careful consideration of the measures that will indicate whether they have been realised. However, using the framework of benefit types in Table 7.2, very few become categorised as intangible.

Care should be taken to avoid defining benefits that cannot be measured. If a benefit cannot be measured it cannot be managed, and so fails one of the critical validation tests of a benefit.

7.9   BENEFITS REALISATION PLAN

Realisation of most benefits will take place within the business operational environment. The programme will deliver a new capability as a new process, function, service or set of working practices, and will enable the business operations to implement these. Realising the measurable effects of the change means embedding the new

capability into the business operations. Realisation of the full set of benefits may not happen until long after the final project in the programme has been completed.

The Benefits Realisation Plan is a complete view of all the benefits, their dependencies and the expected realisation timescales and is derived from the Benefits Map and the Benefit Profiles.

The Benefits Realisation Plan will be developed alongside the Programme Plan (see Chapter 8 'Blueprint design and delivery', Chapter 9 'Planning and control' and Chapter 10 'The Business Case') to ensure alignment and 'do-ability' across:

- Delivery of capability
- Realisation of benefits
- Expected costs
- Attendant risks.

Also, to ensure the right focus on benefits it is sometimes good to integrate the Benefits Realisation Plan and the Programme Plan into one document.

The people aspects associated with change should not be underestimated. Good preparation and adequate lead times are required for those impacted by change to accommodate and accept new ways of working, new systems, new environments, etc. This may well include people outside the organisation. Successful realisation of benefits relies on the total commitment and involvement of those affected within an organisation, as well as understanding from those outside it.

Checklist

Ensuring ongoing applicability and relevance of the Benefits Realisation Plan:

■ The Benefits Realisation Plan should be regularly reviewed and updated throughout the programme, and as a minimum at the end of each tranche

■ The total set of benefits matching the required outcomes from the programme should still be valid

■ All the end benefits necessary and sufficient to achieve the programme's strategic objective should be aligned

■ Any wider benefits or contributions to benefits should be documented.

The development of the Benefits Realisation Plan should be closely integrated with the programme's strategies for stakeholder management and communications. The Benefits Realisation Plan should also identify benefit reviews to formally assess the realisation of benefits.

For details of the content of a Benefits Realisation Plan, see Appendix A: 'Programme information'.

7.10 BENEFITS REALISATION PROCESS

This section describes a generic six-step process for managing benefits realisation on any programme (Figure 7.9).

The Benefits Realisation Process is continuous throughout the programme. The following sub-sections describe steps A to F.

7.10.1 Establish and maintain a Benefits Management Strategy

The Benefits Realisation Process begins with establishing the Benefits Management Strategy.

Creating a Benefits Management Strategy involves the following activities:

■ Establishing the structures and functions required
■ Identifying the roles and responsibilities
■ Defining the frequency of benefit reviews
■ Measurement techniques to be used
■ Stating how benefits double-counting will be avoided
■ Detailing the process to be employed (particularly if it is a standard company practice) down to and including the granularity of detail
■ Establishing ownership and management commitment requirements.

Some organisations establish Benefits Realisation Management at the strategic or corporate portfolio management levels of the organisation. In these cases, a generic Benefits Management Strategy template may already exist, or consistency is driven by a policy or guiding principles for programmes. In this situation the programme management team should review such a Strategy to assess its relevance and sufficiency as soon as possible, and tune and supplement it where necessary and subject it to appropriate approvals.

7.10.2 Identify and map benefits

The next step in the Benefits Realisation Process is to identify likely benefits and map them, preferably by working from the strategic objectives back to the enabling project outputs (Figure 7.3 above).

Benefits are often best identified initially by gathering a group of representatives from key stakeholders to consider

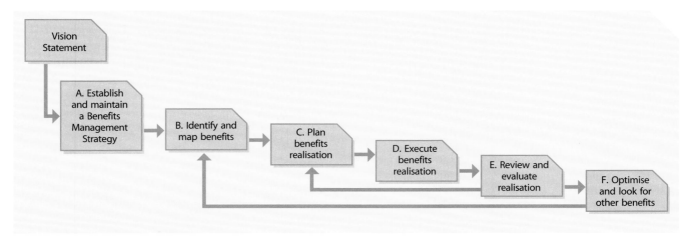

Figure 7.9   Benefits Realisation Process

where the benefits are to be realised. The different perspectives and insights should help generate an initial list.

Benefits may be identified and categorised in a number of different ways:

- By business area
- By stakeholder
- By business impact (e.g. see Figure 7.4).

Table 7.3 shows benefit categories by business area.

Table 7.3   Business areas where benefits may be identified

Business area	Description
Policy or legal requirement (mandatory)	Benefits that enable an organisation to fulfil policy objectives, or to satisfy legal requirements where the organisation has no choice but to comply
Quality of service	Benefits to customers, e.g. quicker response to queries, providing information in a way the customer wants, fewer customer complaints
Internal improvement	Benefits that are internal to the organisation, such as improving decision-making or management processes
Process improvement (productivity or efficiency)	These are 'more with same' type of benefits; benefits that allow an organisation to do the same job with less resource, allowing reduction in cost, or to do more
Personnel or HR management	The benefits of a better-motivated workforce may lead to a number of other benefits such as flexibility or increased productivity
Risk reduction	Benefits that enable an organisation to be better prepared for the future by, for example, not closing off courses of action, or by providing new ones
Flexibility	Benefits that allow an organisation to respond to change without incurring additional expenditure
Economy	These are 'same with less' type of benefits; benefits that reduce costs whilst maintaining quality (often referred to as cost reduction)
Revenue enhancement or acceleration	Benefits that enable increased revenue, or the same revenue level in a shorter timeframe, or both
Strategic fit	Benefits that contribute to, or enable the desired benefits of, other initiatives

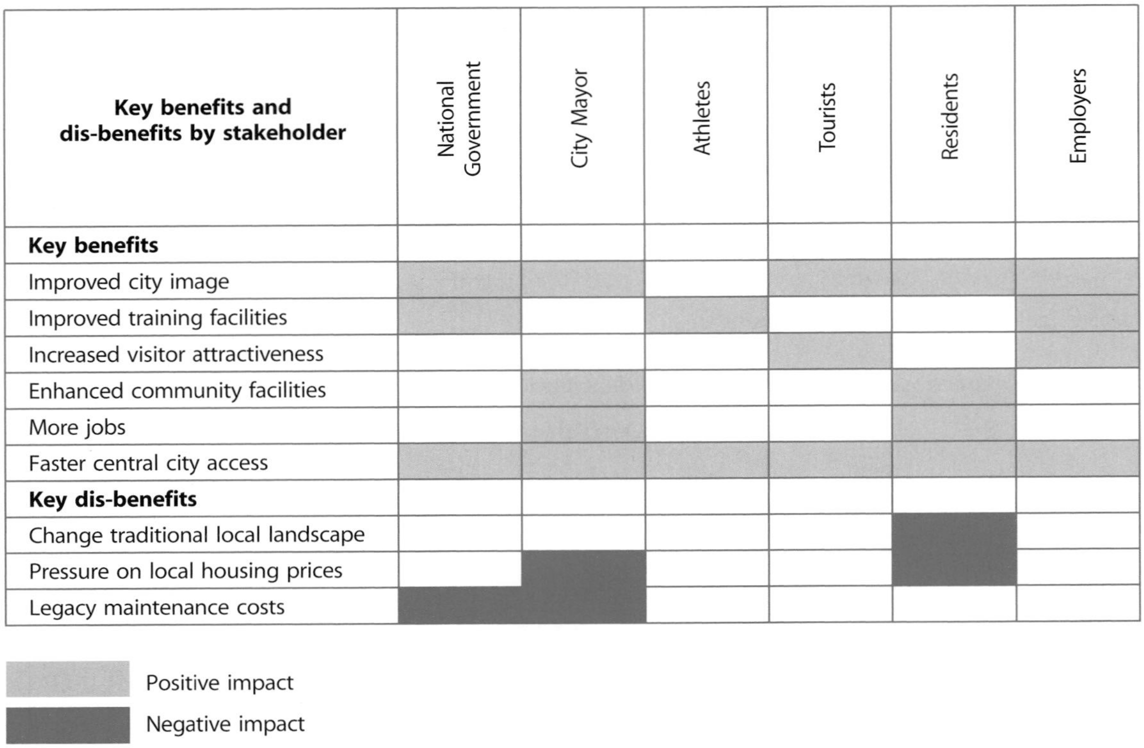
Key benefits and dis-benefits by stakeholder
National Government
City Mayor
Athletes
Tourists
Residents
Employers
Key benefits
Improved city image
Improved training facilities
Increased visitor attractiveness
Enhanced community facilities
More jobs
Faster central city access
Key dis-benefits
Change traditional local landscape
Pressure on local housing prices
Legacy maintenance costs
Positive impact
Negative impact

Figure 7.10 Benefits distribution matrix of stakeholders (sports-complex example)

Figure 7.10 shows benefit categories by stakeholder.

Since the Benefits Realisation Process will have an impact (positive and negative) on stakeholders, this should be closely integrated with Stakeholder Engagement and communications. With a benefit distribution matrix it is easier to identify potentially resistant stakeholders (where the perceived balance of benefits against dis-benefits is either marginal or negative), and plan engagement accordingly.

Figure 7.11 shows benefit categories by business impact. Each small square (within each quadrant) represents a benefit located in terms of a) its estimated value, and b) its complexity or difficulty to realise. The small square P1 is a **speculative** benefit (e.g. savings from installing wireless communications instead of land lines), which does have

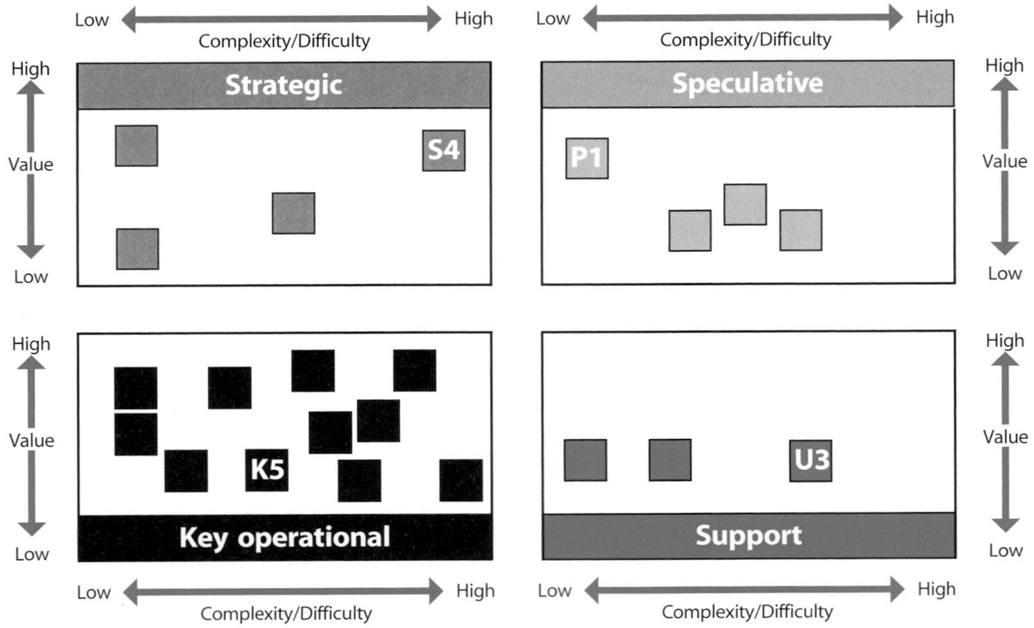
Low
High
Complexity/Difficulty
Strategic
Speculative
S4
P1
Value
K5
U3
Key operational
Support

Figure 7.11 Benefits by business impact

significant value as well as low difficulty in realisation, whereas the more strategic benefit S4 (e.g. more firms attracted to the area) might well has a higher value, but its realisation is expected to be more complex.

This analysis is helpful in assessing the overall mix or balance of types of identified benefits, and possibly adjusting the scope/balance of the portfolio/programme to ensure it will deliver the expected balance of benefits. In Figure 7.11 there are a high number of **key operational** benefits compared to expected benefits across **strategic**, **support** and **speculative**. This could be an early indication that the programme might not be as radical as first thought. The team should use this analysis to consider how well the programme will address the targeted organisational drivers.

7.10.3 Plan benefits realisation

Some benefits will take longer to appear than others. It is important to consider shorter-term (early) benefits as well as the longer-term ones (end benefits and consequential benefits) to ensure there is sufficient ongoing focus and commitment to the programme. Initial shorter-term benefits demonstrate to stakeholders that the programme is making a tangible difference, and that these early benefits are the stepping stones for achieving longer-term benefits. Benefits that are not going to be realised for many years will generate less commitment and enthusiasm. Using the Benefits Map, the focus on longer-term benefits can be improved by identifying those interim activities or benefits that will directly contribute to the longer-term ones (see Figure 7.3).

7.10.4 Execute benefits realisation

This is also discussed in Chapter 18 'Realising the benefits'. It requires benefit owners to:

- Establish benefit measures if they do not already exist
- Prepare for transition, including:
  - Assessing the effect on business-as-usual and the readiness of stakeholders for moving to the 'new'
  - Some stakeholder engagement activities, managing expectations, explaining why the change is necessary, and any necessary preparatory training
  - Establishing a benefit-tracking and -reporting regime/mechanism
- Ensure the ongoing operational performance is not suffering unduly during the changeover
- Provide follow-up support and training
- Ensure the new capabilities are embedded within the operational environment through appropriately managed business change

- Monitor progress of any other related dependencies (e.g. in other programmes).

7.10.5 Review and evaluate realisation

Benefit reviews should cover both expected benefits and those benefits that should have been realised to-date.

With expected benefits it is important to ensure they remain valid and valuable in the:

- Eyes of stakeholders across the programme
- Light of any changes to the business environment – internal and external.

For realised benefits, input from stakeholders, including the Business Change Managers responsible for the changed operations, will provide realistic information and evidence of what has been achieved to-date.

The objectives of a benefit review are to:

- Assess and update the Benefit Profiles and Benefits Realisation Plan to ensure that the planned benefits remain achievable and have not changed in scope or value
- Check that the overall set of benefits included within the Benefits Map remains aligned to the programme's objectives, and to reprioritise or realign them as necessary
- Inform stakeholders and senior management of progress in benefits realisation, and to help identify any further potential for benefits
- Assess the performance of the changed business operations against their original (baseline) performance levels
- Assess the level of benefits achieved against the Benefits Realisation Plan
- Review the effectiveness of the way benefits management is being handled, so that improved ways can be developed and lessons learned for the future, for example, improving the definition of benefits or improving the understanding of the organisation's capability to deliver.

Such reviews are likely to require the Benefits Realisation Plan, along with its Benefits Map and Benefit Profiles, being adjusted or re-worked. If there are fundamental concerns about the effectiveness of benefits realisation, then the Benefits Management Strategy itself should be revisited.

7.10.6 Optimise and look for other benefits

Programmes should be:

- Managed and led as agile, improving ventures
- Always alert to the possibility of new benefits

- Looking to accrue greater benefits, on top of those already realised
- Adjusted if benefits do not appear to be reaching their target levels.

New benefits could be those that were overlooked in early analysis. Changing strategy and possibly new organisational drivers mean that the programme must be responsive to these in looking for the opportunity for identifying benefits in the same way as risks are continually being reviewed and identified.

At the tactical level, the Business Change Manager will be in dialogue with different stakeholders during transition and realisation. A common phenomenon is that when such stakeholders are won over to the programme and its benefits, they are informed and creative enough to identify new benefits and to optimise the realisation of existing ones.

7.11 CHANGE READINESS

Organisations preparing to embark on a change programme should consider the broad implications. Delivering the benefits of the programmes and projects will require high organisational focus and high resource commitment. It may well need additional skills, resources and capabilities. It is good to remember that delivering the beneficial changes and realising the benefits requires a level of commitment that is beyond that required to deliver project outputs or the programme capability.

When considering an organisation's capacity to change, the following should be considered:

- Level of change already being undertaken, and how this new initiative will fit in
- Resources available to support the change within the organisation
- Levels of internal competence and experience within the organisation to achieve the goals
- External market experience of delivering this type of change and costs of using it
- Mobility of labour, availability of additional skilled labour to support the operations during the change
- Previous experience of change – negative or positive
- Type of change – growth or contraction
- Consequence of the change on individuals; is it likely to positive or negative
- Nature and style of the organisation and the individuals within it.

The answers to these considerations will help clarify the realism of the change being considered and the likelihood of success. It will help the organisation establish realistic timescales and aspirations. In essence, it will help the organisations to establish the level of risk to the ambitions and set expectations accordingly.

7.12 ROLES AND RESPONSIBILITIES

Roles and responsibilities are set out in Table 7.4. The SRO is ultimately accountable for the overall realisation of benefits from the programme.

Table 7.4   Benefits Realisation Management: roles and responsibilities

Role	Responsibilities
Senior Responsible Owner	Owning the Vision Statement that is a beneficial statement of the future organisation
	Owning the Benefits Management Strategy and is responsible for its adjustment, improvement and enforcement
	Leading benefit reviews involving relevant stakeholders, business managers, and possibly internal audit
	Input and approval, along with the Sponsoring Group, of all benefits claimed by the programme and described in the Benefit Profiles.
Sponsoring Group and Programme Board	Showing visible commitment to the Vision Statement and to the realisation of End Benefits
	Supporting the SRO by offering suitable candidate Business Change Managers from the affected parts of the business
	Ensuring the strategic alignment of benefits realisation
	Ensuring commitment to benefits realisation from all relevant stakeholders.

Table 7.4   Benefits Realisation Management: roles and responsibilities (continued)

Role	Responsibilities
Programme Manager	Developing the Benefits Management Strategy on behalf of the SRO with the Business Change Managers and relevant stakeholders from the affected business areas
	Developing, owning and maintaining the Benefits Realisation Plan in consultation with the Business Change Managers, relevant stakeholders and members of the project teams
	Initiating benefit reviews as part of Benefits Realisation Plan or in response to any other triggers.
Benefits Realisation Manager	An optional role, usually a permanent appointment sitting within the organisation separately from the temporary programme roles
	Maintaining a permanent 'centre of expertise' in benefit realisation within the organisation. In some organisations this role would reside in a corporate Programme Office or centre of excellence
	Providing objective challenge of benefits, dependencies, measures, targets and the programme's approach to benefit realisation
	Supporting the SRO, the Programme Manager and the Business Change Managers in executing their benefit realisation responsibilities.
Business Change Managers	Identifying and quantifying the benefits, along with relevant stakeholders, the Programme Manager and members of the project teams
	Owning particular benefits as profiled.
	Benefits realisation as part of their line management role in business operations
	Setting performance deviation levels during realising benefits.
Programme Office	Monitoring the progress of benefits realisation against plan
	Ensuring the information gathered for the benefit reviews and the assessment of benefits is disseminated appropriately.

Blueprint design and delivery

8

8 Blueprint design and delivery

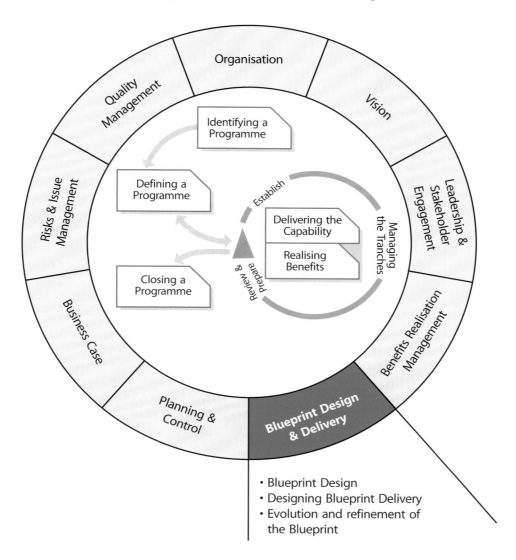

- Blueprint Design
- Designing Blueprint Delivery
- Evolution and refinement of the Blueprint

8.1 INTRODUCTION

The programme's Vision Statement provides early and valuable information as a description of the desired outcomes in customer-focused terms. As it is a description at a summary level it needs to be expanded and developed into a Blueprint. It is the Blueprint that provides a usable basis for modelling benefits and designing the Projects Dossier.

The Blueprint is not concerned with how to get to the future state. The how is dealt with when designing the Projects Dossier (i.e. examining different solutions and routes to get to the defined future state). The optimum set of solutions and routes is selected.

The new capability occurs when the outputs from projects are put into operational use; once transition is completed the outcomes have been achieved. Many programmes

choose not to deliver all the new capability at the same time, as such a major concentrated change is often too big a risk. The UK National Audit Office produced an analysis of programme and project failures that identified this as a major reason for failure, which was independently confirmed by the results of OGC Gateway reviews.

The Programme Plan is designed to show when and how the new capability will be delivered in step changes. These step changes are achieved through a series of tranches. A well designed, tranche-based Programme Plan will be the result of careful consideration of Themes, including:

- Feasibility studies or similar to discover the best way forward where there is uncertainty early in the programme
- Quick wins – benefits realised early are valuable and boost confidence

■ Incremental expansion of capabilities delivered in earlier tranches.

The Blueprint, Projects Dossier, Programme Plan, Benefits Realisation Plan and the Business Case will be developed in parallel and will require close integration to ensure the benefits to be realised are driving the desired transformation. It is often necessary to consider more than one design of the future organisation, and to examine different possible approaches to delivering the capability. Each of these different approaches will have a different mix of time, cost, risk and benefits. It is the responsibility of the SRO and programme team to discover the optimum mix that produces the most acceptable Business Case (see also Chapter 7 'Benefits Realisation Management').

8.2 BLUEPRINT DESIGN

The Blueprint is a model of the organisation, its working practices and processes, the information it requires and the technology that supports its operations. The future organisation is designed to deliver the capability described in the Vision Statement. The detail of this future organisation is described in a Blueprint. When delivered, the future organisation has to be capable of achieving the outcomes desired and realising the benefits expected. The Blueprint is used throughout the programme to maintain the focus on delivery of the new capability.

Blueprints have their origins in other management disciplines such as **business architecture planning** and **enterprise architecture planning**. Some organisations have an overall Blueprint for the entire business. In these contexts, each programme (or standalone project) is briefed to deliver a discrete part of that corporate Blueprint.

Tips

■ Involve staff who are not just subject experts, but are able to envision the future – remember, every programme should aim to produce a good design for the future organisation

■ Make substantial use of knowledge from other appropriate change initiatives, from inside the organisation and from other organisations

■ Use external facilitation to enable radical thinking and challenge existing expectation.

The Programme Manager is responsible for organising activities to ensure the Blueprint is appropriately authored and owned. Where the Programme Manager and Business Change Managers have suitable skills and experience, they can be the authors of the Blueprint. Where they don't, it is the responsibility of the Programme Manager, assisted by the Business Changes Managers, to engage appropriately skilled and knowledgeable people as the authors. (See also in Chapter 2 'Programme management principles', paragraph 2.2.2 'Leading change' – assembling the right people first.)

Whilst the precise format of a Blueprint will depend on the characteristics of each programme, and may contain words and diagrams, a consistent overall structure is recommended.

The POTI model sets a high level scope of what must be included and integrated in an effective Blueprint:

P Processes, business models of operations and functions including changes to operational costs and performance levels

O Organisational structure, staffing levels, roles, skills requirements and changes to organisational culture, style and personnel

T Technology, IT systems and tools, equipment, buildings, machinery, accommodation requirements

I Information and data requirements, changes from existing to future state, including details of any new developments or redevelopments.

8.2.1 Future state

Whereas the primary purpose of the Vision Statement is communication of the intended future, the primary purpose of the Blueprint is specification and ensuring coherence of the entire future state and the solution set that will underpin it. Many programmes do not deliver the desired capability all at once. There can be several defined points in the future, where tranches deliver the change in phases. The Blueprint may show the intermediate future state as it is planned to be at the end of each tranche. This would predicate and support the step-based changes in capability and benefit realisation (see also paragraph 8.3.3 'Step changes through tranches' later in this chapter).

The Blueprint describes the elements of the future organisation. It is the combination of these elements that enable outcomes. These elements have a close relationship with outputs, but a more complex relationship with outcomes. The example in Figure 8.1 below explains this point further.

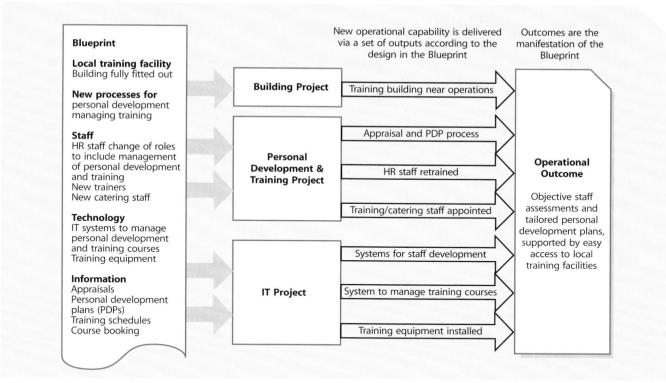

Figure 8.1   Relationship between Blueprint, outputs and outcomes

8.2.2   Current state and gap analysis

Each programme has to plan and manage the journey from where the organisation is today to the future as described in the Vision Statement. An understanding of the current state and the gap (the difference between current and future states) is essential to be able to effectively explore alternative approaches to delivering the new capability.

The initial analysis of the gap is a comparison between the current organisation (described in the current state section of the Blueprint) and the design for the future organisation (described in the future state section of the Blueprint).

Elements of the Blueprint, such as processes, technology etc., are compared as they are now with how they need to be. These are high-level descriptions; more detailed analysis will be carried out by the projects.

In Figure 8.2, the final Blueprint shows a new front-office operational capability. As this does not exist today, the gap to close is establishing this new capability. How that is done should be considered as part of paragraph 8.3.1

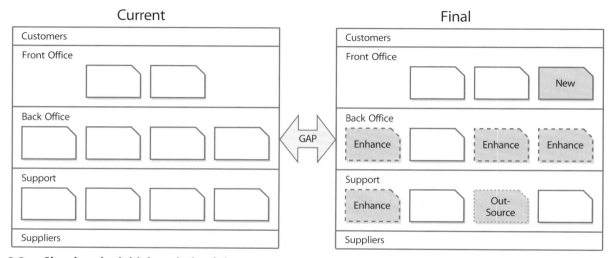

Figure 8.2   Showing the initial analysis of the gap

'Options analysis' and the design of the Projects Dossier, in Chapter 9 'Planning and Control'.

> ### Tip
> Good documentation of the current state is often missing. Use this to encourage programme staff to leave behind good documentation, and not inflict the same problem on future change initiatives.

For programmes that will adopt current projects, and for emergent programmes, where projects are already under way, the programme should analyse each project's definition and current status to:

- Identify its products and their dependencies
- Extract and create abstractions
- Design information.

The programme Blueprint should then be designed to reflect the merging of the project designs, but also to ensure the now validated cohesive future operations are delivered.

The Blueprint is refined throughout the programme at key learning points such as the end of a tranche.

8.3 DESIGNING THE BLUEPRINT DELIVERY

Figure 8.3 shows the nature of collaboration with other Themes. The design of the Blueprint and its delivery is carried out iteratively with Benefits Realisation Management (see Chapter 7) until an acceptable business case starts to emerge.

Output from this work then informs other work done in 'Defining a Programme', and refinements which take place during 'Managing the Tranches', to ensure effective management of the programme.

8.3.1 Options analysis

The project outputs will provide the means to enable the organisation to change, thus delivering the future organisation as described in the Blueprint. In many cases there will be more than one way to create or acquire the outputs. Each approach will have different costs, timescales and risk. Each approach will also enable

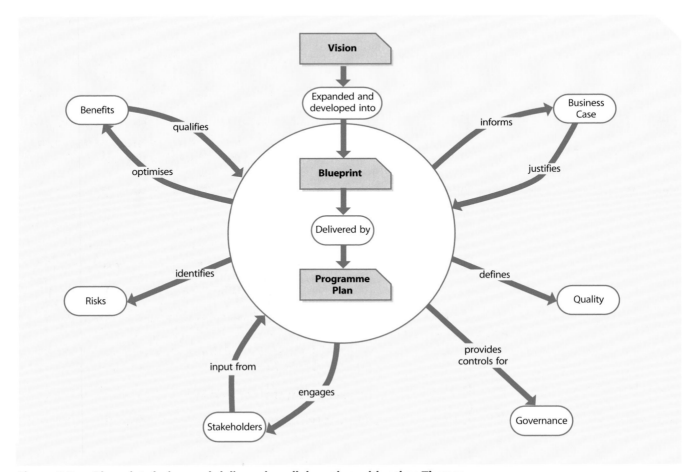

Figure 8.3 *Blueprint design and delivery in collaboration with other Themes*

different degrees of improvement. Before the design of the Projects Dossier is decided on, a range of different solutions (and therefore approaches) should be considered. These then need to be modelled to link outputs as enablers to outcomes which then lead to benefits. These models then need to be assessed to see which option produces the most acceptable business case. The ideal option/model has low cost and low risk, is quick to deliver and produces high benefits.

8.3.2 Optimising the approach

Optimising the approach is about finding the best mix of future state, solutions to deliver the new capability and the timing of that delivery via tranches. This is done by cross-working and iteration between the activities in Chapter 7 'Benefits Realisation Management' and the activities in this Theme.

It is important to test the chosen set of solutions from a number of key perspectives, in order to make sure it is viable, for example:

- Will the organisation be able to acquire adequate funding?
- Will there be sufficient ability available when required, to manage the work?
- Will programme and project staff have appropriate skills and experience?

and

- Have the risks been identified and assessed against the expected benefits?
- Is there an acceptable business case emerging?

If this test shows an acceptable business case is not emerging, it will be necessary to adjust the Blueprint and/or the approach. At this point there are generally only three options available:

- Be less ambitious and design a Blueprint where the gap between the current state and future state is smaller
- Find a different approach and solutions to those already considered, which can deliver the Blueprint addressing the constraints (i.e. more quickly, for less cost, with fewer threats) or with greater benefits
- Close the programme.

See also Chapter 2, 'Programme management principles', paragraph 2.2.4 'Focusing on the benefits and threats to them' and paragraph 2.2.5 'Adding value'.

8.3.3 Step changes through tranches

Only when an acceptable business case seems possible should consideration be given to arranging the solutions into projects. Other factors now need to be considered:

- Large complex work might be split into two or more projects
- Combine several small pieces of work into one project
- Consider:
  - Discipline, skills, knowledge, technology, facilities, etc.
  - Existing teamworking arrangements
  - Geography and culture
  - Current projects.

See the principle in paragraph 2.2.6 'Designing and delivering a coherent capability'.

How and whether to adopt existing projects needs to be considered. Analysing and taking designs from their plans and definitions into a Blueprint can help to provide a first definition of the boundaries of the emerging programme. Treatment of the rest of the preparation of the emergent programme should ideally follow the same process as a new programme. However, as work is already in progress in current projects, there may be overriding practical constraints. The following criteria may be helpful:

- **Proximity to delivery** – Projects close to completion, and where there is a high degree of confidence of successful improvement as a result of their outputs, could be allowed to continue
- **Strategic fit** – Projects which do not closely align with the current organisation policy and strategy, may be candidates for premature closure, especially if they are not close to completion
- **Re-use and adaptation** – Projects that are mid-lifecycle but not a good strategic fit, may have work completed so far that can still be of value if adapted to the vision of the emerging programme. Research results, designs and prototypes are some examples of assets that might be of value.

In MSP the Programme Plan is designed to deliver the new capability in tranches (groups of projects). These step changes in capability should be carefully planned to support the realisation of the appropriate, desired benefit(s). Each tranche delivers part of the final future state described in the Blueprint. A Blueprint document also describes the intermediate future states. There will be an intermediate future state required at the end of each tranche. This part of the Blueprint should provide a clear understanding of what the tranche has to deliver (see also paragraph 8.2.1 'Future state' above). The complete Blueprint document therefore contains several sections:

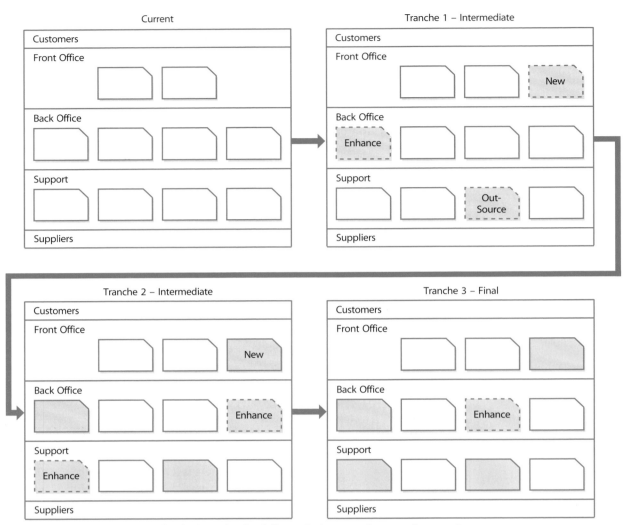

Figure 8.4 *Showing how the final Blueprint is delivered via step changes in tranches*

the current state, sections for the intermediate future state for each tranche and the final future state for the end of the last tranche. Benefits realisation planning (see Chapter 7 'Benefits Realisation Management') should help to identify points during the programme where sufficient projects will have delivered/completed for benefit reviews and progress assessments to take place.

Figure 8.4 shows how Blueprint sections are used to describe the current state, intermediate future states at the end of each tranche, and the final future state at the end of the last tranche. In this example, Tranche 1 is designed to deliver part of the new front-office operational capability and one of the back-office enhancements, and to outsource a support capability. Tranche 2 is designed to deliver the remainder of the new operational capability, the other back-office enhancement and the support enhancement. The final tranche, Tranche 3, is designed to deliver the third back-office enhancement.

Tip

One area sometimes overlooked in Blueprint design work is service arrangements. As the organisation will operate differently in the future, it might have a different infrastructure, IT systems, manufacturing plant etc. As well as designing these new systems it will be necessary to design new service management arrangements to support them.

Projects may cross tranche boundaries, beginning in one tranche and possibly not completing until several tranches later. However, allowing this to happen potentially increases risk and weakens control.

Based on the results achieved so far, if a programme discovers at a tranche boundary that it needs to change direction significantly to achieve the expected outcomes, expenditure in projects already started but not yet closed may be have to be written off.

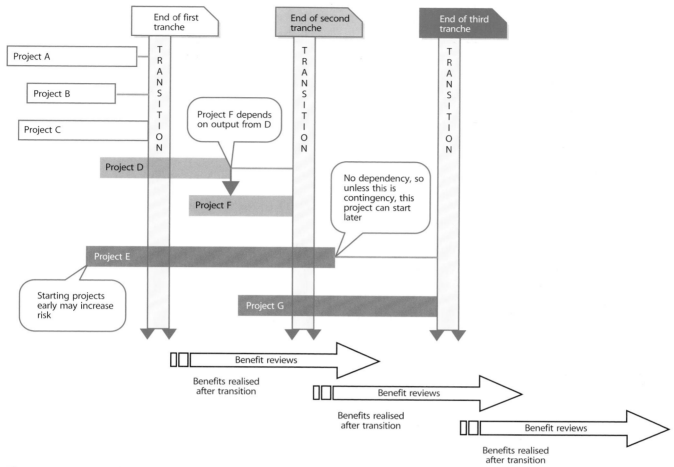

Figure 8.5   Example programme schedule

Figure 8.5 shows an example programme schedule indicating the grouping of projects into tranches and the review points.

Once the overall design of the delivery is accepted, the timing of delivery can be considered (see Figure 8.5). The nature of the change required will determine the thinking at this point. Some programmes need to explore different delivery options, as early in the programme there isn't sufficient data or knowledge to decide which is the best route. The result of this exploration in an early tranche determines the arrangement of the later tranches. Early tranches may be designed as pilots or proofs of concept. The most important outputs from such tranches are the lessons learned that enable the programmes to be refined and steered to success. Some programmes might be driven by a strategic initiative (or similar). Just because an initiative is part of strategy, that does not guarantee it will succeed. A good programme will attempt to prove (or disprove) the hypotheses embedded in the strategy as cheaply and quickly as possible.

A company that sells mobile phones changed its strategy from shop-based to Internet sales. Fortunately they decided to test this hypothesis. A small-scale pilot showed the cost of sales greatly reduced, but the lack of face-to-face contact with customers was a big dis-benefit, as they lost the close understanding of customer requirements. This was their big strength over the competition. They also found that too many phones were being returned, increasing operating costs. The lessons learned from this test enabled them to refine their approach. The Internet became more a means to entice customers into their stores. The cost of this learning was insignificant compared with their original plans to switch to the Internet in one major change, which probably would have put them out of business.

Delivery can be incremental. Early tranches might deliver core changes, with later tranches building on that core. This provides quick wins, and as each change is smaller, it reduces the risk. See also the Transformational Flow chapters in Part 3.

8.4 EVOLUTION AND REFINEMENT OF THE BLUEPRINT DESIGN AND DELIVERY

At each tranche border, and when a major change to the programme is proposed, the definition, scope, delivery status and expected benefits of the programme need to be revisited:

■ Before transition, to check against the Blueprint for that tranche, to ensure that the capability described is ready to be delivered

■ After transition, to test whether the new capability enabled the improvements and benefits required

■ To use the lessons learned to adjust the future state, the delivery approach, and plans for at least the next tranche, to maximise those aspects that worked well, and to minimise (or eliminate) those that didn't enable adequate benefits.

Other aspects of refinement are treated in each of the other Governance Theme chapters and Transformational Flow chapters.

8.5 ROLES AND RESPONSIBILITIES

Table 8.1 shows the roles and responsibilities involved in Blueprint design and delivery.

Table 8.1 Blueprint design and delivery: roles and responsibilities

Role	Responsibilities
Sponsoring Group	Endorsement of and commitment to the programme, demonstrated through active cooperation; for example making appropriate resource available to assist with the design of the Blueprint and analysis of delivery options.
Senior Responsible Owner	Overall responsibility for directing the work of the design of the Blueprint and analysis of delivery options
	Providing the interface with the Sponsoring Group and other key stakeholders, maintaining their buy-in; for example as the design of the future organisation becomes clearer
	Providing advice and direction to the Programme Manager and Business Change Manager(s) as required, including risks or issues identified during Blueprint design and delivery.
Programme Board	Supporting the SRO and assisting with stakeholder engagement
	Assisting the SRO in assessing and making decisions about the designs of the Blueprint and its delivery.
Programme Manager	Ensuring the Blueprint is authored and assembled in collaboration with the Business Change Manager(s)
	Working closely with the Business Change Manager(s) to ensure that the Blueprint, Programme Plan, Benefits Realisation Plan and Benefit Profiles are consistent and able to deliver the Business Case
	Contributing to managing stakeholder expectations.
Business Change Manager(s)	Providing and coordinating essential input to the Blueprint with the assistance of experienced operational staff and specialists, and where appropriate authoring (part of) the Blueprint.
Programme Office	Providing, or directing the programme to, information and resources that can assist with the design of the Blueprint.

Planning and control 9

9 Planning and control

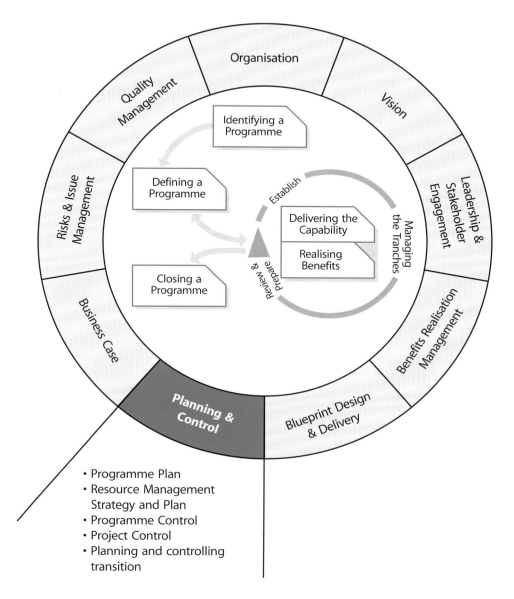

- Programme Plan
- Resource Management Strategy and Plan
- Programme Control
- Project Control
- Planning and controlling transition

9.1 INTRODUCTION

Planning and control are key to the success of any transformation programme and should be seen as distinctly separate concepts and activities.

9.1.1 Programme planning

The preparation of the Programme Plan involves:

- Processing large amounts of information
- Extensive consultation
- Building the plan.

During its early iterations the Programme Plan will include many unknowns and a high level of ambiguity.

9.1.2 Programme control

Programme control provides supporting activities and processes that run throughout the lifecycle of the programme to:

- Refine and improve delivery
- Minimise the impact of ambiguity
- Bring certainty wherever possible

based on the experiences from the previous tranches.

9.2 PROGRAMME PLAN

The Programme Plan is not a master plan that is created and then left on the shelf. It is a key control document for the programme that forms a complete picture of how the

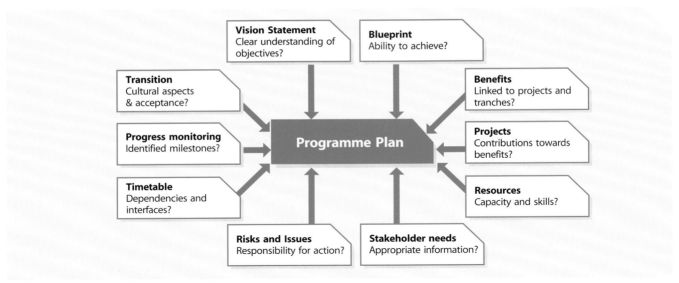

Figure 9.1 Contributions to programme planning and control

programme is going to work. When constituent project plans are developed later, they will be aligned to, but not embedded in, the Programme Plan in all their detail. It enables the Programme Manager, on behalf of the Senior Responsible Owner (SRO), to implement a planned and controlled environment that can be monitored and maintained throughout the life of the programme.

The Programme Plan should include the following core information (see Figure 9.1):

- Project timescales, costs, outputs and dependencies
- Risks and assumptions
- Schedule showing the programme's tranches
- Transition plans
- Monitoring and control activities and performance targets.

For further details of the contents of a Programme Plan, see Appendix A: 'Programme information'.

Developing the Programme Plan requires an understanding of the:

- Level of detail in the Programme Plan needed to:
  - Provide adequate information about progress to enable decision-making
  - Identify pressure points and other issues that may affect progress
- Tools to be used to monitor and maintain the Programme Plan, including how:
  - Information from the Programme Plan will be presented to stakeholders
  - Information from the Programme Plan will be distributed, to whom, and when (see Chapter 6 'Leadership and stakeholder engagement')

- Project-level information will be integrated at the programme level.

Whilst Benefit Profiles and the Benefits Realisation Plan are often initially developed separately from the Programme Plan, collaboration between these activities is critical. The total set of Benefit Profiles, together with the Benefits Realisation Plan, need to be integrated with the Programme Plan to ensure the dependencies on project delivery and transition are properly considered. A close link also needs to be established with risk management activities.

Developing and maintaining the Programme Plan requires the ongoing coordination of all the project plans. The focus for programme planning is on the interdependencies between the projects and any dependencies on external factors outside the control of the programme. This makes programme planning and monitoring a complex task.

The programme's journey is longer and more complex that those of its constituent projects. Some programmes require considerable exploration in the early tranches to discover a successful way forward. Early programme designs will have very little detail for the later tranches and estimates for the duration and cost of these may be based on huge assumptions. Whilst projects may also refine their plans into more detail as they progress, their degree of uncertainty (and their reliance on learning as they complete each phase/stage) is typically much less than in a programme. Decision-makers in programmes will often rely far more on judgement as opposed to the more structured methods employed in projects.

9.2.1 Resources

Any input required by a project or programme is known as a 'resource'. The term covers people, assets, materials, funding and services. Shared resources (those resources that will be used by two or more projects) should be planned and managed by the programme. Developing the Programme Plan will identify those resources that need to be shared between projects. Minimising resource sharing between projects will help prevent bottlenecks occurring. Against that, maximising resource sharing will help promote knowledge sharing, organisational learning and fluent working.

It is important to remember that resources (especially people) have finite availability, skills and experience. The combination of these factors is their capability to contribute to the changes required. This will determine the maximum pace at which work can progress. Programmes must ensure that planning at all levels does not disregard the limits of capability, otherwise unrealistic plans may be developed. Of all the resources that a programme will consume, it is often availability of capability that presents the most compelling constraint.

People, often expected to work together in teams in a programme or its projects, may have no previous working relationships with each other. Corporate HR policies for team building should be employed (or created) to help get such groups up to speed quickly.

Many people (amongst other resources), in addition to being on more than one programme or project at the same time, have operational obligations. The acquisition of such resources needs careful consideration, in particular how conflicts will be resolved when a resource is required in more than one place at the same time. Preparing in advance for such problems will make it easier to prioritise when necessary. If such issues are not quickly resolved with tact and diplomacy there will often be confusion and tension.

The Resource Management Strategy describes how resources will be identified, acquired, and managed. It will provide direction on how to resolve resource problems.

9.2.2 Resource Management Strategy and Plan

A major part of programme planning is to consider what resources the programme will require, and how they will be acquired, used, shared and managed effectively. How this will be approached is defined in the Resource Management Strategy. Programme resources will include the:

- Programme's financial needs as expressed in budgets, expenditure profiles and accounting procedures
- Staff and other personnel involved in the programme. This includes those who will be affected by its outcome(s) even if their involvement may be minimal (as they will need to be available at the right time to change to the new way of working)
- Assets the programme will use, e.g. buildings and equipment
- Systems, services and technology the programme will use as part of delivery.

Resource sharing

Shared resources represent a set of dependencies between the programme and its projects and therefore need to be managed effectively and used efficiently. Scarcity of shared resources often creates more critical constraints on the progress of the programme than even the logical dependencies between project outputs.

Typical examples of resource sharing are:

- **Staff** – where people are involved with more than one project within the programme
- **Infrastructure or facilities** – for example where office space may need to be shared
- **Information** – for example where a group of projects may be updating a shared repository
- **Third-party services** – where several projects make use of the same service provider.

The Resource Management Strategy should be developed alongside the Programme Plan to ensure the resources required match the planned activities and timescales.

The Resource Management Strategy is implemented through the Resource Management Plan, which reflects the timeline for the requirement of the resources, when and who will be implementing them.

For further details of the Resource Management Strategy and Plan, see Appendix A: 'Programme information'.

9.2.3 Risk management

Implementing the Programme Plan will inevitably have risks associated with it. Individual projects may face critical risks that, should they materialise, could affect the entire programme. All assumptions should be regarded and managed as risks. The identification of these, together with suitable responses, should be part of the programme's risk management activities. Such activities and contingency for risk should be included in the Programme Plan, based on the Risk Management Strategy. For further details on risk management, see Chapter 11

'Risk management and issue resolution', and Appendix A: 'Programme information'.

9.2.4 Projects Dossier

The Projects Dossier contains a summary description of all the projects that together, through their combined outputs, will deliver the required future state(s) as described in the Blueprint. These outputs allow the organisation to acquire the capabilities described in the Vision Statement. The Projects Dossier includes information on existing projects to be absorbed into the programme, and new projects to be commissioned by the programme. See Chapter 17 'Delivering the Capability'.

The Projects Dossier should include the following information about each project:

- A description of the project, including its outputs and timescales
- Its dependencies with other projects
- The contribution it will make to benefit realisation
- Risk-related information, the acceptable risk threshold for each particular project, as well as the contribution of each project to the overall risk profile of the programme.

These will form the basis of the Project Briefs that will be developed by the programme to give each project a thorough and rapid start. For further details on the content of the Projects Dossier see Appendix A: 'Programme information'.

One of the objectives for designing the Projects Dossier is to place clear and direct accountability on the projects, while avoiding a spaghetti-like tangle of interdependencies. This can be achieved by ensuring that the delineation of project boundaries maximises the internal consistency of the projects and minimises the number of interfaces and dependencies between the projects.

The following are standard ways of delineating projects:

- **By discipline** (e.g. process engineering) – programmes are typically multidisciplinary, whereas projects are often seen as single discipline. Projects can be defined and scoped such that each involves a single discipline
- **By location** (e.g. designed in the UK built in the Far East) – multi-site projects are inherently difficult to manage, largely because of the communication overheads between members of the project teams. Projects may be scoped by grouping activities that can be achieved on a single site

- **By outputs** (e.g. an IT system or a building) – projects may be defined such that each is responsible for a single set of outputs, or outputs that are closely related.

There may be other business activities outside the scope of the programme that could conflict with the programme's objectives. These should be identified and any possible conflicts defined so that appropriate action can be taken if required. As such conflicts arise from outside the programme, they need to be escalated by the Programme Manager to the SRO, the Sponsoring Group or the management of the corporate portfolio (where this exists).

Projects must be managed by effective teams to achieve success. Potentially all of the following are worth considering when forming good project teams:

- Design smaller projects if the change is big or complex
- Combine work in small packages into one project
- Consider skills, knowledge, technology and facilities that are likely to be available when the work needs to be carried out
- Maintain existing team-working arrangements
- Geography and culture – project teams that are spread across different regions or countries can be difficult to manage.

Critical inputs for this aspect of programme planning come from the Blueprint and its delivery (see Chapter 8 'Blueprint design and delivery').

9.2.5 Deadlines and constraints

The drivers for the programme may include immovable deadlines over which the programme has little or no control. The staging of an Olympic Games is a good example. These time-related drivers will naturally constrain the overall timescales within which the programme must operate. It is important not to lose site of realism when such constraints exist. A programme is obliged to concentrate on the delivery of the high-priority capabilities – those that maximise benefits. It should recommend exclusion of capabilities that cannot be delivered before the deadline.

9.2.6 Scheduling

A key step in the planning process includes constructing a schedule of project delivery that demonstrates realisation of benefits aligned with the strategic objectives that set the context for the programme. In order to achieve this, the programme needs to:

- Integrate the increasing refinement of individual project plans (as each project proceeds through its stages) into the Programme Plan to inform and assess progress

■ Respond to project exception situations (by external influences or internal variances) that mean a reassessment of the Programme Plan

■ Continually monitor and review progress against the Programme Plan, including looking forward to anticipate emerging risks to the Programme Plan.

Treating each project as a black box (being concerned just with key inputs and outputs, not the detail) enables the Programme Manager to schedule projects according to their dependencies, and to assess the impact of any potential slippages. Key elements within individual projects should be revealed within a dependency network diagram (Figure 9.2), especially where this clarifies major interdependencies between projects.

Often there is a combined dependency. Here, until all the outputs from a group of projects are ready for operational use there is not a capability on which to base and complete an operational transition. In Figure 9.2 above, transition cannot start until all the outputs from the four projects are complete and ready for operational use.

The Programme Plan's schedule provides the overall sequence and timetable for the programme by incorporating the dependency network and the timescales for each of the projects.

9.2.7 Priorities

Priorities are a key factor influencing programme scheduling. The effect on staff and the rest of the programme of delaying or bringing forward a particular project can be significant. Prioritisation should focus on critical programme activities, for example:

■ Specific projects, such as procurements, whose outputs are prerequisites for future projects

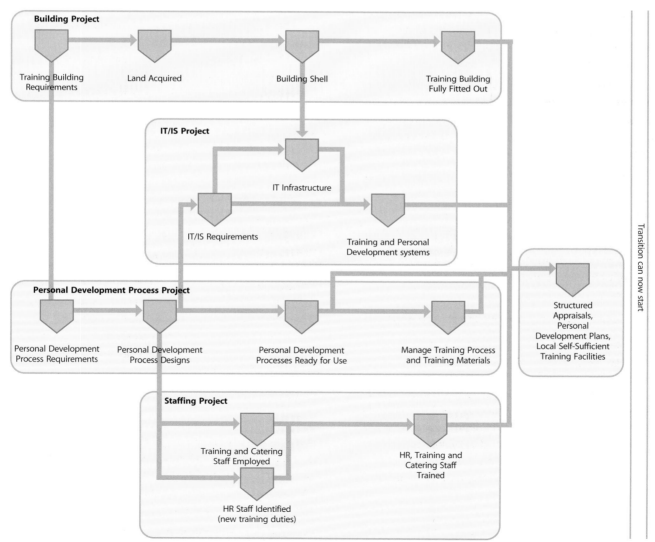

Figure 9.2   Example dependency network showing how projects depend on other project outputs

- Resource requirements, such as specific skills that may be scarce
- Early benefit realisation, such as reduced operational costs, that will help engender continued commitment and enthusiasm for the programme.

9.3 PROGRAMME CONTROL

As soon as the programme is under way and is being managed tranche by tranche, all the definition and planning work comes into play so that there is a fluent, orderly construction and delivery of the new capability, resulting in the new outcomes being achieved.

Managing the programme does not mean micro-management of the projects within it. Communicating the right information between the programme and its projects is a major consideration when establishing programme controls. Projects should be empowered but need clear tolerances and limits, to ensure they do not exceed their delegated authority. Allowing the project managers to manage their projects within the tolerances set by the programme is an essential part of good programme management.

The aim of the programme is, through the achievement of the desired outcomes, the realisation of expected benefits. The aim of the projects is the delivery of the required outputs. This difference may lead to tensions between the project and programme planning and control processes. One of the greatest challenges in running a programme is therefore to reconcile project objectives and accountability with overall programme goals and programme-level consistency and control. Factors such as project management experience, programme risk and available margins should all be assessed when determining how tightly the programme controls its projects. All of these factors are then reflected in the Monitoring and Control Strategy which sets out the approach the programme will take to applying these internal controls (see Appendix A: 'Programme information' for details of the contents).

The communication flow between the programme and its projects should aim to reuse information contained in standards introduced as part of the programme governance. Project documentation such as Project Initiation Documents (PIDs), highlight reports, exception reports, and Issue and Risk Registers will provide much of the information required by the programme. Part of the role of the Programme Office is to support this reporting (see also Appendix C: 'Programme Office').

9.3.1 Starting projects

A programme should have good knowledge about the overall requirements for each project even before the project has started. Projects in a programme should be started with a thorough brief to give them a running start. The Project Brief should:

- State the project's objectives, scope, outputs, constraints and interfaces
- Provide direction and clarity about how the project will contribute to delivering some of the new capability
- Explain how this new capability relates to outcomes and benefits
- Define the authority delegated to the project, with clarity about how and when it needs to escalate to the programme
- State how and in what format the project will report progress to the programme
- Provide guidance on the standards to which the project should conform through its management activities.

Tip

For a PRINCE2 project, a well-prepared Project Brief from the programme may allow the project to effectively meet the requirements of the first process 'Starting up a Project' (SU), enabling it to go straight into 'Initiating a Project' (IP).

9.3.2 Integration of information

Circumstances may require one or more pre-existing projects to be adopted into the programme. In these cases the relevant project information should be integrated into the design of the Blueprint and Programme Plan (see Chapter 8 'Blueprint design and delivery'). The approach to information integration should be defined in the Information Management Strategy.

The main areas to cover under the integration of programme and project information are:

- Strategic level changes that alter the programme's Blueprint, Vision Statement or Business Case and will have an impact on live projects, or those due to start soon
- Responsibilities and ownership of any risks and issues that are managed at the programme level but may have an impact at the project level
- Tolerance levels for project-level costs, timescales and quality
- Project milestones and review points.

9.3.3 Progress monitoring

The programme management team will need to establish monitoring early in the implementation of the Programme Plan (in the first tranche of 'Delivering the Capability'). This monitoring process should cause management intervention to address raised problems, preventing the programme drifting off target.

> **Tip**
>
> Where PRINCE2 is being used, this monitoring can be achieved through the 'Directing a Project' (DP) process.

The end of each tranche is a key review point (or milestone) at which a formal assessment of progress and benefits realisation must be made. The length of a tranche may warrant mid-tranche reviews. For this, there might be something tangible available (for example a prototype) that can be used to assess the likelihood of achieving the benefits required. The prime purpose of these mid-tranche reviews is to answer the question: If we build and use this, will it work well enough in a full operational environment to enable the scale of benefits desired? These reviews may involve internal assurance, peer-level assessors, audit or external scrutiny, depending on the type of programme and its governance requirements. For further details on reviews, see Chapter 12 'Quality management', and Appendix D: 'Health checks'.

The completeness, timeliness and relevance of information are critical if monitoring is to be worthwhile. A programme that has anything more than trivial levels of information that is incomplete, out of date or inaccurate is a programme that is out of control. The design of data collection, information flows and timing of reporting must also be practical and do-able. The Information Management Strategy will describe how this coherent information will be delivered and managed within the programme.

> **Tip**
>
> At the beginning of each tranche, implement a suitable infrastructure for that tranche of the programme, and train and brief programme and project staff to ensure timely adequate information is available.
>
> Keep it as simple as possible, focusing on the information critical to effective control.
>
> Keep information as complete and up-to-date as possible.

9.4 PROJECT CONTROL

Each project should have its own management processes, with clearly assigned responsibilities and owners. Project governance should be formally integrated with programme governance to ensure the projects remain aligned to the objectives of the programme.

As already stated a well-managed programme will start its projects with a clear brief. The Programme Manager should continue to guide the projects, focusing on matters such as project interdependencies, and the impact on projects from strategic or programme risks and issues.

> **Tip**
>
> Test project teams from time to time to assess their understanding of their relationship with the programme, with questions such as:
>
> - How will your project's outputs contribute to enabling change in the organisation?
> - What benefits will the outputs of your project lead to?
> - What is the enabling capability that your project outputs will need to deliver benefits?
> - What other projects are you dependent on to deliver your outputs?
> - What other projects are dependent on your project to deliver their outputs?
> - What benefits will the outputs of their project lead to?
> - What is the current state of these other projects?

9.5 PLANNING AND CONTROLLING TRANSITION

Whilst an estimate of the length of the transition period should be considered when developing the overall programme plan, more detailed transition planning is not practical until sufficient progress has been made in each individual tranche. Detailed transition planning requires both knowledge of the specific project outputs and the state of readiness of the operations which are due to change.

Some organisations have seasonal demands. For example retail outlets that depend heavily on seasonal trade do not normally want to make significant changes over that period. Transition planning needs to take account of such constraints.

Often there will be more than one concurrent programme and several projects, all of which are due to deliver change in a similar period. Careful planning is required to avoid change overload. This is an area where a corporate Programme Office and portfolio control can help the organisation avoid such pitfalls.

Change to an organisation, its people, working practices, and information and technology needs to be planned and managed carefully. This must allow the cultural and infrastructural migration from the old environment to the new one. The planning and control aspects of transition management will go hand-in-hand as the tranche approaches completion and continues until the new business operations are self-supporting and fully embedded. Maintaining existing business operations is an important consideration during transition since new operations will be introduced while the existing ones are still operating. See paragraph 2.2.2 'Leading change' principle.

Successful benefit realisation depends on the identification and effective management of all the business changes stemming from the delivery of the project outputs.

The scope of a project is usually (and rightly) too narrow to include all the necessary activities to embed a change and realise its full benefits.

The Programme Manager and Business Change Managers work closely together to manage all aspects of transition. Figure 9.3 shows an example of the sequence towards realising benefits through pre-transition, transition and post-transition.

9.5.1 Pre-transition

■ Preparing an operational unit to be ready to receive a project output with contingencies for possible roll-back
■ Selling and leading the change; convincing people that the:
  ● Change is necessary
  ● Solution is appropriate
  ● Outcome will be beneficial
■ Identifying specific objections and resistance and preparing responses to these (e.g. simulation training to work through scenarios and reassure)
■ Establishing the system to measure expected benefits and taking an 'as is' measurement ('1' in Figure 9.3).

9.5.2 Transition

In this simple case the transition is a single output from a single project in a single business unit. The project has delivered its output ('2') which is received by the business unit as an enabler ('3'), to take into its operations ('4'). Particular business changes may be required ('5') for this single enabler to embed the enabler into the operations. In most programmes it is more complex, with many outputs relating to many outcomes. Generic transition usually includes:

■ Initiating planned transition activities
■ Abandoning old practices and their associated ingrained habits, plus the disorientation and confusion that often accompanies new environments

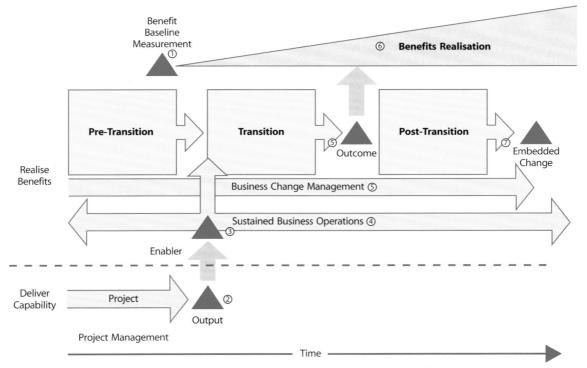

Figure 9.3   *Simple example showing outputs, transition management and benefits realisation*

- Establishing special support arrangements, such as a temporary helpline for people still getting to grips with a new system
- Embedding new service management arrangements supporting the new operations
- Possibly providing a period of parallel operation (this needs careful handling), ensuring the old processes and systems are ruthlessly phased out.

This takes the business unit to a state where there is achievement of the planned operational outcome ('5'). Meanwhile, benefits realisation may sometimes be already under way ('6') and so should be tracked by the Business Change Manager responsible. Such tracking may yield valuable information, for example, about realisation of dis-benefits during transition. Care must be taken, though, that such tracking does not unduly disturb operations and the transition itself.

9.5.3   Post-transition

This is where the following occur:

- Supporting culture and personnel changes. Behaviour change is never an established habit until after a period of conscious, consistent practice. The danger is falling back into old practices. Bedding in to optimise performance requires leadership to make sure the new behaviours become ingrained and new practices viewed as normal, lest gains are only short-term and lost
- Supporting benefit realisation until it gathers sufficient momentum
- Measuring benefits that may only come on-stream after the trauma of transition
- Aligning and attuning the organisation. This may mean a deliberate – and sometimes symbolic – abandoning of old practices. More improvements can be implemented from the experience of transition

- Responding to new requirements. Embedding will bring to light new problems and requirements. These should be fed back to the Programme Manager via the Issue Log
- Monitoring and reporting, particularly against established performance measures and targets
- Managing outcome achievement. It takes time for outcomes to be fully realised. Beware of premature announcements of victory, but once an outcome is achieved it is news for the communications process to exploit
- Above all, guarding existing service level commitments to customers of the operating unit (i.e. sustaining business operations) throughout the disturbance of the change ('4') whilst not allowing this as an inhibitor to commit to the change.

The aim is to achieve a prevailing outcome, a change that sticks ('7') – an embedded change.

Much of this change or transition management happens in Realising the Benefits as part of the Flow, led by the appropriate Business Change Managers. However, in planning these types of change leadership actions, they may identify particular business changes that need to be included in the Benefit Profile and in the Benefits Map. This in turn means that the associated costs of such business changes need to be accounted for by the programme.

All this guards against one of the common reasons for programmes failing to realise their expected benefits: project outputs are planned and accounted for, but necessary business changes are not.

9.6   ROLES AND RESPONSIBILITIES

Table 9.1 shows the roles and responsibilities involved in planning and control.

Table 9.1 Planning and control: roles and responsibilities

Role	Responsibilities
Sponsoring Group	Endorsement of, and commitment to, the programme demonstrated through active cooperation, for example making appropriate resource available to assist projects with the design, development and assurance of their outputs.
Senior Responsible Owner	Providing the interface with the Sponsoring Group and other key stakeholders, maintaining their buy-in, especially preparing for and executing transition
	Providing advice and direction to the Programme Manager and Business Change Manager(s) as required, including risks or issues escalated
	Managing and monitoring any strategic risks facing the programme
	Ensuring the other roles defined in the Programme Organisation are appointed as required for each tranche

Table 9.1 Planning and control: roles and responsibilities (cont.)

Role	Responsibilities
	Leading the ongoing monitoring and review activities of the programme, mid tranche and end of tranche, including commissioning formal reviews, such as audits/health checks, if required
	Monitoring progress across the programme at a strategic level and initiating management interventions where necessary.
Programme Board	Supporting the SRO and assisting with stakeholder engagement
	Ensuring changes are implemented in the business
	Ensuring the business continues to operate effectively during the period of change
	Providing adequate and appropriate resources to the programme and its projects to ensure outputs are designed, developed and assured to give them the best chance of enabling the scale of improvements required.
Programme Manager	Designing the Projects Dossier, Programme Plan, Resource Management Strategy and the required monitoring and control activities
	Working closely with the Business Change Manager(s) to ensure that the Blueprint, Programme Plan, Benefits Realisation Plan and Benefit Profiles are consistent and able to deliver the Business Case
	Establishing and managing the appropriate governance arrangements for the programme
	Updating the key programme documentation
	Managing the programme's risk management and issue resolution activities to ensure barriers to successful benefit realisation are removed/avoided
	Coordinating and integrating the work of the projects and managing the interdependencies
	Progress monitoring against the Business Case, Programme Plan and Blueprint. Adjusting the Project Portfolio, Blueprint and plans to optimise benefit realisation
	Managing stakeholder expectations and participating in communications activities to inform stakeholders of progress and issues.
Business Change Manager(s)	Working closely with the Programme Manager on designing the Projects Dossier and scheduling the tranches and constituent projects to ensure the transition will align with the required benefits realisation
	Making sure operational functions are adequately prepared and ready to change when transition starts
	Maintaining business operations during the change process until transition and handover is complete. Also providing input to the reviews
	Ensuring the projects' outputs can be readily integrated into operational areas.
	Planning the transition within operational areas, accommodating requirements to maintain business operations.
Programme Office	Supporting the development of planning, control and information management arrangements
	Providing, or directing the programme to, information and resources that can assist with the design of the Projects Dossier, Programme Plan, Resource Management Strategy and the required monitoring and control activities

Table 9.1 Planning and control: roles and responsibilities (cont.)

Role	Responsibilities
	Establishing and operating the programme's information management systems, reporting procedures, updating documentation, infrastructure, support tools, configuration management, change control and other procedures for the programme
	Collecting monitoring and measurement data and keeping the information up to date and publicised regularly to ensure all affected and interested parties are kept fully informed and able to provide feedback as appropriate
	Ensuring there are coherent and common project-level standards in place for all document management arrangements for the programme. The Programme Office will often provide the same service to the projects within the Project Dossier.
Project teams	Delivery of the projects to the programme; liaising with the Programme Office.

The Business Case

10

10 The Business Case

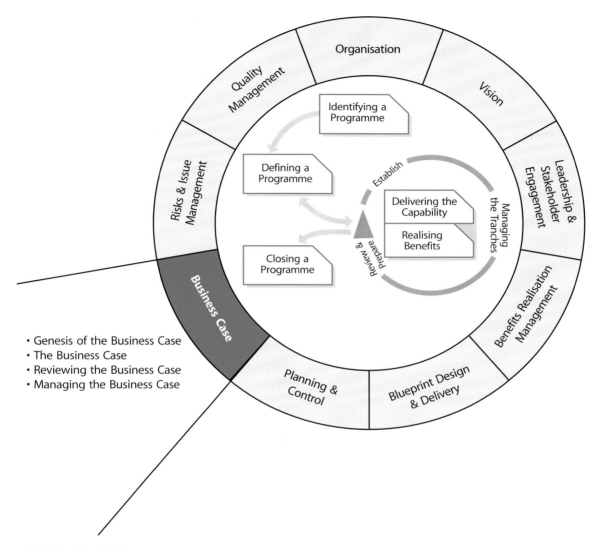

- Genesis of the Business Case
- The Business Case
- Reviewing the Business Case
- Managing the Business Case

10.1 INTRODUCTION

The Senior Responsible Owner (SRO), the Sponsoring Group and the Programme Board must have confidence at every stage that the programme is still viable. In MSP the Business Case provides the vital test of the viability of the programme. It answers the question: Is the investment in this programme still worth it?

Since this viability question is ongoing, the Business Case cannot be static. It provides more than the basis for initial approval to kick off the programme. It is actively maintained throughout the programme, continually updated with new information on benefits, costs and risks.

The Business Case is an aggregation of specific information about the programme:

- Value of the benefits
- Risks to achieving them

- Costs of delivering the Blueprint
- Timescales for achievement.

The Business Case presents the optimum mix of information used to judge whether or not the programme is (and remains) desirable, viable and achievable. It identifies the added value of managing the change as a whole in a programme (see the 'Adding Value' principle, paragraph 2.2.5) as well as the added costs of the programme over and above project costs. The Business Case effectively describes what the value is – including the added value – to the sponsoring organisation from the outcomes of the programme. Managing the Business Case is about making sure the balance of benefits, costs, timescales and risks are optimised throughout the programme.

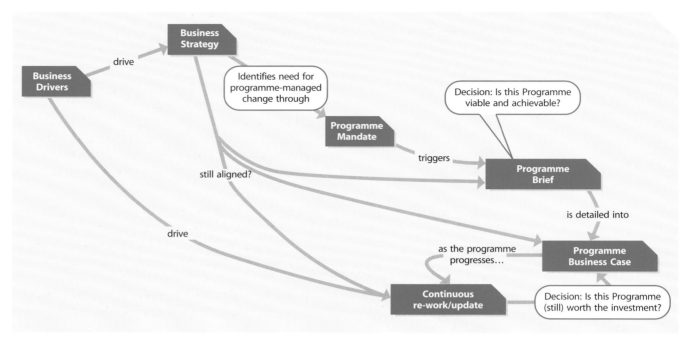

Figure 10.1   Genesis of a Programme Business Case

10.2 GENESIS OF A PROGRAMME BUSINESS CASE

10.2.1   Programme Mandate

A programme begins most effectively when it is launched in the context of a clear corporate strategy. Good strategy is robust enough to cope with continually changing business drivers, both internal and external (see Figure 10.1). Ideally the strategy will suggest the optimum route for programme delivery and the prioritisation of new and existing work against it. The Programme Mandate provides the strategic trigger at the start of a programme. The Programme Mandate articulates the:

- Strategic objectives
- Context
- Boundaries within which the programme will work,
- Optimum approaches for delivery
- Improvements that are expected to result.

The Programme Mandate may be a consolidation of information from a number of documents, policies and directives. Collectively this Programme Mandate informs and directs the activities of programme identification (in 'Identifying a Programme') and definition (in 'Defining a Programme'). A Programme Mandate might contain a suggested Business Case, and should at least provide much of the raw material for outlining one. For further details on what the Programme Mandate should contain, see Appendix A: 'Programme information'.

10.2.2   Programme Brief

If the Programme Mandate provides the trigger and context for a programme, it is the Programme Brief that develops the programme concept and provides the basis for an initial assessment of the viability and achievability of the proposed programme. The Brief sets out:

- Outline Vision Statement
- Anticipated benefits
- Risks and issues
- Analysis of the options available at this point (more may develop later)
- Estimated costs and timescales
- Outline of the current situation.

As such, the Programme Brief does provide an outline Business Case, the formal basis for assessing whether such an investment is viable or achievable before committing to the detailed programme definition work. If the Programme Mandate is flawed, the process of developing the Programme Brief should reveal this.

Achieving success requires a realistic view of the organisation's capability, capacity and culture to accommodate change. Just because a venture looked a good idea in a strategic planning session does not necessarily mean it can stand further scrutiny. The Programme Brief checks for corporate strategic alignment by comparing the outline Vision Statement (future picture of the beneficial future state) and benefits against the outline estimates and risks (broad-based viability and achievability). At this summary level of detail the Programme Brief allows the SRO to consider several scenarios or options in a way that might not be practicable once the programme has narrowed down and detailed some of these options in the Programme Definition. This early work has a freedom to consider sometimes quite radical alternatives to what might be expected – a freedom that is not so present once 'Defining a Programme' begins.

10.2.3   Link with projects

There will be individual project business cases as well as the Business Case for the programme. A project business case is about balancing the costs, timescales and risks relating to delivering the project outputs, and the context and contribution to the realisation of directly enabled benefits.

The programme's Business Case is broader than a project business case. The programme Business Case embraces the wider horizons of strategic outcomes arising from the programme's projects. It is more than a summation of the project business cases (where they exist). It will also include the cost of business changes required in the programme and additional benefits realisation costs, showing how these integrate with the project outputs to achieve the corporate strategic objectives.

The business cases for the programme and the projects are constantly monitored, reviewed regularly, and updated as necessary to ensure that progress remains aligned to the strategic objectives (Figure 10.1). In the most serious case, an escalation of a major issue from one of the projects could result in the programme's Business Case becoming unviable.

10.3 BUSINESS CASE

The programme's full Business Case sets out the overall costs, the planned benefit realisation and the risk profile of the programme, in order to assess its viability and make appropriate management decisions about its continued viability.

The Business Case is developed by iteration through stages of formulation and analysis (see Figure 10.1), and is compiled from other information, including the:

- Blueprint
- Benefits Realisation Plan
- Risk Register
- Resource Management Strategy and Resource Management Plan
- Programme Plan.

The level of detail and completeness of the Business Case will reflect that amount of certainty associated with the programme at that point. Initially, the programme may

tolerate high levels of uncertainty; estimates will be very approximate, with high levels of potential variance. The Blueprint may be going through frequent iterations as well.

There may be options in the outline Business Case (or Programme Brief) that are carried forward into 'Defining a Programme'; these options consider alternative means of how the programme's final capability could be delivered and embedded. Each option will require detailed consideration to be able to compare the likely costs, benefits and risks.

In 'Defining a Programme', the Business Case should be developed in tandem with the early iterations of the Blueprint, Programme Plan and Benefits Realisation Plan (the Business Case is an aggregation of information from these and other sources). These documents will be developed in parallel and will require close integration to ensure the benefits to be delivered are driving the programme's transformation.

Developing the Business Case alongside the Blueprint enables the programme to select the most cost-effective combination of projects and activity work streams. This helps the design of the programme's Blueprint to focus on a target capability that will be the basis for realising the expected benefits within justifiable costs.

Throughout the programme, the integrity of information included in the Business Case and the related documentation should be maintained and kept current – thus providing an auditable trail between it and the progress of the programme.

The Business Case will provide leaders with key information to convince stakeholders to give support and commitment.

10.3.1   Net Benefit Line

The Business Case is where a trade-off is made between:

- The costs associated with delivering the new capability and embedding changes

and

- Realisable benefits, and the value to the organisation(s) of having those benefits.

The concept of 'net benefit' is represented by the net benefit line in Figure 10.2. During the early stages of a programme the cumulative costs of delivery and embedding may outweigh the cumulative benefit to the organisation(s). As the programme continues, more benefits are realised, thus providing greater value, so the cumulative net benefit increases.

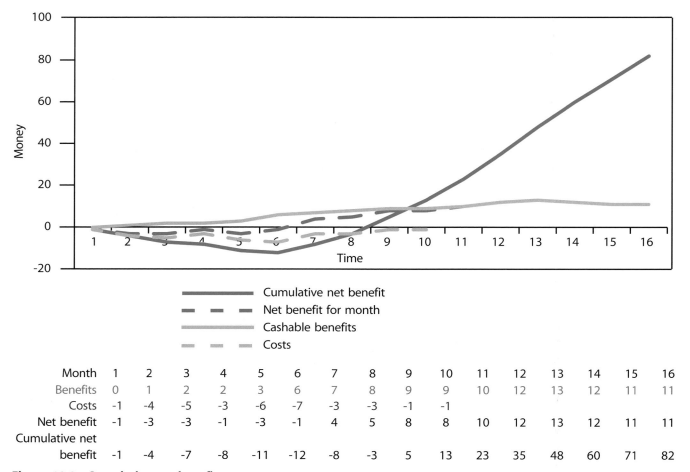

Month	1	2	3	4	5	6	7	8	9	10	11	12	13	14	15	16
Benefits	0	1	2	2	3	6	7	8	9	9	10	12	13	12	11	11
Costs	-1	-4	-5	-3	-6	-7	-3	-3	-1	-1						
Net benefit	-1	-3	-3	-1	-3	-1	4	5	8	8	10	12	13	12	11	11
Cumulative net benefit	-1	-4	-7	-8	-11	-12	-8	-3	5	13	23	35	48	60	71	82

Figure 10.2 Cumulative net benefit

Of course, the analysis illustrated in Figure 10.2 can only meaningfully compare cashable (financial) benefits against financial cost. Other benefits that are listed in the Benefits Realisation Plan will have non-financial measures.

The programme is usually planned to close:

■ Sometime after complete delivery of the full capability (also shown in Figure 10.2)
■ When sufficient transition is deemed to have been achieved from the old capability to the new
■ When changes are so embedded that the target outcome is achieved.

This means that arrangements to continue Benefits Realisation Management and tracking of net benefits (costs and benefits) after the programme close should be made while the programme is still live. Business Change Managers, who will continue in their operational roles, will be central to achieving this post-programme continuity.

Tip

The net benefit line has a value in engaging many stakeholders. For example:

■ The very credibility of the programme may be in the balance for some stakeholders, until there is demonstrable evidence of early realisation of financial benefits
■ The moment the net benefit line rises above zero it could be managed as a communications milestone, with the message that the programme has already achieved its break-even in investment and is now moving into the black
■ As the programme draws to a close, expectations are managed by the message that the benefits still need to be realised
■ Compliance programmes may need to express their benefits as avoided costs (e.g. legal penalties) or foregone reputational damage.

The full Business Case is developed during 'Defining a Programme'. Even though there should be an ongoing

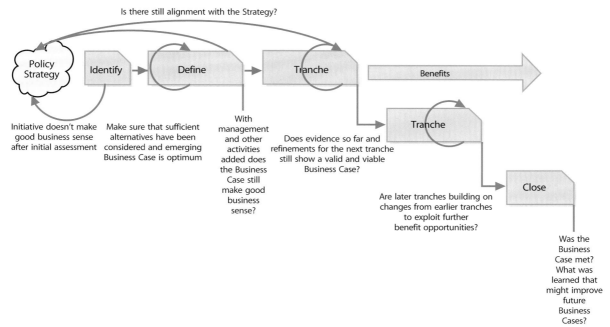

Is there still alignment with the Strategy?

Initiative doesn't make good business sense after initial assessment

Make sure that sufficient alternatives have been considered and emerging Business Case is optimum

With management and other activities added does the Business Case still make good business sense?

Does evidence so far and refinements for the next tranche still show a valid and viable Business Case?

Are later tranches building on changes from earlier tranches to exploit further benefit opportunities?

Was the Business Case met? What was learned that might improve future Business Cases?

Figure 10.3   Validating the Business Case

review by the Programme Manager, Business Change Manager and the Programme Office, it should also be formally validated (reviewed and re-accepted) at the end of each tranche (see Figure 10.3 and section 10.4 below) by the Programme Board and SRO.

10.3.2 Costs

Programme Business Case management means budgeting for the programme's costs; these may be quite varied. The main cost categories are set out in Table 10.1 below.

Table 10.1 Types of programme cost

Type of cost	Description: Costs that are incurred	Information source
Project costs, sometimes referred to as investment or development costs	By the projects in acquiring and delivering the enabling outputs For project and programme contingency and change budget	Blueprint, Projects Dossier, Resource Management Plan, project business cases
Benefit realisation costs	Setting up and implementing measurement, monitoring, and reporting on benefit realisation; costs of activities defined in the 'Realise Benefits' element of the tranche should be included under this heading, including the costs of the Change Team	Benefits Management Strategy Benefit Profiles
Business change and transition costs	Preparing, training, moving and supporting an operational unit until new practices are embedded; these may include interim operational resources required to embed the change	Resource Management Plan

Table 10.1 Types of programme cost (cont.)

Type of cost	Description: Costs that are incurred	Information source
Increased operational costs	Whole-life costs of operating/maintaining new products/equipment – transaction costs – as benefits are realised above the baseline. For example, the benefit 'increased sales' may require more sales people to service the increased volumes	Resource Management Plan Benefit Profiles
Programme management cost	Some programme roles will be full-time – the Programme Office and the Programme Manager. Associated costs for these roles and for programme management activities: e.g. office space, programme tools for tracking and reporting progress	Resource Management Strategy and Plan
Capital cost	One-off set-up costs	Blueprint Resource Management Strategy

10.4 REVIEWING THE BUSINESS CASE

As a minimum, the Business Case should be reviewed at the end of each tranche to assess the continued viability of the programme and any need for realignment. In the UK public sector such reviews are often undertaken as part of Gateway Reviews. It is good practice to formally review the Business Case at least every six months, particularly if tranche ends are spaced over longer periods.

Reviewing the Business Case should provide answers to the following questions:

- Is the programme (still) affordable – is there sufficient funding?
- Is the outcome (still) achievable – is there a realistic assessment of the organisation's ability to cope with the scale of change envisaged?
- Does the programme (still) demonstrate value for money – are the benefits and the costs of realising them in the right balance?
- Have options been considered – is the programme's dossier of projects (still) the appropriate or optimum way of achieving the desired outcome(s)?
- Is the programme still justifiable in terms of its ability to meet strategic objectives?

However, the Business Case is not just refreshed and updated. As a learning organisation (see the 'Learning from Experience' principle, paragraph 2.2.7), the programme management team will seek ways of building in new learning and observations where these can improve the Business Case even further. In effect, the end of each tranche becomes another mini 'Defining a Programme' resulting in an update for the Business Case document. It is tuned and optimised, taking advantage of both data on recent trends and a growing understanding of the possibilities by the management team.

10.5 MANAGING THE BUSINESS CASE

Information presented in the Business Case will serve many purposes during the life of the Programme – all focused on ensuring successful delivery and strategically aligned outcomes.

The key questions here are:

- To what extent can the programme realise the expected benefits?
- Will changes to the cost/benefit profile (as in the net benefit line) alter the status and relative priority of the programme in relation to meeting the corporate strategic objectives?

The Business Case will be used to assess the impact of:

- Accommodating any strategic change or any changed business driver
- Proposed revisions to the programme's boundary and target capability
- Revised benefit and cost estimates from the Business Change Managers and the projects
- Any major new issue identified
- Any significant new risk identified.

Delivering the Business Case should not end with the Programme. The SRO should continue to champion the:

- Values and principles that underpinned the change initiative
- Desired outcomes
- Continued leveraging of the benefits after the programme closes.

10.6 ROLES AND RESPONSIBILITIES

In the case of programmes involving more than one sponsoring organisation, each organisation will have its own Business Case. The Sponsoring Group may not be able to easily select the SRO of the overall programme and its Business Case. One approach to resolving this issue is to consider the financial input to the programme. Since the financial investment underpins the viability of the programme, the organisation with the largest financial stake usually nominates the SRO to own the overall Business Case.

The development of the Business Case and the input of specific information will inevitably require expertise from other members of the programme management team and, in some cases, input from external specialists.

On larger programmes, it may be necessary to appoint a programme accountant to carry out this responsibility on behalf of the Programme Manager.

Table 10.2 Business Case: roles and responsibilities

Role	Responsibilities
Senior Responsible Owner	Ultimately accountable within the Programme Board to the Sponsoring Group for the successful delivery of the programme and will therefore own the Business Case
	Securing investment for the programme
	Ensuring the Business Case is monitored, reviewed regularly and updated with more detailed information as the programme develops and progresses. This involves scanning the business horizons surrounding the programme and will often lead to realignment of the programme in some way
	Ensuring that the progress of the programme remains aligned to the Business Case.
Sponsoring Group	Delivering the programme changes
	Working with the SRO to keep the Business Case strategically aligned
	Providing early warning of any changed or new business drivers that might affect the business case.
Programme Board	Helping the senior responsible owner to identify significant costs and benefits
	Supporting the SRO and the Programme Manager in the ongoing validation and review of the Business Case
	Helping the senior responsible owner to optimise the Business Case.
Programme Manager	Preparing and updating the Business Case
	Managing the programme's expenditure against the overall investment defined in the Business Case.
Programme Office	Supporting the SRO and the Programme Manager in compiling and updating the Business Case. There may be financial planning and control expertise in the Programme Office
	Collecting and maintaining Business Case information
	Facilitating Business Case reviews.
Business Change Manager(s)	Profiling the benefits and dis-benefits and their associated costs
	Assuring operational stability is maintained during delivery
	Benefits continue to be valid through regular Business Case review
	Operational risks to the Business Case validity are controlled

Table 10.2 Business Case: roles and responsibilities (cont.)

Role	Responsibilities
	Measuring benefits at the start of the programme and tracking throughout
	Managing transition costs
	Realisation of the benefits profiled
Programme Accountant	This is an optional role, usually within the Programme Office reporting to the Programme Manager, who can provide assistance in:
	■ Developing and refining Business Cases (programme and project)
	■ Creating and distributing financial reports
	■ Development and maintenance of the Resource Management Plan
	■ Advice on cost control and opportunities for savings
	■ Adherence to accounting procedures
	■ Capitalisation of capital assets.

Risk
management
and issue
resolution

11

11 Risk management and issue resolution

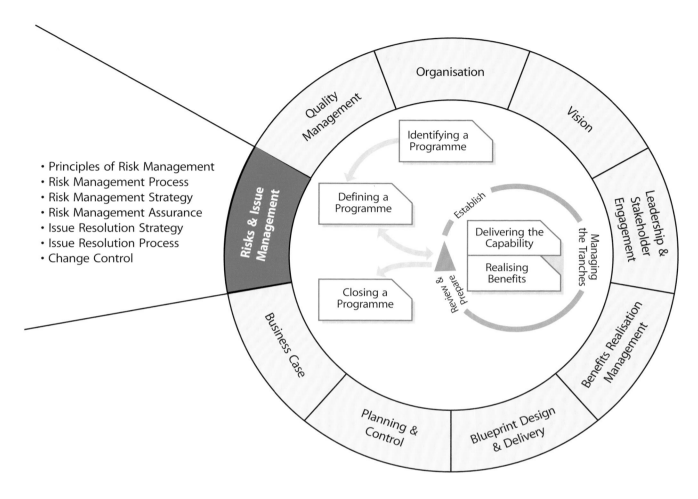

- Principles of Risk Management
- Risk Management Process
- Risk Management Strategy
- Risk Management Assurance
- Issue Resolution Strategy
- Issue Resolution Process
- Change Control

11.1 INTRODUCTION

Programmes are established to deliver change through the coordinated execution of multiple projects and other business activities. Programmes typically involve diverse groups of stakeholders, together with contributions from service providers, suppliers and other third-party organisations. At any point during a programme, there will be events or situations that may affect the direction of the programme, the delivery of its outputs, realisation of expected benefits or the achievement of desired outcomes. These events or situations are the risks and issues that the programme has to manage and resolve.

Successful programme management has at its core the need to both manage and tolerate uncertainty, complexity and ambiguity. Risk management and issue resolution are the vehicles for achieving this.

A risk is an uncertain event or set of events which, should it occur, will have an effect on the achievement of objectives. These effects need not all be detrimental. A risk

can be either a threat (i.e. an uncertain event that could have a negative impact on objectives or benefits) or an opportunity (i.e. an uncertain event that could have a favourable impact on objectives or benefits).

Issues are events that have happened, were not planned, are currently affecting the programme in some way and need to be actively dealt with and resolved. Risks, should they occur, become issues.

The task of programme risk management is to ensure that the programme makes cost-effective use of a Risk Management Process that includes a series of well-defined steps. The aim is to support better decision-making through a good understanding of risks and their likely impact.

Issues can arise at any time during the programme and will require specific and usually immediate management action. The task of issue resolution is to prevent the issue from threatening the programme's chances of achieving a successful outcome.

The programme's approach to managing risks and issues should be derived from, and be consistent with, any organisational standards that exist, and both programme risk management and issue resolution should be formally incorporated into standards for the projects operating within a programme. These standards should also include rules of engagement between the projects and the programme level. Projects will need to have mechanisms for escalating risks or issues to the programme and for participating in the management and resolution activities associated with these risks and issues. Risks and issues in the projects will typically be handled by the project's problem/incident reporting mechanisms, only being escalated to the programme level should the project be unable to resolve them. For example, there may be a one-off issue facing a particular project, which if left unresolved, could effectively undermine the entire programme. These killer issues will need to be escalated and resolved at the programme level or higher.

11.2 PRINCIPLES OF PROGRAMME RISK MANAGEMENT

This section describes the proven principles that should underpin successful risk management within the programme, and within the organisational context of the programme:

- Understand the programme's context
- Involve stakeholders
- Establish clear programme objectives
- Develop the programme risk management approach
- Report on risks regularly
- Define clear roles and responsibilities
- Establish a support structure and a supportive culture for risk management
- Monitor for early-warning indicators
- Establish a review cycle and look for continual improvement.

Application of these principles is essential for the development of good programme risk management practice. They are derived from proven corporate governance principles and recognise that programme risk management should be aligned to the organisation's internal controls, extended and applied to the context of the programme. Adherence to these principles enables programmes to tailor the organisation's risk management practices to meet their specific needs.

11.2.1 Understand the programme's context

A key step of programme risk management is the identification of threats, opportunities and other areas of uncertainty. Effective identification of these is dependent on an understanding of the context of the programme to avoid blind spots and subsequent unpleasant surprises. Hence programme risk management must reflect the context of the programme and the activity being undertaken. The context includes the political, economic, social, technological, legal and environmental backdrop but also commonly includes the industry, markets, locations, technologies and regulatory regimes the programme's organisation(s) operate in. Whilst programme risk management must take cognisance of the current context, it must also consider how it may change over time.

11.2.2 Involve stakeholders

As the trend for increasingly complex, large and costly programmes of change continues unabated, so does the effort required for the engagement of stakeholders. Large public-sector programmes in particular have a vast number of stakeholders who are typically a combination of the ultimate end users plus organisations that are providing funding, approval, scope definition, guidance, design, information, management and financial advice. The lack of timely engagement of these stakeholders can be detrimental to establishing, agreeing and achieving a programme's objectives. Hence programme risk management should involve all stakeholders.

11.2.3 Establish clear programme objectives

The success of any programme is measured by whether it accomplishes its objectives and also whether they are achieved in a satisfactory and responsible way. As the purpose of programme risk management is to understand and manage the threats and opportunities arising from these objectives, programme risk management can only commence when it is clear what these objectives are. In simple terms, risks should be identified against programme objectives. However, as these objectives are continually evolving, evaluation of the exposure to risk should be conducted on a regular basis.

11.2.4 Develop the programme risk management approach

Programmes should develop an approach to the programme risk management which reflects the programme's unique objectives. Programmes describe their approach through their Risk Management Strategy. This document describes the specific risk management activities that will be undertaken within the programme. It should reflect the organisation's risk management policy and risk management process guidance (where these exist). These two corporate documents show the organisation's commitment to risk management, are signed up to by senior (board-level) management and effectively set the tone for the organisation's risk appetite and culture. They set out how risks will be identified, assessed and controlled. They indicate when risk management will be carried out by whom and for what purpose. They describe risk tolerance levels, escalation rules, methods for calculating contingencies and the approach to be adopted for insurance and reporting cycles. They describe what should be examined, reflect the context of the organisation and describe the reports to be produced to satisfy governance, shareholders and the regulatory regime, where one exists. Building on these corporate standards, the programme will set its own appetite and culture for managing its risks in the programme Risk Management Strategy.

11.2.5 Report on risks regularly

The Senior Responsible Owner (SRO), the Programme Board and the governing body of programmes (Sponsoring Group or something akin to a corporate portfolio board in a multi-programme or portfolio environment) should receive, review and act on programme risk reports. As a result, a fundamental aspect of programme risk management is the timely communication of programme risk information to management to enable them to make informed decisions. All significant planned programme activities should be evaluated from a risk perspective. The benefit a Programme Board will derive from reports will depend on the quality of the reports, the interval between the preparation of the report and its receipt and the window of opportunity to act on that report.

11.2.6 Define clear roles and responsibilities

When a Sponsoring Group or SRO establishes the programme roles to be performed (and the programme structure to enable those roles to function and deliver the programme objectives), it has to decide on the level of commitment it is going to make to programme risk management. Hence for programme risk management to perform and contribute effectively there must be a clear understanding of the need for and responsibilities of risk management. As a consequence, the Programme Board is instrumental in providing leadership and direction for programme risk management. Without a focus, supported by the Programme Board, the aims of programme risk management are unlikely to be delivered. Programmes should establish clear roles and responsibilities for the programme risk management in terms of leadership, direction, controls, day-to-day management of the risks, reporting and reviewing.

11.2.7 Establish a support structure and a supportive culture for risk management

For the benefits of risk management to be realised, the process needs to be led, directed, driven and encouraged through the creation of a support structure. This may be provided by the Programme Office ensuring that policies are adhered to, the process is followed, appropriate techniques are adopted, reports are issued and best practice is followed – all at the appropriate time. The Programme Office can also facilitate the embedding of risk management in the programme. The benefits of risk management must be described and communicated across the programme along with the steps required to achieve those benefits. The programme's risk culture will reflect that of the organisation and should enable all those involved in the programme to take opportunities for innovation as well as allowing timely responses to threats. To gain the most value from risk management, the programme should look to creating an environment of trust where information about risks is willingly shared and discussed.

11.2.8 Monitor for early-warning indicators

An aim of programme risk management is to be proactive and to anticipate potential problems. Hence programmes should establish early-warning indicators to provide information on the potential sources of risk. Early-warning indicators can be used as a way of tracking sensitive issues, so that should certain predefined levels be reached, corrective action will be triggered. Whilst these early-warning indicators could measure a number of diverse wide-ranging issues, they are only of value if they are measuring critical symptoms, are reviewed on a regular basis, and the information is accurate, reaches decision-makers and is acted upon.

11.2.9 Establish review cycle and look for continual improvement

An organisation's system of internal control has a key role to play in effective programme risk management. A sound system of internal control provides a firm platform for the governance and control aspects of the programme, as the two should go hand-in-hand. However an organisation's objectives, its internal organisation and the environment within which it operates are continually evolving. Alongside this, the programme itself will evolve and change. As a result the internal and external risks the programme faces are continually changing. A sound and effective risk management process therefore depends on a regular review of the risks the programme is facing in its context, and the policies, processes and plans it is adopting to manage them.

Although risk management reviews will enable the programme to understand the effectiveness of risk response planning on current or recently completed activities, it will not equip management with an adequate understanding of their risk maturity to enable them to plan and implement a step change in their risk management practices. Because programmes tend to be long-lived, there is an opportunity for them to develop an interest in continual improvement and develop strategies to improve their risk management maturity. The Programme Office would be ideally placed to adopt this role for risk as well as other management practices and feed lessons learned back into the control framework of the organisation.

11.3 PROGRAMME RISK MANAGEMENT APPROACH

The above principles provide a base on which risk management practices can be developed. However, the way in which they are implemented will vary from programme to programme. A major factor determining how risk management is undertaken within any given programme will be the way in which risks are managed across the organisation. A starting point, therefore, will be to review the organisation's risk management policy and/or risk management process guidance (or similar documents).

The organisation's risk management policy communicates how risk management will be implemented throughout the organisation to support the realisation of its strategic objectives. This will include information such as the organisation's risk appetite and capacity, risk tolerance thresholds, procedures for escalation, and defined roles and responsibilities. The risk management process guidance describes the series of steps and their respective associated activities necessary to implement risk management. This guide should provide a best practice approach that will support a consistent method of risk management across the organisation. Such a process is placed into a programme context below.

The programme approach to risk management is a combination of the programme's documented strategy, processes (including planning for implementation), and means of delivery (such as the Risk Register), as outlined in this section. The programme's risk management approach will set the framework for the interrelationship of managing risks across the different organisational perspectives outlined below, particularly between the programme and its projects, and from the projects into

the operational environment where benefits will be realised.

11.3.1 Programme Risk Management Strategy

Having reviewed these documents, and before embarking on any risk management activities, a Risk Management Strategy should be developed for the programme. The purpose of this strategy is to describe the specific risk management activities that will be undertaken to support effective risk management within the programme. The strategy will typically include:

- **Introduction**: states the purpose and owner of the strategy
- **Outline of the programme**: provides a summary of the programme to which the plan relates
- **Roles and responsibilities**: describes the main roles and responsibilities within the programme
- **Process**: this will be based on the Risk Management Process Guide but may be adapted as necessary depending on the nature of the programme
- **Scales for estimating probability and impact**: these should be developed for each programme to ensure that the scales for cost and time (for instance) are relevant to the cost and timeframe of the programme. These may be shown in the form of probability impact grids giving the criteria for each level within the scale, e.g. for very high, high, medium, low and very low
- **Expected value**: provides guidance on calculating expected value, which is done by multiplying the average impact by the probability percentage. By totalling the expected values for all the risks associated with a programme, an understanding of the total risk exposure faced by the programme can be calculated.
- **Proximity**: provides guidance on how this time factor for risks is to be assessed. Proximity reflects the fact that risks will occur at particular times and the severity of their impact will vary according to when they occur
- **Risk response category**: the responses available will depend on whether the risk is a perceived threat or an opportunity. Table 11.1 describes the alternative responses for a threat and Table 11.2 describes those for an opportunity
- **Budget required**: describes the budget required to support risk management throughout the life of the programme
- **Tools and techniques**: refers to any preferred techniques to be used for each step of the process described above
- **Templates**: these might include a Risk Register; a Risk Register is described in Appendix A

- **Early-warning indicators**: these will be selected for their relevance to the programme
- **Timing of risk management activities**: will state when formal risk management activities are to be undertaken, as part of end-of-tranche reviews

- **Reporting**: describes the reports that are to be produced and record their purpose, timing and recipients.

Table 11.1 Threat responses

Threat response	Description
Reduction	Proactive actions taken to reduce: ■ The probability of the event occurring, by performing some form of control ■ The impact of the event should it occur.
Removal	Typically involves changing some aspect of the programme, i.e. changing the scope, procurement route, supplier or sequence of activities.
Transfer	A third party takes on responsibility for an aspect of the threat (for example through insurance or by means of appropriate clauses in a contract).
Retention	A conscious and deliberate decision is taken to retain the threat, having discerned that it is more economical to do so than to attempt a risk response action, for example. The threat should continue to be monitored to ensure that it remains tolerable.
Share	Modern procurement methods commonly entail a form of risk sharing through the application of a pain/gain formula: both parties share the gain (within pre-agreed limits) if the cost is less than the cost plan; or share the pain (again within pre-agreed limits) if the cost plan is exceeded. Several industries include risk-sharing principles within their contracts with third parties.

Table 11.2 Opportunity responses

Opportunity response	Description
Realisation	Identifying and seizing an opportunity The realisation of an opportunity ensures that potential improvements to the programme are delivered. For example, if there is an opportunity to complete a project early and reduce the headcount, the realisation of the opportunity would be to achieve the reduced costs possible through a lower-than-planned headcount.
Enhancement	Seizing and improving on an identified opportunity Enhancement of an opportunity refers to both the realisation of an opportunity and achieving additional gains over and above the opportunity. An example may be negotiating a lower rental figure for existing occupied premises and restructuring the organisation to reduce the floor space required. Or it may include achieving financial gain from finishing a project early and gaining additional revenue from deploying the released resources on another project.
Exploitation	Identifying and seizing multiple benefits Exploitation refers to changing the programme's scope, supplier or specification to achieve a beneficial outcome without changing the objectives or specification. An example is where a contractor on a fixed-price contract manages to obtain a lower price from an alternative supplier on multiple subcontracts, while maintaining the desired specification.

11.4 PROGRAMME RISK MANAGEMENT PROCESS

This section describes the risk management process. It is divided into four primary risk management processes known as:

- Identify:
  - Context
  - Risks
- Assess:
  - Estimate
  - Evaluate
- Plan
- Implement.

Figure 11.1 shows these basic elements of the programme risk management process, which are described in the following sections.

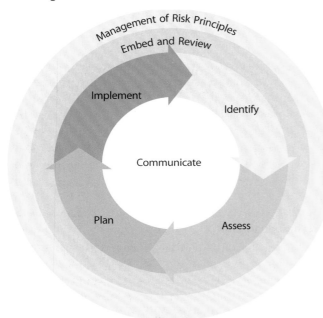

Figure 11.1 Programme Risk Management Process

11.4.1 Identify – Context

The primary process goal of the Context step within the Identify process is to obtain information about the programme. This will include understanding:

- What the programme's objectives are
- What the scope of the programme is
- What assumptions have been made
- How complete the information is
- Who the stakeholders are and what their objectives are
- Where the programme fits in relation to the organisational structure

- The organisation's own environment (industry, markets, products and services etc.)
- The organisation's approach to risk management as described by the risk management policy.

11.4.2 Identify – Risks

The primary goal of this step within the Identify process is to identify the risks to the programme that would reduce or remove the likelihood of the programme reaching its objectives, while maximising the opportunities that could lead to improved performance. This will include:

- Identifying the threats and opportunities to the programme
- Preparing a Risk Register
- Preparing key performance indicators
- Understanding the stakeholders' views of the risks.

An important aspect of identifying risk is being able to provide a clear and unambiguous expression of each risk. A useful way of expressing risk is to consider the following aspect of each risk:

- **Risk cause**: this should describe the source of the risk, i.e. the event or situation that gives rise to the risk. These are often referred to as risk drivers. They are not risks in themselves, but the potential trigger points for risk. These may be either internal or external to the programme.
- **Risk event**: this should describe the area of uncertainty in terms of the threat or the opportunity.
- **Risk effect**: this should describe the impact/s that the risk would have on the programme should the risk materialise.

Using a car journey as a simple example: a nail in a tyre is the cause, a flat tyre from the puncture is the risk event (threat) and the effect is arriving late at the destination.

11.4.3 Assess – Estimate

The primary goal of the Estimate step within the Assess process is to assess the threats and the opportunities to the programme in terms of their probability and impact. The risk proximity will also be of interest to gauge how quickly the risk is likely to materialise if no action were taken. This will require an understanding of:

- The probability of the threats and opportunities in terms of how likely they are to occur
- The impact of each threat and opportunity in terms of the programme objectives. For example, if the objectives are measured in time and cost, the impact should also be measured in units of time and cost
- The proximity of these risks and opportunities.

11.4.4 Assess – Evaluate

The primary goal of the Evaluate step within the Assess process is to understand the net effect of the identified threats and opportunities on a programme when aggregated together. This may include preparing, for example, the following:

■ An estimated monetary value (EMV) calculation, which records the weighted average of the anticipated impact
■ A risk model, which aggregates the risks together using a simulation technique
■ A net present value (NPV) calculation using an accepted discount rate.

11.4.5 Plan

The primary goal of the Plan process is to prepare specific management responses to the threats and opportunities identified, ideally to remove or reduce the threats and to maximise the opportunities. Attention to this process ensures as far as possible that the business and its staff are not taken by surprise if a risk materialises.

The usual types of response are listed in Tables 11.1 and 11.2.

It is common for risk responses not to be fully effective, in that they do not remove the risk in its entirety. This leaves a residual risk remaining. If the original risk was significant and the risk response was only partially successful, the remaining risk can be considerable.

11.4.6 Implement

The primary goal of the Implement process is to ensure that the planned risk management actions are implemented and monitored as to their effectiveness, and corrective action is taken where responses do not match expectations.

An important part of this is to ensure that there are clear roles and responsibilities allocated. The main roles in this respect are:

■ **Risk owner**: this will be a named individual who is responsible for the management and control of all aspects of the risks assigned to them, including the implementation of the selected actions to address the threats or to maximise the opportunities
■ **Risk actionee**: a risk actionee is the individual assigned the implementation of a risk response action or actions to respond to a particular risk or set of risks. They support and take direction from the risk owner.

11.4.7 Communicate

Rather than being a distinct stage in the Risk Management Process, communication is an activity that is carried out throughout the whole process. A number of aspects of communication should be recognised and addressed if risk management is to be effective.

A programme's exposure to risk is never static: effective communication is key to the identification of new threats and opportunities or changes in existing risks. Horizon scanning in particular depends on the maintenance of a good communications network, including relevant contacts and sources of information to facilitate the identification of changes that may affect the programme's overall risk exposure.

The implementation of risk management is dependent on participation, and participation, in turn, is dependent on communication. It is important for management to engage with staff across the programme as well as wider stakeholders.

11.5 EMBEDDING AND REVIEWING PROGRAMME RISK MANAGEMENT

A programme that effectively and visibly manages its risks demonstrates part of that programme's core values and should therefore improve stakeholder confidence in the programme's ability to deliver the required outcomes and expected benefits. The programme therefore needs to ensure that risk management has been integrated successfully, has the necessary support, is addressed in an appropriate way and is successful. A key component of the risk management integration within a programme is the cultural acceptance and change required to embed the risk management principles and values within the programme. This can be best achieved through a structured set of activities that lead to the achievement of risk knowledge, understanding and education within the programme.

A programme needs to be able to measure the effectiveness and appropriateness of risk management, including the programme's progress in embedding risk management, and also its ability to develop its risk management capability and maturity. The latter can be assessed using a maturity model approach. See Appendix B (section B6) for more details on using maturity models in programmes.

11.6 RISK MANAGEMENT PERSPECTIVES

Programmes interface with other organisational perspectives as can be seen by Figure 11.2.

Figure 11.2 Interrelationships between different organisational perspectives

The nature of the interfaces between these perspectives can be a source of significant risks to the programme.

11.6.1 Strategic risks

Considered risk-taking can enable an innovative approach to seeking greater opportunities for realising benefits. Within the strategic perspective, there are drivers (such as political or regulatory pressures, emerging technologies and new initiatives) arising while the programme is under way, which may alter the programme's scope and lead to changes in direction – a source of further risk to the programme.

The failure to achieve a common understanding among members of the Sponsoring Group, Programme Board and other stakeholders about the definition and value of a programme's objectives is a risk in itself. Not having a common understanding means not only that success is unlikely, but that it is not possible to tell whether success has been achieved. Such failure will, of course, affect the direction and chances of success of the entire programme.

There are also likely to be risks around programme interdependencies that need to be considered at a corporate portfolio level as new programmes are scoped and planned. Changes at the strategic perspective, such as new initiatives that the organisation must respond to

quickly, can affect programme interdependencies and the associated risks. Areas to consider include:

- Political, economic, social, legislative, environmental and technical impacts
- Other programmes including inter-programme dependencies
- Cross-organisational initiatives, including working with third-party suppliers or partners
- Other initiatives within the organisation
- Internal political pressures.

11.6.2 Programme risks

Programmes focus on delivering benefits to the organisation and often affect a wide variety of stakeholders both internally and externally. Risk management for a programme must be designed to work across organisational boundaries in order to accommodate these differing interests and ensure that stakeholders are engaged appropriately.

Typically the principal areas of risk within a programme relate to:

- Lack of clarity about the expected benefits and the buy-in from key stakeholders
- The complexity and complications associated with working across organisational boundaries, which also tends to lead to a larger and more diverse group of stakeholders
- The management of interdependencies between the programme and its projects, and between the programme and its wider context
- Funding
- Organisational and cultural issues and the higher likelihood of changes to the organisational environment due to the naturally longer timescales programmes operate under; e.g. a change of personnel in key roles, such as the SRO, is more likely in a programme than a change of equivalent key roles in a project
- The quality of the benefit-enabling outputs from the projects within the programme.

Other risks to the programme may arise if the underlying assumptions of the programme's Business Case (or the business cases of the projects within the programme) change. Given this broader and more diverse risk profile, it is often helpful to include explicit statements of any assumptions made within the Risk Register, in order to flag up potential impact and monitor the ongoing validity of the assumptions. If objectives are vague the programme is likely to be exposed to considerable dangers during implementation, especially if a new initiative causes the programme's objectives to alter.

Key early-warning indicators for the programme relating directly to the programme's objectives might include:

- The achievement of key programme milestones
- Impact of the establishment of new capabilities on timings and budgets
- Changes to vision, Blueprint etc. that set the agenda for the programme
- Reduction or delays in the delivery of expected/planned benefits on time and on budget
- Availability of required skills
- Interproject dependencies
- Impact on business continuity
- Level of aggregated risk resulting from project and operational risks.

11.6.3 Project risks

The project outputs within a programme are the vehicles for delivering the programme outcomes and benefits; therefore much of the focus of risk management within a programme is at the project perspective. The programme should set the risk management standards and framework for the projects. The projects are then given the authority to manage their risks within these parameters. Risks may be identified before the projects are underway, for example when the programme is being set up. When project teams identify and assess risks, they may gain clearer insight into risks affecting the programme, necessitating a revision of the programme's risks. Further risks may be identified due to non-availability of skills and resources that will affect the project's capability to deliver its products or services. Project risk management must be integrated into the programme's risk management processes, typically with the support of the Programme Office.

To manage the risks to projects well, it is necessary to:

- Ensure each Project Brief outlines the risks from the perspective of the programme
- Provide, as individual projects progress, regular feedback to the programme's risk management activities.

Engaging and managing third-party resources should be carefully considered from the project perspective, as the engaging activities may have a broader impact that merits a higher profile and more senior level of ownership (either within the programme or possibly the Sponsoring Group). The parameters for the project interaction and management of associated risk with third-party suppliers should be set by the programme within the programme's Stakeholder Engagement Strategy.

Typically the areas of uncertainty within the project perspective include risks arising from lack of clarity of customer requirements, the timely availability of skills and expertise, procurement and acquisition, scope creep and scheduling – all of which are areas where the programme can offer support to the projects.

11.6.4 Operational risks

As projects deliver their outputs of products and services (new capability), the transition to new ways of working and new systems can lead to further sources of risk. For example, during a handover process, risks could arise from the need to maintain operational stability as well as the integrity of the systems, infrastructure and support services.

Transition must be properly planned, managed and resourced. There may be projects required to achieve soft deliverables (for example, changes in staff behaviour) as well as physical outputs. Will new ways of working introduce new risks, such as fraud or abuse of financial arrangements?

Areas to consider include:

- Business continuity
- Transfer of outputs to operations
- Acceptability within business operations
- Stakeholder support
- Rate and volume of change across the corporate portfolio
- Availability of resources
- Organisational track record of managing change.

11.7 ISSUE RESOLUTION

In a similar way to the formality necessary for managing risks, resolving issues also requires the programme to determine how issues will be handled and resolved efficiently. The purpose of issue resolution is to build a mechanism for the programme to efficiently deal with anything that arises by having processes and responsibilities in place. It is impossible to anticipate everything that could possibly happen during the programme, so planning how to deal with the unknown, and usually unplanned, is important.

11.7.1 Issue Resolution Strategy

The Issue Resolution Strategy sets out how issues will be captured and assessed prior to the appropriate resolution activities being carried out. Information is a necessary prerequisite for effective assessment of the potential impact of an issue. The Issue Resolution Strategy defines how the relevant information for assessment will be collected, who will be responsible for resolution activities and how ownership of the issues raised will be allocated.

The Issue Resolution Strategy will define how issues will be managed within the programme; in particular it must define how the Issue Resolution Process will include projects and operational issues to ensure that they are captured and processed effectively.

In addition to defining responsibilities, it will also describe how priorities will be assessed, the tools and systems. It is critical that it defines how exceptions that take the programme outside the boundaries set for it by the Sponsoring Group, i.e. when it exceeds its margins, will be escalated and resolved.

Some organisations may chose to merge their Issue Resolution Strategy into their overall Risk Management Strategy if this fits their organisational governance arrangements.

For further details on the Issue Resolution Strategy, see Appendix A: 'Programme information'.

11.7.2 Sources of issues

Issues are likely to arise from a wide variety of sources, for example:

- Benefits Management, transition activities, costs, scope and timescales
- Dependencies, quality of operations, resources and programme deliverables
- Anything that cannot be resolved by the project, or issues common to more than one project
- Stakeholders, organisation and programme staff, and third parties
- Operational performance degradation beyond acceptable levels
- Other projects and programmes under way within the organisation.

All issues raised, from whichever source, should be captured and logged on the programme's Issue Log. The Issue Log provides a management tool for the Programme Manager in the ongoing tracking and monitoring of issue resolution.

Appendix A 'Programme information' provides a full description of the Issue Log contents.

11.7.3 Issue Resolution Process

Issues may suggest some kind of change to the programme. The options for change should be considered and actioned appropriately as part of the programme's change control process.

Assessing issues typically classifies them into one of the following three types:

- A previously identified risk that has now hit and requires the appropriate issue management action
- A required change to some aspect of the programme
- A problem or question affecting all or part of the programme in some way.

Prioritisation of issues is a key part of issue resolution. The volume of issues facing programmes can be huge. It may be helpful to develop prioritisation criteria (e.g. cost impact, time delay caused, possible reputational damage etc.) to provide a filter to focus on critical issues.

When identified, issues may in fact turn out to be possible future events rather than present concerns (i.e. the issue identification process may in fact identify risks). Such issues should be moved to the Risk Register and managed under the Risk Management Strategy.

Issues that are not dealt with through change control or programme risk management should be prioritised in terms of their actual impact on the programme. Some issues – for example, queries from stakeholders or requests for information – should be responded to as quickly as possible. Other issues may not be resolvable within the limits of the current resources, timeframe or scope of the programme. These issues should be escalated to the appropriate top management level for resolution.

The status and resolution of issues should be included in the Issue Log for audit trail and future reference. For further details on the Issue Log, see Appendix A: 'Programme information'.

Figure 11.3 overleaf shows the Issue Resolution Process.

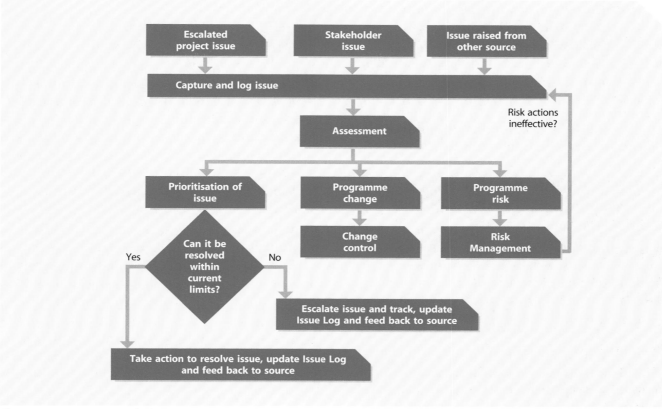

Figure 11.3   Issue Resolution Process

11.7.4 Cross-programme issues

Some issues may, individually, have an impact across many parts of a programme or across more than one programme. The resolution of these issues should still be handled within the programme's formal Issue Resolution Process. However, the priority given to these issues will inevitably be high because of the need to consider the wider implications of any management action or intervention.

Cross-programme issues may involve any aspect of the programme, for example internal or external resources, suppliers, stakeholders, changes to requirements or escalation in costs. As with all issues, they should be captured and formally assessed in terms of their impact (whether actual or potential) on the programme. Typically, cross-programme issues need to be escalated to top management for resolution (often via the SRO to the Sponsoring Group). It is important to establish and maintain effective communication channels between top management and the appropriate members of the programme management team, particularly during the resolution of cross-programme issues (see paragraph 4.9.3, 'Cross-organisational programmes').

11.8 CHANGE CONTROL

A critical aspect of resolving issues is the process of making changes to the programme. Change control is the process of managing and controlling changes to any aspect of the programme, the projects or the project outputs. In a programme context, change control should be applied to at least the key sets of information about the programme, such as the Blueprint, the Business Case and the Programme Plan. The process may also be applied to products during their development stages on a project. In this case, change control would be applied at the project level.

There will be a close link between change control and the exception procedures that a programme designs for dealing with issues that take it outside of its boundary.

Defining the procedures for change control on a programme requires consideration of the following:

- Maintaining a central log of potential changes – the Issue Log
- Establishing a mechanism for prioritising the potential changes
- Carrying out formal impact assessments of the potential changes against the programme's Business Case, Programme Plan, Project Portfolio, Blueprint etc.

- Assessing the impact of the change on the risks to the programme, or the expected benefits
- Re-evaluating the priority status
- Decision processes for deciding which changes to accommodate
- Updating the Issue Log with the decision and maintaining an audit trail
- Implementing the approved changes appropriately and communicating the outcome to those affected.

11.9 INTEGRATION BETWEEN THE PROGRAMME, ITS PROJECTS AND OPERATIONS

All project-level issues and risks must also be visible at the programme level, since individual projects may not be able to perceive their wider implications to other projects or the programme itself. Responsibility for all the risks and issues within the projects lies with the project managers, ensuring their resolution with escalation to the programme level and specifically the Programme Manager.

The Programme Manager must also engage actively with the Business Change Manager and other key stakeholders to ensure that they are part of the risk management arrangements. Often problems occur in the broader stakeholder community that could have been dealt with had broader engagement been in place. If a corporate Risk Management Process is in place, the programme must have visibility of risks being raised and managed to ensure that their impact is understood within the programme.

Each project team within the programme is responsible for its own change control procedures. However, certain changes will have an impact outside the project, either on other projects within the project portfolio or on the Programme Plan. The programme should specify the tolerance levels for any such changes at the project level so that only those changes that matter to the programme are escalated to the programme level. It is important for all the project teams to have a common understanding of the change control process for the programme. The programme and the projects within the programme should be using a singular consistent process (with layers, escalation paths etc.) using singular and consistent language to manage risks and issues. Likewise the programme and the projects within the programme should be using a singular consistent process (with layers, escalation paths etc.) using singular and consistent language for change management. This should allow clear communication to all interested and affected parties without the overhead of too much administration.

An integrated Risk Register, spanning the programme, operations and its projects is an appropriate tool for ensuring a cohesive programme-wide management of risks.

The Programme Office should play a central role in building and maintaining efficient, effective and consistent two-way flows of information between the programme and its projects. The Programme Office should own the Risk Management and Issue Resolution Processes for the programme.

11.10 ROLES AND RESPONSIBILITIES

Table 11.3 shows the roles and responsibilities involved in risk management and issue resolution.

Table 11.3 Risk management and issue resolution: roles and responsibilities

Role	Responsibility
Senior Responsible Owner	Approving the Risk Management and Issue Resolution Strategies
	Ensuring the programme risk management and issue resolution activities are operating effectively
	Initiating assurance reviews of risk and issue management effectiveness
	Ownership of strategic risks and issues and ensuring mitigation actions are dealt with at the appropriate senior level.
Programme Manager	Developing and implementing the strategies for handling risk and issues
	Designing and establishing the Risk Management Process
	Programme adherence to the risk management principles
	Allocation of risks is appropriate
	Ensuring that issue resolution is undertaken by individuals with the correct authority
	Maintaining the programme Risk Register
	Maintaining the programme Issue Log
	Ensuring that the impact of individual and aggregated risks is understood by the relevant stakeholders.
Business Change Manager	Managing and coordinating the resolution of risks relating to operational performance and benefits achievement
	Ensuring that the Risk Management Process includes operational risks
	Ownership of risks that impact on business performance and transition.
Programme Office	Managing and coordinating the information and support systems to enable efficient handling of the programme's risks and issues
	Providing support and advice on the risk and issues processes.

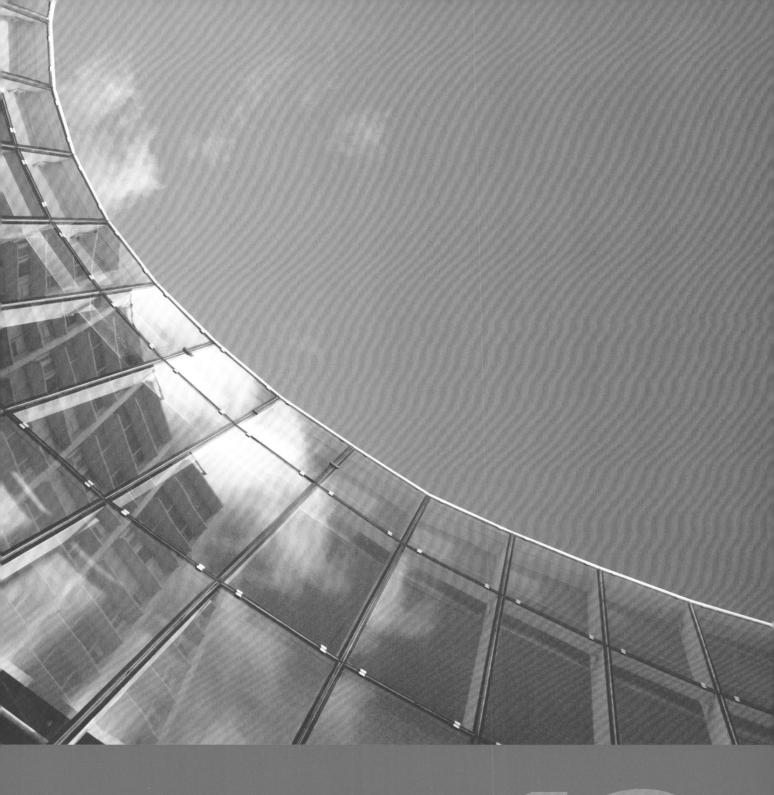

Quality
management

12

12 Quality management

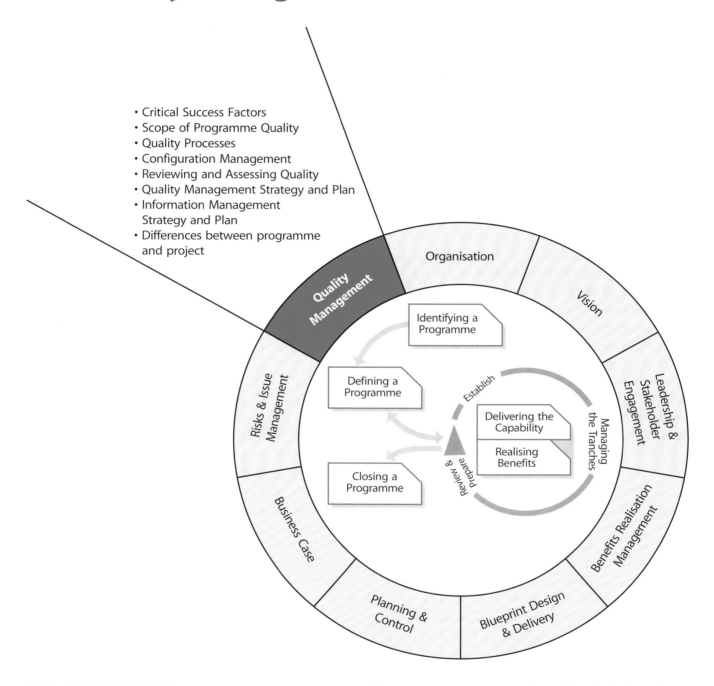

- Critical Success Factors
- Scope of Programme Quality
- Quality Processes
- Configuration Management
- Reviewing and Assessing Quality
- Quality Management Strategy and Plan
- Information Management Strategy and Plan
- Differences between programme and project

Quality Management

Organisation

Vision

Leadership & Stakeholder Engagement

Benefits Realisation Management

Blueprint Design & Delivery

Planning & Control

Business Case

Risks & Issue Management

Identifying a Programme

Defining a Programme

Closing a Programme

Establish

Delivering the Capability

Realising Benefits

Managing the Tranches

Review & Prepare

12.1 INTRODUCTION

Quality management in a programme ensures that stakeholders are satisfied that their planned benefits have the best chance of being realised and will meet their expectations. Quality management must be an activity that runs continuously throughout the life of a programme and beyond (the organisation continues to realise benefits after the programme has ended). Therefore, achieving quality must be an integral part of all the day-to-day activities of the programme.

If a programme does not apply quality effectively to its activities, its assets and outputs are less likely to be fit for purpose, with the consequential detrimental impact on the outcomes and desired benefits.

The management of quality within a programme is different to that within a project. In a programme the focus of quality is helping the programme with the achievement of strategic goals. These goals may themselves change during the life of the programme to reflect the organisation's changing strategic priorities.

Quality management in a programme must ensure there is a full understanding of these corporate priorities, and that the programme's Blueprint and schedules remain aligned to them. By contrast, the management of quality within a project is generally more straightforward, being focused on ensuring that the outputs will meet acceptance criteria (in a PRINCE2 project environment this includes meeting specifications as given in pre-agreed product descriptions).

12.2 CRITICAL SUCCESS FACTORS

Critical Success Factors (CSFs) are the limited number of areas that, if fully addressed, will ensure successful completion of the programme. They are the few key areas where things must go right for the desired improvement in the business to be achieved. If results in these areas are not adequate, there will be significantly less improvement and fewer benefits than desired or expected. CSFs are areas of activity that should receive constant and careful attention from those responsible for management of the programme.

By identifying and communicating these CSFs, you can help ensure everyone is focused on those specific areas and activities that are most important. As the characteristics of every programme are different, the specific nature of (and attributes of successful delivery for) each CSF should be identified as part of developing the Quality Management Strategy (in 'Defining a Programme'; see Chapter 15).

The identification of CSF activities requires considering and including the implications from a wide range of areas, including:

- **Wider environment**: the more extra-organisational changes threaten the programme, the more attention should be given to closely monitoring this
- **Policy and strategy**: programmes exist to help deliver change and benefits that are important to the organisation. Where policy or strategy might be subject to (frequent) change, programmes need to be agile enough to avoid delivering what is no longer important to the organisation.
- **Organisational culture**: if change is not well accepted or if the organisation is in a state of 'change overload', engaging successfully with stakeholders will need more time
- **Resources**: if the change skills and experience of the people who will manage and deliver the change is limited, these might need to be supplemented with external help, or the programme might need to be more modest in its ambitions.

Close alignment between CSFs and stakeholders is important to make sure everyone understands the areas of critical importance which must be protected to ensure success.

12.3 SCOPE OF QUALITY IN A PROGRAMME

Quality as applied to a programme embraces a number of different aspects, such as in Figure 12.1.

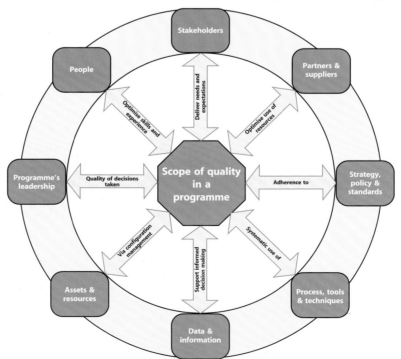

Figure 12.1 How quality in a programme ensures best use of resources

Quality activities are set out in the Quality Management Plan, which schedules and directs the ongoing review and improvement of a programme's activities.

12.4 STAKEHOLDER RELATIONSHIPS

Stakeholders more directly affected by the programme can be considered its customers. Quality in a programme needs to ensure these customers are as satisfied as the operational part of the organisation would want its customers to be.

In order to truly understand the requirements for change and deliver them, people in programmes will need to:

- Segment the programme's stakeholders and get to know and understand them by developing sound working relations
- Maintain those relations throughout the life of the programme in order to remain responsive to stakeholders' present needs and expectations
- Anticipate what stakeholders' future needs and expectations will be and act accordingly in order to meet or exceed them
- Monitor and review the experiences and perceptions of their stakeholders and, where deliverables do not meet the required quality, respond quickly and effectively to rectify the situation.

Quality assurance activities will need to be focused clearly on testing the perceptions of (expected) success of the stakeholders, and the quality of the relations with them, to ensure that there are no surprises for either side.

See also Chapter 6 'Leadership and Stakeholder Engagement'.

12.5 LEADERSHIP

Good leadership is critical to programme success. As with any other programme activities, the application of the Quality Management Plan must ensure that good, effective leadership is taking place.

The leaders of successful programmes provide clear direction and communicate that direction to people inside and outside the programme. This communication is critical to establishing unity and constancy of purpose. The programme's leadership must establish a governance framework that provides adequate levels of control for the programme, including the delegation of unambiguous authority and responsibility (covered in Chapter 4 'Organisation'), which quality review activities will evaluate regularly.

In order to inspire and motivate people to create the necessary culture of quality in the programme, it is critical that the programme's leaders perform and behave as role models of a quality-driven approach. This can be promoted by creating and modelling appropriate behaviours, shared values and ethics at all levels of the programme, and by leaders recognising people's contributions as the programme's performance is evaluated.

> **Tip**
>
> For the Senior Responsible Owner (SRO) and others who provide leadership:
>
> - Near the end of 'Defining a Programme' get the programme team to demonstrate that the planned quality arrangements will be adequate
> - Ask the programme team to explain how contingency will work as part of issue resolution
> - At reviews, such as that at the end of a tranche, ask for evidence that quality is working
> - Use the services of a quality expert, independent of the programme, to verify this
> - If the programme is under time, cost or similar pressure to skimp on quality, defend it appropriately.

12.6 INVOLVEMENT OF PEOPLE

Several of the principles for good programme management are particularly concerned with people (see Chapter 2 'Programme management principles'):

- Leading change
- Envisioning and communicating a better future
- Learning from experience.

Quality activities should make sure these are appropriately applied to get the best out of the people deployed on the programme.

A programme's main asset is the people within it. A programme may adopt the best processes and have access to considerable funds but if it does not deploy the right number of people with the right skills, attitude and experience at the right time, it is unlikely to be successful in the eyes of its stakeholders.

As people are assigned to their particular roles, they will need to understand the importance of their contribution to the programme and be told what will enable them to fulfil their role (within its constraints), for example:

- Their degree of accountability and level of authority
- What the prevailing policy, processes and standards are to which they must adhere

- What resources are (or are not) available, including facilities, equipment and materials
- Their rights to create, access, use or delete data, information and records.

Reviews of individual and team performance will need to take place regularly and feed into the SRO or Programme Board to ensure that all aspects of people management, including specific quality-related elements, are reviewed and the appropriate preventive or corrective action is taken.

Tip

If some people who join the programme may have limited experience, make sure:

- There is either a plan to help them learn and develop, or
- The pace they are expected to perform at is consistent with their ability.

Where the staff development option is chosen, verify their improved capability, after learning events, as part of assessing their performance.

12.7 ADHERENCE TO STRATEGIES, POLICIES AND STANDARDS

Programmes are always driven by the organisation's policies and strategies. Quality activities in a programme need to ensure that the planned changes continue to be correctly aligned to the relevant parts of these corporate strategies and policies. It is particularly important to remember that most organisations review and change their policies and strategies at intervals that are unlikely to coincide with a convenient review point in a programme. A monitoring and informing mechanism to alert programmes of pending policy or strategy will help in two ways:

- The programme can provide input to the policy and strategy makers, to explain how well it is progressing in line with current policy and strategy. This can help strategy makers avoid changing direction because they have not seen evidence that current strategy is working
- It enables programmes to assess the impact of proposals to change policy and strategy. What might be gained and what will be lost can be fed back to the strategist or policy-maker, so their decisions are made on an informed basis. The case study in section 12.16 shows an example of where this mechanism failed, resulting in the overall failure of the programme.

Many organisations have a quality management system that supports operations to ensure their products and services satisfactorily meet their customers' requirements. Where such a system exists programmes need to be aware of how quality standards relate to planned changes in the programme. New improved operations may still need to comply with these standards, or the quality standards may need to be adjusted to suit the amended process, products or services.

There are few business activities that are not subject to some aspect of legislation and/or regulation. Programmes need to be aware which laws and regulations are relevant to ensure their projects' outputs, and the changed operations, comply correctly. Similar to the reasons explained above for policy and strategy, programmes need to monitor these external standards to detect and assess the impact of any pending changes. This point is also important in the context of technical or professional standards. For example, if an organisation advertises itself as complying with ISO 9000 then it must ensure it can still comply after changes have been embedded.

12.8 PARTNERS AND SUPPLIERS

Just as many operational parts of an organisation depend on their suppliers providing goods or services that are fit for purpose, so too is a programme dependent on its suppliers. Quality in a programme also has to ensure that its suppliers deliver fit-for-purpose products. A programme's suppliers are internal and external:

- Internal – for example, its projects or business units providing services
- External – for example, providers of temporary offices and infrastructure for the duration of the programme.

An organisation and its suppliers are interdependent and a mutually beneficial relationship increases the inclination of both parties to create greater, shared value.

Key benefits:

- Increased ability to create value for both parties
- Flexibility and speed of joint responses to changing market or customer needs and expectations
- Optimisation of costs and resources.

Applying the principles of mutually beneficial supplier relationships typically leads to:

- Relationships that balance short-term gains with long-term considerations
- Pooling of expertise and resources with partners
- Identifying and selecting key suppliers more effectively
- Clear and more open communication

- Sharing information and future plans, allowing better response from both parties
- Establishing joint development and improvement activities
- Encouraging and recognising improvements and achievements by suppliers.

12.9 QUALITY PROCESSES

A process is a set of related activities that are carried out in a defined order. A system contains several processes and requires good management infrastructure and control mechanisms for all of its parts to work together properly. MSP can be thought of as a system, with parts of it as processes, for example 'Managing the Tranches'.

Good systems and processes have in-built measurement and control to monitor against deviation. Process control approaches are equally applicable to a programme as to operational activities. Programmes are managed through activities that need to be carried out in a defined order, and success is only achieved if the customers of the programme (the operations that will change) are fully satisfied with the result. In projects and programmes the Quality Management Process should provide the control to ensure customers are satisfied by the products and services that are their outputs.

Applying the principles of a systems and process approach typically leads to:

- Achieving the organisation's objectives in the most effective and efficient way
- Understanding well the interdependencies inherent in a processes
- Integration and alignment of the processes that will best achieve the desired results.
- Structured approaches that harmonise and integrate processes
- Better understanding of the roles and responsibilities for achieving common objectives (and thereby reducing cross-functional barriers)
- Ability to focus effort on the key processes
- Taking into account capability and resource constraints prior to action
- Fully defining how activities should interoperate to obtain desired results
- Continually improving systems through measurement and evaluation
- Establishing clear responsibility and accountability for managing key activities
- Identifying the interfaces of key activities within and between functions

- Focusing on the factors that will improve key activities of the organisation.

Quality in a programme needs to make sure that MSP processes are appropriately adapted (Chapter 15 'Defining a Programme') and used effectively (Chapter 17 'Delivering the Capability').

Identifying, understanding and managing processes as parts of an interrelated system can contribute to the organisation's effectiveness and efficiency in achieving its objectives.

12.10 CONFIGURATION MANAGEMENT

No organisation can be fully efficient or effective unless it manages well those assets that are vital to the running of the organisation's business.

Configuration management is a well-established discipline that ensures a set of components fit together to function properly as an assembly. It is widely used in manufacturing and computer software development.

The purpose of configuration management is to identify, track and protect the programme's assets (i.e. anything that is of material value to its success). These can be grouped as follows:

- Assets of the programme itself, for example the Blueprint and the Programme Plan
- Interfaces between the projects and the programme, for example project progress reports
- Project outputs.

Programme information should be seen as a critical asset. Appendix A: 'Programme information' (Programme information evolution) explains the four information baselines that the programme team must manage:

1 **Boundary**: those that set out the direction of the programme
2 **Governance**: those that set the standards and frameworks within which the programme will be delivered
3 **Tools**: those that are created and actively managed and updated throughout
4 **Programme**: those that take the scope and put the detail specification around how the end game will be achieved.

Baselines interrelate; if one document is changed, configuration management should help assess the impact on the others. Change should be made under control. Please see section 11.8 for more information on change control and details on Information Management Strategy in Appendix A.

Success in a programme is often reliant on the satisfactory functioning of a combined set of project outputs and operational functions. The failure of one component can mean failure of the whole assembly. Changed operations are depending on that complete assembly, and if it malfunctions the desired improvements may well not be achieved, leading to failure for all or a large part of the programme.

For these reasons it is important that programmes have a process of ensuring that all individual components or sub-products of a complete system (the configuration) are identified, understood and maintained, with any changes to them assessed, tested and their release controlled.

See also Appendix A: 'Programme information' (Information Management Strategy and Information Management Plan) and Appendix C: 'Programme Office' for more information on configuration management.

There is a two-way relationship between quality and configuration management:

- Quality makes sure effective configuration management is in place
- Quality is dependent on configuration management, for example to make sure quality reviews are provided with the correct information.

12.11 MEASUREMENT AND ANALYSIS

Effective decisions are based on the accurate measurement of data and the analysis of reliable information. This is as true for programmes as it is for any part of an organisation. In order for people in a programme to measure progress and assess performance, measures of inputs, resources, activities and outputs will need to be taken prior to any change and throughout the programme. The data and information from these measures will need to be analysed and reviewed at the regular meetings set out in the schedule in the Quality Management Plan. Contrary to many people's perceptions, this approach will enable the programme to be more flexible to changes in the business environment and prevent fire-fighting. This is because the programme's leaders will be responding to hard facts and figures, and relying less on intuition.

Measurements in a programme can be considered in two ways:

- Those concerned with the management and control of the programme, for example cost and budget reports
- The measurement of the programme's outcomes to assess whether acceptable benefits are materialising.

Unsuitable measures or misinterpreted analysis are likely to lead to poor control. Quality should ensure measurement and analysis procedures and systems are effective.

12.12 REVIEWING AND ASSESSING QUALITY

12.12.1 Audit

Audit is a generic activity, not one confined solely to the audit of financial accounts, and is often used to assess the management and conduct of a programme. Audit involves examination of the activities of a programme with the aim of determining the extent to which they conform to accepted criteria. The criteria may be internal standards and procedures or external codes of practice, accounting standards, contract conditions or statutory requirements. Audits may be carried out by internal audit staff or by external audit bodies.

> *Tips*
>
> Audit is more about ensuring the programme is doing things right as defined in its control framework (covered in Chapter 15 'Defining a Programme'); i.e. is it following its own rules?
>
> However, it might be right to expect an audit to also check evidence that the programme is doing the right things (relative to its Business Case), that its progress so far is on track to achieving benefits that are in alignment with strategy.
>
> It is not unheard of for the programme audit to also assess the inherent do-ability of the Business Case.
>
> Make sure the audit staff are briefed clearly.

Programme auditors should be able to provide the programme with particular information needs, and be able to assist the Programme Manager to build in any specific audit requirements to the governance procedures and plans for the programme.

Programme audits will consider any or all aspects of the programme, its management and delivery capability. While audits tend to focus on conformance and compliance, health checks may be used as a programme assurance tool by senior managers to determine whether a programme should continue. Health checks can also be used to provide an impartial view of a programme during its lifecycle to assess whether or not it will meet its objectives. See Appendix D: 'Health checks' for more details.

12.12.2 Review

Review is an important activity that is often forgotten or ignored. Without review, the findings of audits or other forms of programme assessment cannot be evaluated properly by the programme's leaders. This will lead to ill-informed decisions about the real performance and direction of the programme and what actions are needed to keep it on course.

Review activities include meetings between the SRO and the Programme Manager, Programme Board meetings, business change meetings and any meeting where decisions are taken that affect the effectiveness and efficiency of the programme. It will be useful to set out these key meetings in the Quality Management Plan.

> *Tips*
>
> Review and programme assurance is more about ensuring the programme is doing the right things, for example as defined in the Blueprint, Projects Dossier, Programme Plan and Benefit Profiles, which are produced in 'Defining a Programme' (Chapter 15).
>
> However, it might be pertinent to require a review to also check evidence that the programme is doing things right, and that its activities so far comply with the management strategies that make up the control framework.
>
> Make sure the review staff are briefed clearly.

Many programmes in the UK Public Sector will be subject to the OGC Gateway Review 0. This strategic level review provides assurance to the Programme Board that the scope and purpose of the programme has been adequately researched; that there is a shared understanding of what is to be achieved by the main players; that it fits within the organisation's overall policy or management strategy and priorities; and that there is a realistic possibility of securing the resources needed for delivery. The review will, in addition, examine how the work-strands will be organised (in sub-programmes, projects etc.) to deliver the overall programme objectives, and that the programme management structure, monitoring and resourcing is appropriate.

In short, the first OGC Gateway Review 0 aims to test whether stakeholders' expectations of the programme are realistic, by reference to costs, outcomes, resource needs, timetable and general achievability. Subsequent OGC Gateway 0 Reviews revisit the same questions at appropriate points in the programme's life to confirm that the main stakeholders have a common understanding of desired outcomes and that the programme is likely to achieve them.

There is high value in an organisation (possibly the SRO, Sponsoring Group or corporate portfolio) subjecting its programme(s) to such rigour. The cost and effort saved by refocusing or cancelling a programme that is no longer strategically aligned far outweighs the cost and inconvenience of the activity.

12.13 QUALITY MANAGEMENT STRATEGY

The Quality Management Strategy is used to define and establish what the activities are for managing quality and, when these are triggered, a description of the quality assurance, review and control processes together with the roles and responsibilities for taking these actions across the programme. See Appendix A, 'Programme information' for more details.

Programmes involving formal contracts with third parties for delivery of products or services to the programme will need to consider the relevant contractual requirements concerning quality management. Quality requirements specified in contracts should be consistent with the programme's overall Quality Management Strategy.

12.14 QUALITY MANAGEMENT PLAN

The Quality Management Plan can be used to explain the arrangements for implementing the Quality Management Strategy, and should include:

- A schedule of the activities required to implement the Quality Management Strategy
- Plans and dates for audits and reviews
- The resources needed for the successful execution of specific quality activities.

The Quality Management Plan provides input to the planning of a programme to ensure the required resources and time commitments are built into all relevant plans. See Appendix A: 'Programme Information' for more details.

12.15 INFORMATION MANAGEMENT STRATEGY AND PLAN

Information is at the core of any programme. Decisions at the outset must be made on reliable and robust information. During the lifecycle, assessing the ongoing viability of the programme and its ability to achieve the outcomes will depend on rigorous management of information about the progress of projects and stability and performance of the business.

It is easy for a programme to become overwhelmed with data, and in fact become a data-generating machine which creates a deluge of documents, templates and reports but fails in the core purpose of providing the right information, in the right format to the right people to enable effective decision-making.

Critical Success Factors that underpin the information management system of any programme include:

- **Compliance**: information storage and retention should be compliant. In particular, consideration should be given to Data Protection, Freedom of Information legislation and requirements in terms of length of retention for personnel and financial records.
- **Integrity**: information stored should be under change and release management control. This should ensure that the right versions of information are in circulation and use. Audit should be considered for checking that the distribution systems are working.
- **Availability**: decision-makers should have access to the information and documentation they require.
- **Confidentiality**: levels of confidentiality should be set within the programme. Documents are allocated appropriate levels of sensitivity and their distribution is limited accordingly. This may also require an audit trail and certification.
- **Currency**: information being used should reflect the current situation. Any gaps in reporting from projects or concerns about accuracy of business performance data should be acknowledged, together with limitations that this brings to decision-making.

Based on such factors, quality reviews should ensure that adequate, timely information is produced, correctly communicated and properly understood by the recipients.

The Information Management Plan sets out how the governance designed in the strategy will be achieved.

See Appendix A: 'Programme information' for more detail on the contents of the Information Management Strategy and Information Management Plan.

Tips

A major problem in many programmes (and projects) is incomplete and out-of-date information, severely compromising management and control.

Early in the programme (for example at the start of the first tranche) pay close attention through quality to validating information flows to check they are complete and up to date.

Establishing such a rigorous regime early will provide not just good information but reinforce the importance of quality.

12.16 DIFFERENCES BETWEEN QUALITY IN PROGRAMMES AND PROJECTS

Whilst the quality of the various programme outputs are tested by its projects, other programme attributes can only be assured by programme staff using their judgement and experience. An IT project can ensure an e-service system functions correctly through technical testing, but the programme has to judge if enough of the target customers will find it useful to make the investment worthwhile.

This very vagueness and uncertainty makes the management of quality within a programme environment of paramount importance. The objective of this management function is to provide assurance that all aspects of the programme are working to achieve results of sufficient quality to achieve the objectives of the programme to the satisfaction of the stakeholders. Given that these objectives may change during the life of a programme, programme quality management requires a full understanding of these corporate priorities and hence it has a strategic dimension.

By contrast, the management of quality within a component project is generally more straightforward, being focused on ensuring that the project outputs will meet their agreed acceptance criteria and thus achieve sign-off on time and within budget.

The case study overleaf of an IT supplier shows how quality in a project can indicate success but in reality the programme has failed.

A large IT supplier was contracted to deliver an IT system to support a mission-critical programme. Because the contract was for a substantial fixed price, the supplier appointed a highly experienced project manager, who employed best-practice project management methods. The completed system was delivered on time and fully in accordance with the contract and specification.

All had not been plain sailing. The cost of developing the software turned out to be significantly higher than originally planned, but by delaying the procurement of hardware until the last possible moment, the project manager was able to make savings that almost exactly matched the cost of overruns on the software development.

The customer was less happy. During the development period one of the main programme sponsors had retired. His successor had different ideas. By the time the new system arrived, working procedures had changed and were no longer consistent with what was delivered. As a result, the new system was abandoned after six months of struggle.

The supplier was blamed for the failure and a replacement IT system, based on different technology, was procured by the customer from elsewhere. The supplier did things right, but did not do the right things. The fault actually lay with the programme for not communicating the consequences of the sponsor's changes.

12.17 SUPPORTING OTHER PARTS OF PROGRAMME MANAGEMENT

Good-quality management helps ensure that other programme activities are effective, for example:

- **Governance**: making sure the processes and rules are being followed and are working effectively. Re-enforcing the importance of using the correct versions of documents and ensuring the content is complete, up to date and timely.
- **Blueprint and Delivering the Capability**: ultimately making sure project outputs are fit for purpose, and that they will enable the scale of improvements needed to achieve the desired benefits. Checking continued alignment of the Blueprint with policy and strategy, so the change is still relevant and important to the organisation. Overseeing projects so that when outputs are combined they are not compromised by the lack of quality of one component.
- **Risk and Issues**: ensuring the programme is appropriately managed and protects its core activities (see section 12.2 'Critical Success Factors' earlier), which will help reduce threats and maximise opportunities. Quality is directly relevant to detecting and managing issues (whilst assurance reveals items are not fit for purpose). It is also relevant as some issues are requests to change the programme. A change to the programme will require changes to planned quality activities.

12.18 ROLES AND RESPONSIBILITIES

Table 12.1 shows the roles and responsibilities involved in quality management.

Table 12.1 Quality management: roles and responsibilities

Role	Responsibilities
Senior Responsible Owner	Ultimately responsible for all aspects of quality in the programme.
Programme Manager	Developing and implementing the Quality Management Strategy and Plan and the setting up, running and delivery of outputs from the projects fit for the purpose of achieving the desired outcomes and benefits.
Business Change Manager(s)	Implementation, transition, realisation and review of benefits from the outputs of the projects.
Programme Office	Establishing and maintaining the programme's Quality Management Plan and for ensuring the establishment of the appropriate audit, assurance and review processes for the programme in accordance with the Quality Management Strategy.
Specialist roles	Often needed for such as audit, compliance, design authority, business and systems architects, legal, procurement etc. These roles can be used to bench-test designs, prototypes etc. to predict whether the Blueprint and project outputs will operate well enough to achieve the scale of improvement needed for the desired benefits. They are also important to help check that the new operations, its products and services will comply with relevant standards, regulations and legislation.

Part 3
The
Transformational
Flow

Transformational
Flow overview

13

13 Transformational Flow overview

13.1 INTRODUCTION

MSP programmes are all about delivering transformational business change. This part (Part 3) looks at how this transformation is achieved through a series of iterative, interrelated steps. Figure 13.1 shows the Transformational Flow through an MSP programme with the main processes and key control documents involved in delivering an MSP programme. Each process may require more than one iteration before the next one begins. This is particularly true for 'Delivering the Capability' and 'Realising Benefits', as programmes often deliver their change through more than one tranche.

Typically, the Programme Mandate pulls together the high-level, strategic objectives of the programme from the organisation's strategic drivers and relevant policies, plus the outline vision statement. This summary of the objectives is then developed into the Programme Brief.

Not all programmes start at the beginning of the process with a strategy/policy-driven mandate. Some programmes emerge due to a better understanding part way through the project(s) lifecycle (as discussed in section 1.6):

■ The organisation may discover a proposed change is bigger and more complex than originally thought, and decide that it should be converted into a programme to give a better chance of success
■ It may become apparent that several projects are trying to achieve similar changes to the same part of the organisation, resulting in duplication and conflict. Combining the projects into a programme may well achieve focus, synergy, solve the duplication and conflict, and maximise benefits.

For emerging programmes, entry to the programme process is now much more than just a mandate. Consideration needs to be given to what has been achieved so far in each project.

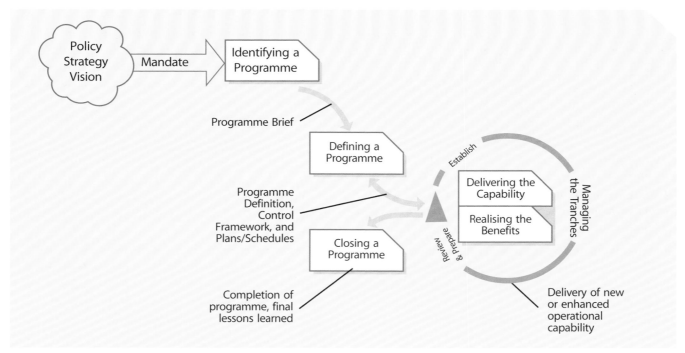

Figure 13.1   Overview of the Transformational Flow

The approved Programme Brief is the key input to 'Defining a Programme'. It provides the basis for development of the:

- Programme Definition document
- Plans/schedules
- Control framework.

This document requires formal approval by the Senior Responsible Owner (SRO) and Sponsoring Group before the programme moves into the next part of the Flow, 'Defining a Programme'.

The Programme Definition can be used to assemble and summarise all of this information into one document. Programmes often produce substantial volumes of information during 'Defining a Programme', and the Programme Definition can be useful for busy executives who only need an overview of the programme. As a form of consolidated executive summary, it can help to prepare the Sponsoring Group so they are adequately informed before they are asked to approve the programme.

The programme's governance arrangements are established in 'Managing the Tranches'. The Programme Definition, management framework and schedules are the basis for 'Delivering the Capability' and 'Realising Benefits'.

Governance arrangements are developed in 'Identifying a Programme' as part of the Programme Preparation Plan for 'Defining a Programme', to manage and control the work in that process. They are developed further in 'Defining a Programme' for 'Managing the Tranches'. As the programme progresses, especially at the end of each tranche, it reviews the effectiveness of its governance arrangements and the continued viability of the programme's Business Case. As the programme moves to later tranches its characteristics might change. For these reasons governance arrangements are often refined as part of the preparation work for the next tranche.

The projects and activities are grouped into tranches. Each tranche delivers a step change in capability after which benefits realisation can be assessed. Tranches can run in parallel, though this can increase the risk. The activities of 'Delivering the Capability' and 'Realising Benefits' are repeated for each tranche. The end of each tranche provides a major review point at which the programme can be formally assessed in terms of its progress towards achieving the desired outcomes and measurable realisation of benefits. Whilst all programmes should have clear vision, the precise route to that vision is often not clear early in the programme. Early tranches might be dedicated to exploring options and discovering a successful route to the vision.

Throughout the programme, monitoring progress and the external environment provides continual assessment of crucial questions such as

- Are we still on track?
- Are the benefits still achievable?
- Is the Business Case still valid and relevant?
- Do we need to change anything to realign the programme, based on lessons learned so far, or because of changes external to the programme, such as from strategy?

'Closing a Programme' is done when the Blueprint is delivered. This means the capabilities required to achieve the Vision Statement are all implemented, and sufficient benefits have been realised to:

- Objectively judge whether the programme was successful
- Be confident the full benefits of the programme will be delivered in the business-as-usual environment.

Further reviews may be required following closure to assess and measure the continuing realisation of benefits.

Programmes close for many different reasons that can be considered under six groups:

- **Planned closure** because the programme has completed all planned work within its scope
- **External environment changes** dramatically and unexpectedly render the programme invalid and therefore it needs to close prematurely
- **Strategy changed** by the organisation for internal reasons, not because of external environment changes; this renders the programme invalid and therefore it needs to close prematurely
- **Evidence** so far predicts that the Business Case cannot be achieved, corrective action is not practical, the programme is unrealistic and therefore needs to close prematurely
- **80/20 rule** shows the cost of the remainder of the programme compared with additional benefits it will realise are disproportionate to what has been achieved so far; it does not make good business sense to complete the rest of the programme
- Evidence that the outcome is being achieved through **alternative actions/events**.

13.2 COLLABORATION WITH THEMES AND PRINCIPLES

The Governance Themes in Part 2 of this manual are used at specific points in the Flow. Cross-references to them are contained in the rest of this chapter. The principles for good programme management are described in Chapter 2. These are universally applicable, at all times and for all types of activities.

13.3 STRUCTURE OF THE TRANSFORMATIONAL FLOW CHAPTERS

There is a chapter that follows for each of the MSP Transformational Flow processes. There is a diagram at the start of these chapters, summarising inputs, activities, outputs, controls and roles. Typical responsibilities are summarised in a table at the end of each of the chapters. These need to be adapted and extended for each programme.

Identifying a Programme

14

14 Identifying a Programme

14.1 INTRODUCTION

The concept (corporate strategy, initiative, policy or emerging programme) and the resulting vision that is driving the change generates the Programme Mandate – the trigger for initiating the overall programme management process. The signing-off of the Programme Mandate allows the 'Identifying a Programme' process to begin, where the Programme Brief is developed. 'Identifying a Programme' (see Figure 14.1) is typically a short process, perhaps taking only a few weeks or less, that turns the concept into a tangible business proposition.

The Programme Brief defines the expected benefits, costs, timescales and risks, allowing:

- Clarification of what is to be achieved, and the desired benefits
- A management decision to be made on whether the programme is desirable and appropriate
- Commitment to the investment and resources required to proceed to the next process of 'Defining a Programme'
- Confirmation that the change should be managed as a programme.

Where a programme has emerged from other change initiatives, work in 'Identifying a Programme' can be used to quickly assess which of these current change initiatives could be practically merged into a programme. This may well reveal duplication, conflict and gaps in the current initiatives, leading to recommended initial actions. It may be necessary to act quickly to avoid further unnecessary expenditure.

14.2 SPONSOR THE PROGRAMME

A programme requires initial and ongoing top-level sponsorship to gain and maintain the necessary commitment to the investment, resources, timescales, delivery and operational changes that will be involved. Those senior executives who are responsible for delivering the strategic objectives or policy requirements form the programme's Sponsoring Group. The Sponsoring Group provides the Programme Mandate.

The Sponsoring Group is made up of those senior executives who:

- Have a strategic interest in the programme
- Have responsibility for the investment decision-making
- Will be significantly impacted by the programme
- Will be required to enable the delivery of the change.

Each member of the Sponsoring Group should:

- Clarify their perspective on the programme and particular interests
- Define the levels of engagement support they will be able to give to the programme
- Confirm their acceptance of, and commitment to, their roles and the programme.

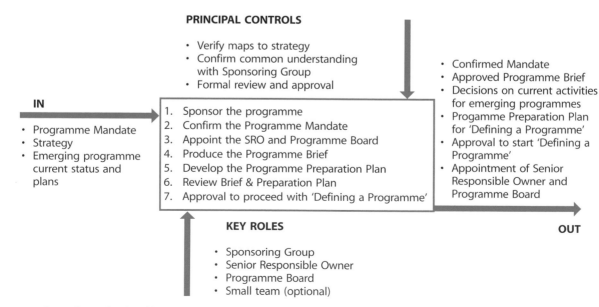

Figure 14.1 Overview of 'Identifying a Programme'

Undertaking stakeholder analysis is necessary to understand who:

■ Will be most impacted by the programme
■ Can provide useful input when considering the composition of the sponsoring group.

See Chapter 6 'Leadership and stakeholder engagement' for more on stakeholder analysis.

14.3 CONFIRM THE PROGRAMME MANDATE

The Programme Mandate articulates:

■ The strategic objectives for the programme
■ Optimum strategies for delivery
■ Improvements and benefits that are expected to result
■ How the programme fits with other initiatives.

This information sets the scene for a controlled start-up for the programme and should be confirmed at its outset.

The Programme Mandate may be a documented output from corporate strategic planning or policy development. However, it may not initially exist as a single, cohesive document. In this case, the information for the Programme Mandate will need to be drawn together into a single document derived from:

■ Facilitated workshops
■ Interviews and discussions with:
  ● The Sponsoring Group
  ● Key stakeholders
  ● Members of the organisation's executive
  ● Senior management teams.

The consolidated Programme Mandate is reviewed and confirmed by the Sponsoring Group.

Information on the content of the Programme Mandate can be found in Appendix A: 'Programme information'.

14.4 APPOINT THE SENIOR RESPONSIBLE OWNER AND PROGRAMME BOARD

The Senior Responsible Owner (SRO) will have ultimate accountability and personal responsibility for the programme's success. The SRO, chosen from the Sponsoring Group, should be the individual with the most appropriate and required authority, credibility, experience and skills to lead and direct the programme.

The individual should be appointed by the Sponsoring Group at the earliest opportunity to be a focal point for the programme, providing leadership and direction, and countering ambiguity.

A specific role definition should be prepared for the SRO, approved by the Sponsoring Group, and then the SRO should confirm understanding and acceptance of the role. Large programmes may impose a workload on the SRO that is too great; in such cases the SRO can be assisted by other persons with appropriate expertise.

The SRO will appoint and chair the Programme Board, which may be formed now or early in 'Defining a Programme'. See also Chapter 4 'Organisation' for details on roles that should be covered by the Programme Board.

A small team is appointed to assist with producing the Programme Brief and the Programme Preparation Plan. It may be helpful to identify and involve the likely Programme Manager and Business Change Manager(s) during this process. Early involvement will help to build commitment from the individuals who will be tasked with executing the programme. See also paragraph 2.2.2 'Leading change' principle.

14.5 PRODUCE THE PROGRAMME BRIEF

The Programme Brief provides the formal basis for assessing whether the proposed programme is viable and achievable. Using the Programme Mandate, the programme's specific objectives, required benefits, potential risks, outline costs and timescales are fleshed out. Options for delivery can also be developed.

It should restate 'where we are now', refining and expanding the input from the Mandate. The assumptions about 'where we will be at a defined point in the future if we do nothing' should be re-examined, especially if some time has passed since the organisation's strategy was approved.

The typical content of a Programme Brief is described in Appendix A: 'Programme information'.

All those involved in the programme will need to gain a summary understanding of the current change initiatives, identifying:

■ Areas of potential overlap that may give rise to duplication
■ Conflicts where activities in one initiative may diminish the outcomes of another
■ Gaps where there are no (or insufficient) activities,

ensuring all these areas are directly related to the strategic objectives in the mandate.

The Programme Brief for an emergent programme will additionally need to clearly state what, if any, current work will be stopped (to resolve issues associated with duplicate/conflicting activities). It will also need to provide guidance for the re-shaping of the current change initiatives into a coherent programme.

The use of a Programme Brief (rather than a complete, highly detailed Business Case) at this early stage of a programme helps to avoid futile, and often time-consuming, work on detailed cost analysis, investment appraisals, expenditure profiles and so on, when the overall concept of the proposed programme may not be viable for reasons other than financial justification. For example, if the initial expectations of benefit realisation are unlikely to be achieved within a sensible timeframe, it may not be worthwhile taking the proposed programme any further.

The Programme Brief (once approved) provides the basis for development of the programme's full Business Case and other Programme Management information in the 'Defining a Programme' process.

14.6 DEVELOP THE PROGRAMME PREPARATION PLAN

'Defining a Programme' involves the detailed planning and design of all aspects of the programme. A Programme Preparation Plan for this work is produced, so the Sponsoring Group are fully aware of, and willing to commit to, the cost, time and resource that will be required in the next part of the programme, 'Defining a Programme'.

It is essential to plan sufficient time and resources, and to identify individuals with the right skills and experience, for the development of a detailed Programme Definition document.

At this point in the life of a programme there will be much uncertainty and ambiguity over the detail of what the programme will involve. Planning sufficient time and resources for 'Defining a Programme' will help to clarify and reduce this uncertainty and ambiguity. The Programme Preparation Plan will explain how governance will be applied to manage the expected complexity of 'Defining a Programme'.

A key element of the Programme Preparation Plan should be an explanation of how stakeholders will be engaged and communications will be managed during 'Defining a Programme'. See Appendix A: 'Programme information' for details of the content of the Programme Preparation Plan.

14.7 REVIEW OF PROGRAMME BRIEF AND PROGRAMME PREPARATION PLAN

It is highly advisable to conduct an independent formal review of the Programme Brief to assess the scope, rationale and objectives of the programme. The review should assess the extent to which the organisation(s) involved have the capacity and capability to deliver and realise the expected benefits. The reality, impacts, possible mitigations of identified risks and assumptions should be challenged.

14.8 APPROVAL TO PROCEED

The Programme Brief and Programme Preparation Plan set the context and direction for the Programme during 'Defining a Programme'.

Formal approval of these mean:

■ The SRO confirms that it meets the business requirements
■ The Programme Board commits to supporting delivery
■ The Sponsoring Group commit to resource and support the SRO in delivery of the programme.

This approval is based on a confirmed understanding of, and commitment to, the proposed programme's vision, and the preliminary view of its expected benefits, risks, issues, timescales, resources and costs. There must be clear justification for the investment of resources in the programme, including:

■ Estimated benefits outweighing the sum of costs and dis-benefits
■ The expected outcomes and end state outweighing the expected risks and challenges.

14.9 RESPONSIBILITIES

Responsibilities Flow Steps	Sponsoring Group	SRO	Programme Board	Identified (small) Team	Business Change Managers	Programme Office
Identifying a Programme						
Sponsor the Programme	AR					
Confirm the Mandate	A					
Appoint the SRO and Programme Board	A					
Produce the Programme Brief		A	R	C		C
Develop the Programme Preparation Plan		A	R	C		C
Review of Brief and Preparation Plan	C	R	R			
Approval to proceed	A	R	C			I

KEY
R – Responsible; get the work done
A – Accountable; make decisions; R reports to A
C – Consulted; supports, has information or capability required
I – Informed; notified but not consulted

Figure 14.2 Typical responsibilities for 'Identifying a Programme'

Defining a
Programme

15

15 Defining a Programme

15.1 INTRODUCTION

The 'Defining a Programme' process (see Figure 15.1) provides the basis for deciding whether to proceed with the programme or not. This is where the detailed definition and planning for the programme is undertaken.

The Programme Brief is used as the starting point for creating the Programme Definition Document. It will be developed to explain:

- What the programme is going to do
- How it is going to do it
- Who is involved
- How it will be controlled
- The justification for going forward.

The Business Case and governance for the programme will now be developed. The governance defines the strategies for quality, stakeholders, risks and issues, benefits, resources, planning and control. The various programme approaches contained in the strategies, plans and schedules (covering risk management, communications, benefits realisation, resources, quality etc.) are developed to provide information on the resources, dependencies, and timescales for delivery and realisation of benefits. This framework will be further developed and applied in 'Managing the Tranches'.

The inevitable trade-off between resources, costs, quality, timings and benefits requires agreement between the Sponsoring Group and Senior Responsible Owner (SRO). At the completion of 'Defining a Programme', formal approval is required from the Sponsoring Group and SRO to proceed with the programme.

PRINCIPAL CONTROLS

- Review of (emerging and final) Business Case by SRO
- Sponsoring Group, approval to proceed

IN

- Programme Brief
- Strategy
- Programme Preparation Plan
- Emerging programme current status and plans
- Decisions on current activities for emerging progammes

1. Establish the infrastructure
2. Establish the team to define the programme
3. Identify the stakeholders
4. Refine the Vision Statement
5. Develop the Blueprint
6. Develop the Benefit Profiles
7. Model the benefits and refine the Profiles
8. Validate the benefits
9. Design the Projects Dossier
10. Identify tranches
11. Design the programme's organisation
12. Develop governance arrangements
13. Develop the Programme Plan
14. Consolidate the Programme Definition Document
15. Develop and confirm programme Business Case
16. Prepare for first tranche
17. Approval to proceed

- Emerging programmes; current activities stopped
- Risks and Issues logged
- Programme Definition Document
- Governance arrangements
- Plans for benefits, communications and programme
- Approved Business Case
- Approval to start first tranche, or stop

OUT

KEY ROLES

- Senior Responsible Owner
- Programme Board
- Sponsoring Group
- Programme Manager
- Business Change Manager
- Team appointed for 'Defining a Programme'

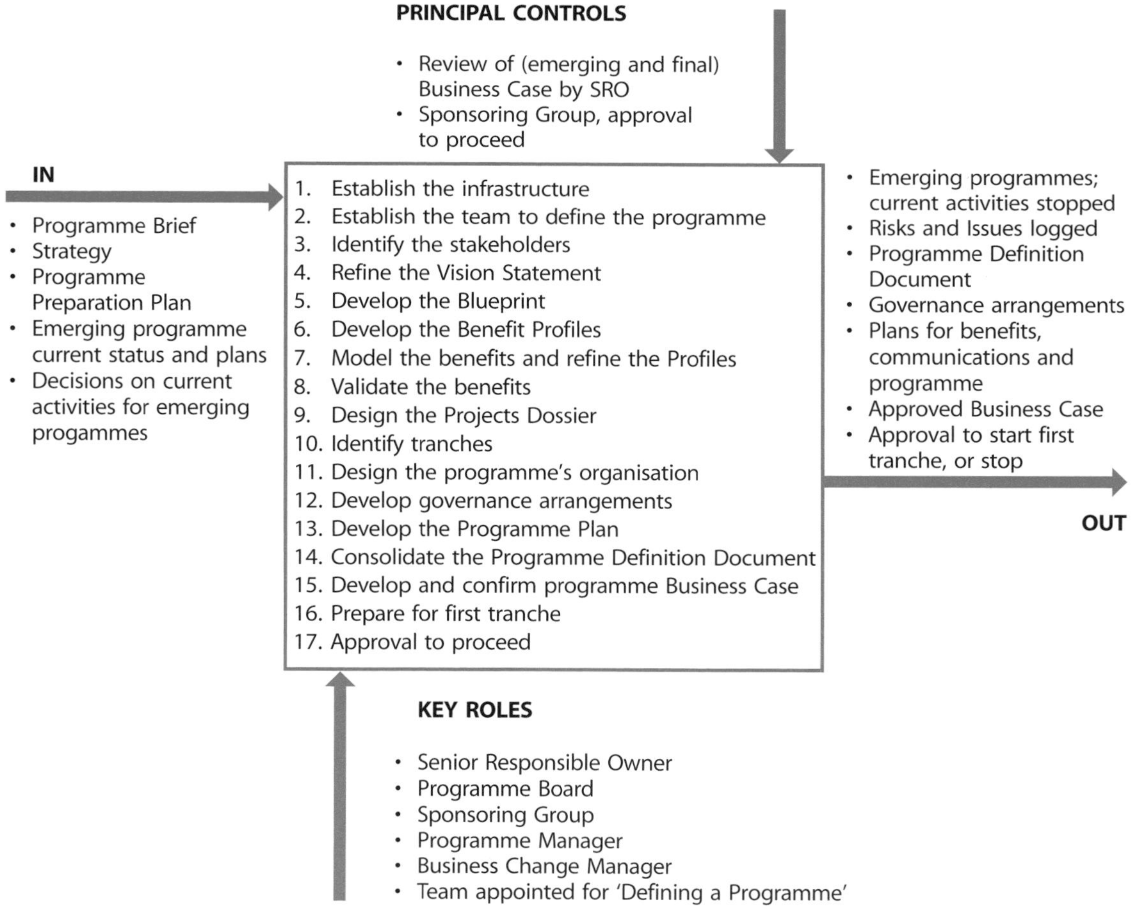

Figure 15.1   Overview of 'Defining a Programme'

15.2 ESTABLISH THE INFRASTRUCTURE FOR DEFINING A PROGRAMME

It is important to establish a programme infrastructure at the beginning to give the team the means to successfully conduct the necessary activities.

This infrastructure might cover items such as:

■ Offices
■ Configuration Management
■ Software tools
■ Computers and other office equipment.

At this stage in the programme the information volumes are relatively small. As 'Defining a Programme' progresses these volumes will increase significantly. Many documents produced in this process are dependent on information in other documents. Some parts of 'Defining a Programme' iterate through more than one cycle, as described in the sections that follow. Document content will be frequently changing as the programme is designed and prepared. It is essential to have a mechanism to keep these co-dependent documents synchronised, otherwise the programme team and stakeholders may be misled. Configuration management provides this control and is an important tool in establishing an effective infrastructure.

15.3 ESTABLISH THE TEAM TO DEFINE THE PROGRAMME

The SRO will typically require the support of a small team. The Programme Preparation Plan produced in 'Identifying a Programme' is used to select and appoint the team.

The team will need appropriate skills, knowledge and experience in areas relevant to the programme and its management. Members of the team may subsequently fulfil formal roles, such as Programme Manager or Business Change Manager, within the programme organisation structure. See Chapter 4 'Organisation' for more detail on programme organisation, roles and responsibilities.

For an emergent programme, careful consideration should be given to making best use of the resources on the current change initiatives relative to the new demands that the emergent programme will place on these projects. Some of these resources may be appropriate for the newly defined needs of this programme and others may be better deployed elsewhere.

15.4 IDENTIFY THE STAKEHOLDERS

All the programme's stakeholders (internal and external) should be identified, together with their particular interest in the programme. It is also important to identify any stakeholders who are likely to be worse off as a result of the programme, as their interests and influence may prevent the programme's successful outcome.

The analysis of stakeholders will identify the various information needs and communication flows that should be established as part of programme communications. The results of this analysis are contained in the Stakeholder Profile document (see Appendix A: 'Programme information'). It contains information such as:

■ Stakeholder Interests Map
■ Impact assessment
■ Analysis information.

This work needs to be started at the beginning of 'Defining a Programme', as the programme team will need to engage stakeholders in these activities. The manner in which this early engagement takes place can have a critical effect on stakeholders' attitude to the programme. It is important that the engagement of stakeholders does not create early barriers to the progress and development of the programme.

For further details see Chapter 6, 'Leadership and Stakeholder Engagement'.

15.5 REFINE THE VISION STATEMENT

The outline Vision Statement contained in the Programme Brief is refined into the programme's Vision Statement. It provides the basis for communicating and encouraging the buy-in and commitment from stakeholders.

The purpose is to communicate the transformed, beneficial future state to the programme's wide audience of stakeholders. When any organisation goes through transformational change, different stakeholders will not necessarily understand the big picture without such a Vision Statement. The Vision Statement is written as a future state, and not as an objective or trend or mission, all of which are commonly written beginning with the word 'To'.

Example: simple Vision Statement for a higher education institution

When this programme is completed we will be able to offer our students a greater range of higher education courses than our competitors, enhancing our reputation as the foremost school for language studies in the world. A student will be able to choose from traditional courses, as well as IT-supported distance learning from anywhere in the globe, all leading to internationally recognised qualifications. Our students will also have the flexibility to progress through their chosen course at a speed to suit themselves.

For further details on the Vision Statement, see Appendix A: 'Programme information'.

15.6 DEVELOP THE BLUEPRINT

Developing the Blueprint involves many concepts of organisational design. It may encompass all dimensions of the organisation or business – its cultural aspects as well as its structure, processes and activities – and how they need to change. Business analysis and design techniques may also be required to explore fully the opportunities and options for achieving the capabilities described in the Vision Statement. There are typically many options for achieving the required changes, with associated costs and impacts. Exploring these options and assessing the implications on the investment required is an important aspect for designing the optimum Blueprint for the programme.

The key drivers behind the Blueprint are the benefits (including dis-benefits) and outcomes required. The scope of change defined in the Blueprint should remain closely aligned to the required benefits and not start to 'creep' to embrace other (possibly beneficial) changes that could distract the programme from achieving its defined objectives.

Designing the Blueprint to realise the required benefits needs to be balanced against the costs of realising those benefits. The programme's Business Case is developed in parallel with the Blueprint to ensure consistency between the proposed changes to the organisation, the costs of doing the changes and realisation of the benefits being realistic.

The Blueprint, Benefits Maps and the Projects Dossier are designed together, with the emerging Business Case acting as the moderator.

Some organisations have an overall Blueprint for the entire business. In these contexts, each programme is briefed to deliver a discrete part of that corporate Blueprint.

The initial cut of the Blueprint might just describe the final future state of the new organisation. This statement of what the organisation will look like needs to be complemented with an explanation of how to get there. This journey is explained in the Projects Dossier and in the Programme Plan. As work in 'Defining a Programme' progresses, this final future state will be refined (see Figure 15.2). Events such as end of tranche (the mini 'Defining a Programme' Business Case review) and Benefits Reviews should give better understanding, and therefore clearer direction for the rest of the journey. The Blueprint is therefore regularly refined, reflecting this continual programme evolution.

The gap, the difference between the current and future organisation, will need to be analysed. It provides a critical input to designing the Projects Dossier and Programme Plan. The Blueprint does not normally need to be expressed in detail. It will be the responsibility of the projects to develop more detailed designs for the future organisation. The programme must own the integration and cohesiveness of the project-level designs, assuring the Blueprint.

The first Benefits Maps can be developed from the first cut of the Blueprint. They will need to be enhanced when estimates of the time and cost are available from the Programme Plan. The merging of this information into the Business Case provides the control to judge if the programme designs are getting good enough in terms of an acceptable balance between time, cost, risks and benefits.

Figure 15.2 is an example showing how the Blueprint, Benefits Maps and Projects Dossier might be developed together until an acceptable Business Case emerges. Through each iteration the SRO will judge whether the developing Business Case is likely to be good enough for formal approval by the Sponsoring Group at the end of 'Defining a Programme'. For more detail see Chapter 8, 'Blueprint design and delivery'.

Involving the target business community, who will be part of the future organisation, in the development of the Blueprint is a powerful method for improving the quality of the information and increasing the sense of ownership and buy-in to the change.

For further details on the Blueprint see Appendix A, 'Programme information'.

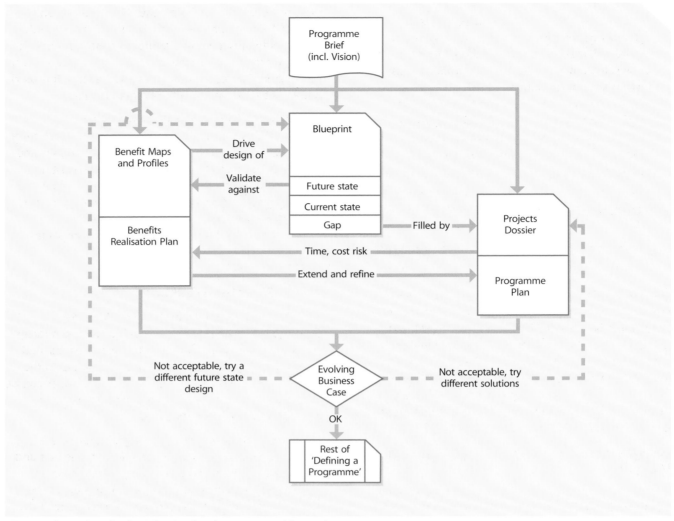

Figure 15.2 Developing the basis of an acceptable Business Case

15.7 DEVELOP THE BENEFIT PROFILES

The Vision Statement and Programme Brief identify the required benefits from the programme. Each benefit (and dis-benefit) requires a complete definition, known as a Benefit Profile.

The total set of Benefit Profiles provides a planning and control tool to track progress on the delivery and realisation of the benefits. The Benefit Profiles will be further refined as the detailed definition of the programme is developed.

Each benefit needs to be measured. As the business prepares to go through the change cycle it is important for it to understand its starting point. To do this it will have to establish what KPIs reflect the overall performance of the organisation at this time.

These indicators will be tracked to assess the business stability during the lifecycle of the programme and the

delivery of benefits resulting from the changes being applied.

It is tempting for a programme to select indicators that are directly related to the outcomes that it will enable. However, it is important that a holistic range of relevant indicators is used for monitoring. It is no use cutting the costs of products if customers leave because of poor quality, or adopting mechanistic processes that cause creative staff to become disillusioned and leave.

The following should be considered when selecting benefit measure and performance baselines:

■ Some KPIs may not be suitable for measuring benefits
■ Some KPIs may need to change as a result of operational changes. The programme may have an obligation to define new KPIs and provide processes and tools to support them
■ Current KPIs may need to be supplemented by other measures to assess the benefits realised

- Performance criteria from contracts, service levels agreements, compliance targets etc. may also need to be taken into account and re-negotiated, particularly to understand any penalties that can occur because of performance deterioration
- Some measures may be subject to deviations as a result of normal process variation (e.g. seasonal trends). It is important this is understood and defined, otherwise actual benefit measures may be misunderstood.

For further details on Benefit Profiles see Chapter 7, 'Benefits Realisation Management'.

15.8 MODEL THE BENEFITS AND REFINE THE PROFILES

The first Benefit Profiles for end benefits are initially created from information in the Vision Statement and the Programme Brief. As the Blueprint is designed these can be extended and refined. Benefits Maps are initially modelled (driven by the Blueprint) and then extended by information from the Projects Dossier and Programme Plan. The mix of benefits, dependencies on project outputs, and other intermediate benefits becomes clearer. Benefit Profiles are refined as a result.

For further details see Chapter 7, 'Benefits Realisation Management'.

15.9 VALIDATE THE BENEFITS

A realistic assessment of the inevitable trade-off between the cost of realising and measuring the benefit against the value of having that benefit should be made, so that trying to realise unrealistic benefits does not happen.

Each benefit should represent some aspect of the programme's desired outcomes. Benefits that are not linked to strategic objectives may actually be unhelpful. Furthermore, they may distract from achieving the desired outcomes. Chapter 7, 'Benefits Realisation Management', explains the tests that should be applied to validate a benefit.

The first validation of benefits is via the test of the emerging Business Case, as described above in section 15.6, 'Develop the Blueprint', and in Chapter 8, 'Blueprint Design and Delivery'.

15.10 DESIGN THE PROJECTS DOSSIER

The Blueprint, Benefit Profiles and Benefits Maps provide the basis for designing the projects, and any other activities necessary to deliver the new capabilities

expressed in the Vision Statement. These projects and activities form the programme's Projects Dossier, which represents the programme's approach describing how it will deliver the future organisation, the operation of which will result in the desired outcomes and benefits. It is used as the basis for developing the Programme Plan.

There may be different options for achieving improvements to business operations, in which case these should be explored in terms of timing, content, risks and benefits. Some projects and activities may be existing, ongoing work that will need to be adopted into the programme as part of the Projects Dossier; alternatively they may be new initiatives that will require commissioning by the programme at the appropriate point.

15.11 IDENTIFY TRANCHES

The outcome(s) described in the Vision Statement, expressed in more detail in the final Blueprint, can rarely be delivered in a single pass; it will typically be reached through progressive refinements or step changes in the capabilities of the organisation. These step changes can be used to define the ends of successive tranches, where formal reviews can be carried out.

The projects and activities in the Projects Dossier are scheduled together showing their relative timescales and dependencies. The schedule is grouped into tranches reflecting the step changes in capability. It may not be possible to define all of the required projects fully at this point. Further analysis may be required to complete the scoping of later projects after the results from early tranches have been assessed.

Some programmes are more vision-led that specification-led. Early in the programme the route to the vision is often unclear. Early tranches may be designed to explore and prove (or disprove) different approaches to get to the vision. The most valuable output of these types of early tranches will be the information that enables the Sponsoring Group to decide whether to continue with the programme, and if so, to have confidence that the best route has been identified. If the results of early discovery work shows the vision is not attainable at reasonable cost, time and risk, the programme must be stopped or significantly changed. Failure to do this will almost certainly result in significant expenditure being wasted.

For further details on scheduling and tranches see Chapter 8, 'Blueprint Design and Delivery'.

15.12 DESIGN THE PROGRAMME ORGANISATION

The organisation for directing, managing, controlling and supporting the programme has to be designed. Successful programme delivery requires sufficient resourcing of the programme and change management activities. The structure must enable effective decision-making and efficient communication flows around the various members of the programme team and stakeholders. The nature and size of the programme will influence the design of an appropriate Programme Organisation. The structure will need to integrate with, and operate alongside, the existing management structures of the organisation(s). The Organisation should reflect the management levels appropriate to the visibility and significance of the programme.

See also paragraph 2.2.2, 'Leading change' principle, and Chapter 4, 'Organisation'. For more details on the contents of the Organisation Structure document see Appendix A, 'Programme information'.

Each role within the organisation should be defined with its specific accountabilities, responsibilities and tasks, together with the skills and competencies required. Individuals with the appropriate skills and experience to take on these roles should be identified.

It is usually not possible to assemble internally all the people required with adequate competencies. This must be addressed, perhaps using those resources with greater skills and experience to coach and mentor others. This situation should also be reflected by the programme and project risk analysis. Where the lack of skills and experience is significant, this must be reflected in the Programme Plan, to allow people sufficient time to learn and develop. It may be necessary to supplement internal resources with external expertise.

Many individuals assigned to programme roles will also have operational responsibilities. Prioritisation of workloads is an important consideration. The work required of each role needs to be balanced against the time the individual is able to commit. It is important that there is understanding and agreement between the programme and line managers about:

- How the time (from, to, how long, which days of the week, percentage of working week etc.) resource will be allocated to programme or project work
- Who will manage the resource when working on the programme or project
- How conflict will be resolved.

It may be necessary to procure external resources for the programme, providing specialist skills and experience to fulfil some of the roles. It is important to remember that procurement is typically lengthy and sufficient time and resources should be planned for procurement. Routes to procure additional resources include secondment, contract, delegate or sub-contract the work, and share with other initiatives.

For further details on Programme Organisation see Chapter 4, 'Organisation'.

15.13 DEVELOP THE GOVERNANCE ARRANGEMENTS

The programme's governance arrangements should cover how the programme is going to handle the inevitable complexity and interdependencies, and bring the different aspects together. The governance framework must be designed to integrate with the corporate governance of the organisation where this already exists.

The various strategies required are described in detail in the Governance Themes chapters:

- Benefits Management Strategy
- Information Management Strategy
- Risk Management Strategy and Issue Resolution Strategy
- Monitoring and Control Strategy
- Quality Management Strategy
- Resource Management Strategy
- Stakeholder Engagement Strategy.

The governance elements underpinning these strategies and plans are discussed further below.

For further information on each of the documents see the chapters on Governance Themes in Part 2 and Appendix A, 'Programme information'.

15.13.1 Benefits management

Benefits Management activities and responsibilities define what needs to be done and who is involved in order to ensure the identified benefits will actually be realised. A Benefits Management Strategy is produced describing the functions, roles and responsibilities for benefit planning and realisation. It also describes the measurement, assessment and review processes for monitoring benefit realisation.

The Benefits Realisation Plan should show the benefits will be achievable following the delivery of new capability from the projects within the Projects Dossier. The tranches identify where step changes in capability will be delivered. Priorities for delivery should be considered to maximise opportunities for early benefits.

The Benefits Realisation Plan and the Programme Plan are closely linked plans and may be combined into one plan showing projects and transition plans together with benefit realisation activities.

15.13.2 Information management

Without good, complete, timely information any programme will struggle to succeed. The Information Management Strategy and the following Information Management Plan describe the work to be done to put in place systems, processes, policies and supporting tools so that adequate information can be produced, communicated and stored to meet the needs of the programme. It is important to consider whether information requirements will change as a programme progresses. Systems, processes, policies and supporting tools might need adapting in such cases.

15.13.3 Risks and issues

The Risk Management Strategy defines how risks to the programme will be identified, analysed, monitored and controlled. It should also encompass the processes required for the management of risks on projects within the Projects Dossier and should define how any project risks that affect other parts of the programme will be escalated, managed and controlled.

The Issue Resolution Strategy defines how issues will be captured, assessed, resolved and communicated. As with risk management, procedures for issue management at the project level need to be integrated at the programme level. Resolving issues on programmes often involves handling complex problems that impact across the entire programme. Escalation routes to senior levels must be efficient and effective.

Risks and issues revealed during 'Defining a Programme', either via a formal assessment or as part of other work, will be recorded in the Risk Register and Issue Log, to include decisions and actions agreed.

This information is considered in finalising the Business Case and informs the 'Managing the Tranches' process (Chapter 16).

15.13.4 Monitoring and control

The arrangements for monitoring and controlling progress of the programme are developed and included in the Monitoring and Control Strategy.

15.13.5 Quality management

A Quality Management Strategy is developed to define the approach the programme will take to ensure that quality is built into all aspects of the programme from the outset.

It should also cover how quality will be assured in the programme's deliverables, and by whom. The Quality Management Plan will include details of when and by whom activities relating to managing quality will be undertaken.

15.13.6 Resource management

A Resource Management Strategy is developed to identify the resources required for the programme and define how they will be acquired and managed. Resources will include finances, people, assets and technology. The Resource Management Plan sets out the activities required to implement the Resource Management Strategy and help ensure resources are available in alignment with the Programme Plan.

15.13.7 Stakeholders and communications

A Stakeholder Engagement Strategy is developed to define how the programme will engage with all stakeholder groups and what information flows will be established and maintained during the programme.

The Programme Communications Plan indicates when, what, how and with whom information flows between the programme and its stakeholders will be established and maintained.

In addition to information about change and the implications for the programme, there is a wide range of subject material to be communicated in any programme.

15.14 DEVELOP THE PROGRAMME PLAN

The Programme Plan is developed by bringing together the information on projects, resources, timescales, risk, monitoring and control. The amount of information available and the level of detail required will develop as the programme progresses. An outline Programme Plan showing the estimated relative timescales for the projects should be developed at this stage. It should identify the tranches where formal reviews of progress and benefits realisation can be carried out.

For further details on developing the Programme Plan see Chapter 8, 'Blueprint Design and Delivery'.

15.15 CONSOLIDATE THE PROGRAMME DEFINITION

All of the information produced in 'Defining a Programme' can now be consolidated into one document. This can be produced as a complete set of information, with an executive summary, or can just be a summary that references the other detailed documents. See Appendix A,

'Programme information', for more details on the Programme Definition Document.

The full set of programme documents should now have been produced. These are assembled into information baselines that reflect the emerging nature of the documentation. More information can be found on the baselined documents and the information that should be contained in them in Appendix A, 'Programme information'.

15.16 DEVELOP AND CONFIRM PROGRAMME BUSINESS CASE

The Business Case will have started to emerge in 'Identifying a Programme' and it is developed further (see section 15.6, 'Developing the Blueprint'). This emerging Business Case is transformed into the final Business Case as the arrangements for managing the programme are developed.

The Business Case brings together information about the programme covering the costs, benefits, timings and risks so that the overall value for money and achievability of the programme can be assessed and appropriate management decisions made about the viability of the programme.

The Business Case will need to be further refined as the programme proceeds, especially at the end of tranches where formal reviews objectively judge the success (or shortfalls) achieved so far.

For further details on the Business Case see Chapter 10, 'The Business Case'.

15.17 PREPARE FOR FIRST TRANCHE

As the programme now has more clarity about the way forward it can prepare for the first tranche(s). It is usually not sensible to prepare in detail for later tranches until near the end of the first tranche and there will then be greater confidence about the programme's approach to achieving the desired benefits. Activities include:

■ Prepare to establish the programme's governance and organisation
■ Specify the physical environment and infrastructure required for managing the next tranche
■ Develop plans for:
  ● Communications
  ● Benefits realisation
  ● The programme (as a summary for all of the rest of the programme, and in more detail for the next tranche)

● Resources
● Quality.

Similar preparations need to occur as the programme approaches later tranches. See Chapter 16, 'Managing the Tranches', for more detail.

15.18 APPROVAL TO PROCEED

The Programme Definition is assembled and the information produced in 'Defining a Programme' is summarised and consolidated into one document to enable easy assimilation by stakeholders.

Approval to proceed is a four-stage process:

1 **SRO (and Programme Board) approves**

   The complete set of documentation describing the programme, its governance, plans and Business Case should be approved by the SRO as suitable to submit for review and formal Sponsoring Group approval and authorisation.

2 **Sponsoring Group endorse**

   A formal endorsement is sought from the programme's Sponsoring Group to confirm that the programme is designed to meet their expectations and requirements.

3 **Independent review**

   Reviews may involve independent scrutiny, such as an OGC Gateway Review. An unbiased objective independent review of the programme may be a contractual obligation in partnership programmes where several organisations are sharing the investment and the risk and later hope to share the benefits. See also Chapter 12 'Quality management'.

4 **Sponsoring Group authorise the SRO**

   The Sponsoring Group must give their approval on behalf of the organisation to proceed with the programme, including their commitment to the investment required for the programme. In many programmes it is not possible to clarify total investment requirements at the start. In such cases the SRO obtains further formal approval from the Sponsoring Group when more information becomes available or at the end of further tranches.

On many programmes, it may not be possible to clarify the total investment at this point. In this situation, the approval could be to proceed only to the end of the first tranche, at which point further formal approvals would be required and more detailed information would be available.

15.19 RESPONSIBILITIES

Responsibilities Flow Steps	Sponsoring Group	SRO	Programme Board	Programme Manager	Business Change Managers	Programme Office
Defining a Programme						
Establish the infrastructure		A		R	I	C
Establish the team		AR	C	I	I	C
Identify the stakeholders	C	A	C	C	R	C
Develop the Vision Statement	C	AC	C	R	C	
Develop the Blueprint		A	C	R	C	C
Develop Benefit Profiles		A	C	C	R	C
Model benefits and refine Profiles		A	C	C	R	C
Validate benefits		A	C	C	R	
Design the Projects Dossier		A	C	R	C	C
Identify tranches		A	C	R	R	C
Design the Programme Organisation		A	C	R	C	C
Develop governance arrangements		A	C	R	C	C
Develop the Programme Plan		A	C	R	C	C
Consolidate the Programme Definition		A	C	R	C	C
Confirm programme Business Case		A	C	R	C	I
Prepare for first tranche		A	C	R	C	C
Approval to proceed	A	R	C	I	I	I

KEY
R – Responsible; get the work done
A – Accountable; make decisions; R reports to A
C – Consulted; supports, has information or capability required
I – Informed; notified but not consulted

Figure 15.3 Typical responsibilities for 'Defining a Programme'

Managing the Tranches

16

16 Managing the Tranches

16.1 INTRODUCTION

The purpose of the 'Managing the Tranches' process (see Figure 16.1) is to implement the defined governance for the programme. This accepts that, as the programme progresses, this will need to be adapted and refined to assure the effective delivery of the tranches and the final outcomes. 'Governance' in MSP means the functions, processes and procedures that define how the programme is set up, managed and controlled.

16.2 ESTABLISH THE TRANCHE

16.2.1 Programme Organisation

The Organisation Structure for the programme is now implemented, with the identified individuals appointed. In particular, the appointment of staff for the Programme Office should be completed. Each role should have a clearly defined set of responsibilities that the appointed individual has understood and accepts.

See also Chapter 7, 'Benefits Realisation Management'.

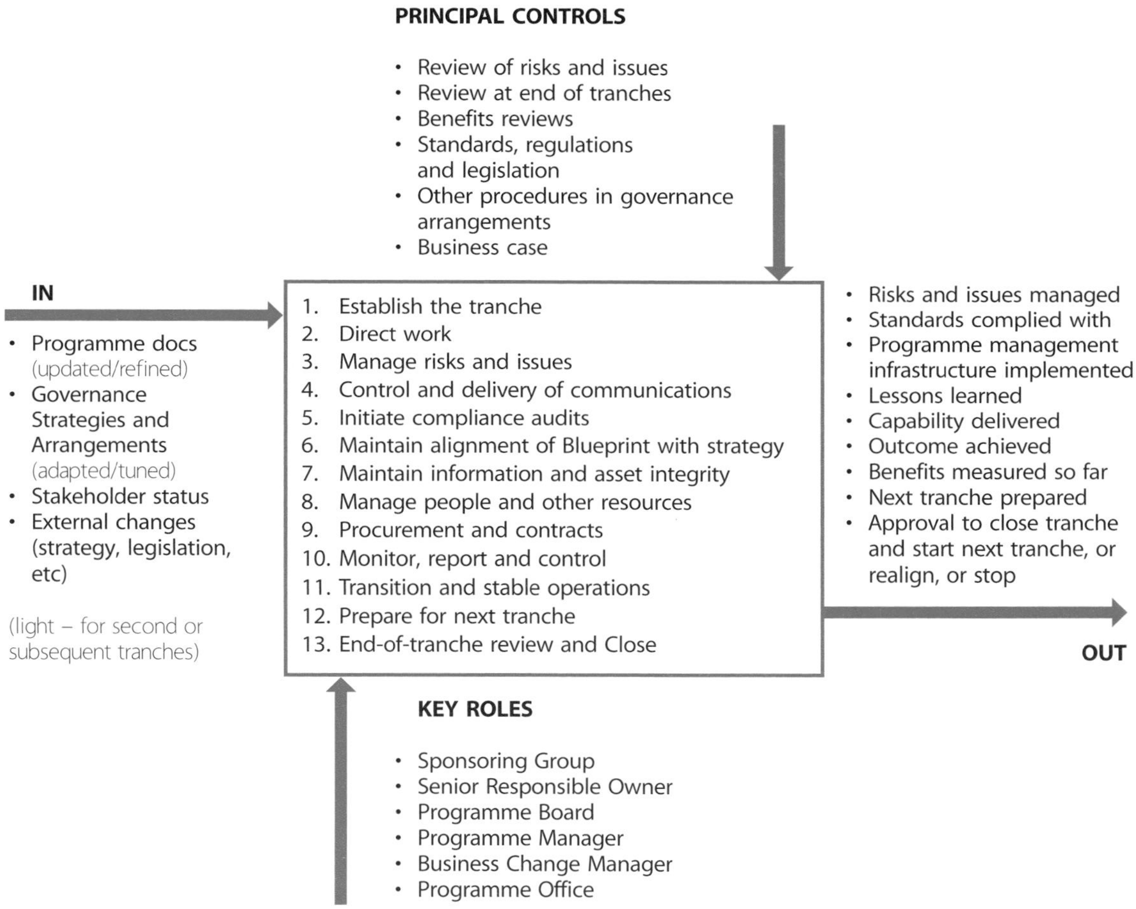

PRINCIPAL CONTROLS

- Review of risks and issues
- Review at end of tranches
- Benefits reviews
- Standards, regulations and legislation
- Other procedures in governance arrangements
- Business case

IN

- Programme docs (updated/refined)
- Governance Strategies and Arrangements (adapted/tuned)
- Stakeholder status
- External changes (strategy, legislation, etc)

(light – for second or subsequent tranches)

1. Establish the tranche
2. Direct work
3. Manage risks and issues
4. Control and delivery of communications
5. Initiate compliance audits
6. Maintain alignment of Blueprint with strategy
7. Maintain information and asset integrity
8. Manage people and other resources
9. Procurement and contracts
10. Monitor, report and control
11. Transition and stable operations
12. Prepare for next tranche
13. End-of-tranche review and Close

- Risks and issues managed
- Standards complied with
- Programme management infrastructure implemented
- Lessons learned
- Capability delivered
- Outcome achieved
- Benefits measured so far
- Next tranche prepared
- Approval to close tranche and start next tranche, or realign, or stop

OUT

KEY ROLES

- Sponsoring Group
- Senior Responsible Owner
- Programme Board
- Programme Manager
- Business Change Manager
- Programme Office

Figure 16.1 Overview of 'Managing the Tranches'

16.2.2 Change Team

The programme team delivers the means to change the operational part of an organisation. The operational functions need to receive and effectively use the outcomes the programme delivers to achieve the benefits. A Change Team represents the interests of the part of the organisation to be changed, and will ensure those parts are appropriately involved and thoroughly prepared for the transition. It will be especially active during transition when operational staff need supporting.

See also Chapter 7, 'Benefits Realisation Management', and Chapter 6, 'Leadership and stakeholder engagement'.

16.2.3 Programme Office

The Programme Office should as a minimum provide an information hub for the programme and may also have skilled resources able to provide consultancy-style specialist assistance to the programme management team and the projects, as required. The Programme Office's functions and procedures are established and operated throughout the programme.

If the Programme Office is dedicated to the programme, its lack of independence means it cannot carry out audits or similar reviews of the programme. In such cases arrangements need to be established with a different body that is independent of the programme and can therefore provide unbiased assessments.

16.2.4 Support for governance

The various governance strategies define the required arrangements, information and procedures that need to be put in place. The Programme Office provides support for the governance requirements of the programme, for example the collection, aggregation, analysis and reporting of detailed data, to enable the programme team to easily assess the overall state of the programme.

See also Appendix C, 'Programme Office'.

16.2.5 Physical environment

The physical programme environment, including buildings, office space, office facilities and services, should be established, as defined in the Resource Management Plan.

The technology and tools required to support the programme also need to be acquired and implemented, and staff trained in their use. Typical tools used to support the programme include:

- Intranet and/or Internet websites
- Planning, estimating and scheduling tools

- Tools to support risk management, quality management, financial management, and change control
- Document management and record management tools
- Configuration Management tools.

16.2.6 Communications

The Programme Communications Plan defines how the programme will inform the stakeholders about the programme and how to encourage feedback. The required mechanisms are set up.

Programme staff are briefed on communications, to include those informal communications that are often by-products of other programme activities. They are also briefed on how to get and interpret feedback from stakeholders. Every contact with a stakeholder is a valuable opportunity to influence them and to understand their attitude to the programme.

16.3 DIRECT WORK

Projects and other activities will need to be started according to the schedules and plans prepared in the 'Defining a Programme' process. Starting the projects is managed by the programme team in the 'Delivering the Capability' process, but other management activities are executed in this process.

16.4 MANAGE RISKS AND ISSUES

Risks and issues are actively managed (added, assessed, reviewed, updated and closed) throughout the programme, and the overall risk and issues profiles continually monitored.

Managing risks and issues in a programme has three perspectives:

- The programme's own risks and issues
- Those that arise outside the programme (e.g. from a change of strategy) and those that arise from outside the organisation (e.g. change of legislation)
- Risks and issues escalated from the programme's projects.

As well as careful monitoring of the programme and its projects, the Programme Manager needs a mechanism to scan the environment external to the programme. It can be useful to get help with this from those who monitor the external environment as part of their day-to-day role, for example legal and marketing staff.

See also Chapter 11, 'Risk management and issue resolution'.

For any given tranche, after an initial risk assessment, the overall risk for that tranche should gradually decline. As transition is about to start, open risks should only be related to transition itself (i.e. the embedding of the new operations, achievement of the outcomes and the benefits measurement arrangements). Issues will increase as quality assurance activities take place. As transition approaches, the number of open issues should also be rapidly decreasing. Any patterns contrary to these are causes for concern and should be investigated.

16.5 CONTROL AND DELIVERY OF COMMUNICATIONS

Use the Programme Communications Plan as early as possible by notifying the stakeholders of the individuals appointed to specific roles on the programme. Thereafter, the communication activities should ensure the stakeholders are kept informed and engaged in the work of the programme, its projects and the benefits expected.

When stakeholders have received new communications it is important to check they have understood them in the way the programme team intended. Misunderstanding in programmes can give rise to significant problems. Communications are intended to generate and maintain support from stakeholders. Communications, formal and informal, will affect how they feel about the programme. Stakeholders' attitudes needs to be continually assessed, and any significant decline in attitude will need attention.

It is essential to ensure that feedback channels between the programme and its stakeholders are working effectively to ensure that both maintain alignment.

Stakeholders will often change during the life of a programme. The Stakeholder Engagement Strategy will provide guidance on how to detect stakeholder changes, and how to assess new stakeholders (see Chapter 6, 'Leadership and stakeholder engagement').

16.6 INITIATE COMPLIANCE AUDITS

The programme must ensure that mechanisms are in place to assess the performance of its processes and its projects. These must be used regularly to ensure the actual performance is acceptable. Stakeholders will require reassurance of this, and may initiate an audit to verify and validate progress and performance so far.

These audits may be extended to review the business operations that have undergone transition, to ensure that the new systems and working practices are being embedded and that the change is established.

16.7 MAINTAIN ALIGNMENT BETWEEN PROGRAMME BLUEPRINT AND BUSINESS STRATEGIC OBJECTIVES

As an organisation's strategy changes, monitoring arrangements should detect pending strategy changes. An impact assessment should take place, with the results fed back to the strategy makers. When corporate strategy changes are approved, the programme may also need to change (possibly including the Blueprint, Business Case and other dependent documents) to ensure strategic alignment.

Programmes and their projects sometimes drift off course. Regularly checking these activities against the Blueprint will be needed to maintain the ongoing alignment of the programme with the corporate strategy. If the programme becomes significantly out of alignment with the strategy, the consequential impact on the Business Case can render the programme invalid and lead to closure.

16.8 MAINTAIN INFORMATION AND ASSET INTEGRITY

As projects are started, information volumes will increase significantly. It is vital that Configuration Management is in place to track new items and changes to existing items. Configuration Management plays an important role in supporting issue resolution by helping to assess the impact of change requests. These activities link closely with quality activities.

Configuration baselines should be updated at the end of each tranche.

See Chapter 12, 'Quality management', for more detail.

16.9 MANAGE PEOPLE AND OTHER RESOURCES

The Resource Management Plan identifies rules of engagement for acquiring and using resources.

Resources are often shared across programmes, projects and operational work. Issues can arise if the resource required is not going to be available. A corporate Programme Office can be helpful here, as they can provide a complete picture of the utilisation resource and the status of potentially competing activities.

There are critical points in a programme when careful attention needs to be paid to managing people. As a tranche end approaches, people typically get concerned as they are soon going to have to change the way they do their work. It might help, for example, to provide extra support for staff as they prepare for transition and as they start to take on their new roles and use new systems.

For further details see Chapter 6, 'Leadership and stakeholder engagement', Chapter 8, 'Blueprint design and delivery', and Appendix C, 'Programme Office'.

16.10 PROCUREMENT AND CONTRACTS

The Resource Management Plan identifies the requirements for procurement and contract management within the programme, which are consequently set up. Managing suppliers and maintaining the alignment of their activities with the overall direction of the programme requires specific management attention and intervention if things go off track. Procurement and contract management activities must be aligned to corporate policies and standards, and may require tailoring to suit the particular needs of the programme.

As part of this activity, there should be regular scheduled reviews of suppliers and their performance against expectation and the contract.

16.11 MONITOR, REPORT AND CONTROL

Arrangements defined in the Monitoring and Control Strategy are implemented. Regular progress reporting from the project level informs the formal progress monitoring which keeps the programme on track. Monitoring progress may identify problem areas requiring management intervention. These issues should be escalated and actioned as soon as possible to prevent the programme losing momentum and moving off track.

A key aspect of control is ensuring the Blueprint and the delivery of new capabilities defined within it remain internally consistent and coherent. Programmes involving major technical infrastructures may require a dedicated design authority function.

The following summarises monitoring and control activities that are important enough to warrant the attention of the SRO and Programme Board:

- Information must be complete, timely, accurate and relevant for the control and decision-making it supports. Any significant gaps in information, or if it is out of date, will mean the programme is out of control. Significant amounts of information come from the programme's projects. Reporting mechanism from projects must be checked regularly to ensure they are functioning correctly
- Decisions – planned and exceptions, definitions of and instructions for – are contained in the Monitoring and Control Strategy

- Approve major exceptions from projects
- Approve outcome achievements, accepting deviations
- Approve benefits achievements, accepting deviations
- Deal with benefits realisation exceptions
- Deal with capability delivery escalations
- Benefits realisation, tracking business performance, benefits achievements and instigating ad hoc Benefits Reviews.

16.12 TRANSITION AND STABLE OPERATIONS

Transition plans prepared earlier in the tranche will be activated when all the tranche outputs have been combined and tested, and operations are ready to use them, changing their ways of working. Transition can sometimes be very disruptive, and these plans may need to be very detailed in order to minimise the impact on ongoing business operations. Consider providing extra support to people who may be legitimately concerned at this difficult time.

Transition ends when the outputs are implemented and the new capabilities embedded. Measurement of the performance of the current state of operations must have been completed before transition starts. Performance measures should be tracked during transition and after to make sure that operations progress to a stable state and do not drift back to the old ways of working. Such measures are also important during this period to help minimise dis-benefits and spot opportunities to realise additional benefits.

However, in most cases overall measurable improvements in operations are unlikely until the new processes are stable and the changes are significantly embedded. Assessing overall success by comparing the performance of new operations with the old operations should not be attempted until acceptable stability is achieved. Whereas the start of transition is usually a clearly identifiable event authorised by the SRO, moving from transition to a stable state is more of a grey area and requires the judgement of experienced senior management.

If everything and everyone is not thoroughly prepared, the change to the new ways of working will take longer and might be less successful. This can produce undesirable downsides:

- Disruption to operations will be more severe, leading to loss of output and/or quality
- Improvements resulting from the new operations might be less pronounced, and delivery of benefits will be reduced or delayed

■ Operations may revert to the old ways of working and lose faith in the programme.

The SRO and the Programme Board should provide formal authorisation to proceed into transition, and ensure appropriate criteria are in place for speeding up or slowing down the transition rate based on the performance of the organisation during this period. This control encourages the programme team and Change Teams to check that preparations are adequate, and helps gain commitment from operational staff that will be critical during this period.

For more detail on transition see Chapter 9, 'Planning and control'.

16.13 PREPARE FOR THE NEXT TRANCHE

As the programme progresses, there is increasing clarity about the way forward. This should occur at the end of each tranche. Changes to the programme's approach may now be needed as a result of the learning from the tranche now ending:

■ Learning from what this tranche has achieved to inform the next tranche, especially where the programme is designed for incremental delivery of change

■ Adapting governance and the Organisation Structure

■ Different skills and experience might be needed, for example if the programme is moving from exploratory to more of a rollout, this should be reflected in the Resource Management Plan

■ Specifying the physical environment and infrastructure required for managing the next tranche

■ Refining and developing the Blueprint, Benefits Maps, Benefit Profiles and Projects Dossier for the next tranche, building on and complementing the change already delivered by previous tranches

■ Reviewing and refining Information Baselines (see Appendix A, 'Programme information').

The programme's Business Case will need to be refined as the plans for the next tranche(s) unfold. The emphasis, as described in 'Defining a Programme' is to consider alternative approaches to develop the best Business Case. Ideally the Business Case should be improved at each tranche end, with the programme concentrating on change that is working well, and reducing that which is not.

The SRO consults with the Sponsoring Group to approve the start of the next tranche.

16.14 END-OF-TRANCHE REVIEW AND CLOSE

Programme information is updated, refined and maintained as the programme progresses. In particular this should be done at the end of each tranche, as preparations for the next tranche need to be informed about what is working well and areas that need attention or adjustment. Successive refinements to the Blueprint will highlight any adjustments that may need to be made to the Projects Dossier to keep the programme on track. The Programme Plan and Benefits Realisation Plan should be refined as completion and delivery dates from the projects are known.

At the end of each tranche there should be a full review to assess the ongoing viability of the programme and ensure that the delivery options and strategy remain optimal. The programme's Business Case, benefits and the benefits management process must be reviewed at the end of each tranche. The Business Change Manager(s) should plan for at least one review after the tranche has closed to assess the realisation of post-tranche benefits. The end-of-tranche reviews may also include a formal assessment of the effectiveness of the programme management activities.

It may be useful to consider the assessment of benefits from both an internal and external perspective. The internal perspective will involve measuring reduction in costs, for example. The external perspective, for example via a programme audit function, will involve assessing whether the potential for realisation of benefits remains on track and ensuring all the possible benefit dependencies are considered.

If the tranche end has been designed to prove whether hypotheses embedded in the strategy can work satisfactorily, in order to collect and analyse sufficient benefit measures to reach a conclusion, there may be a planned delay before the next tranche starts. See Figure 16.2 for a diagrammatic example.

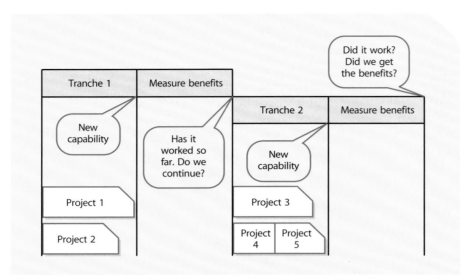

Figure 16.2 Example of a programme where Tranche 1 is a pilot to test the strategy

16.15 RESPONSIBILITIES

Responsibilities Flow Steps	Sponsoring Group	SRO	Programme Board	Programme Manager	Business Change Managers	Programme Office
Managing the Tranches						
Establish the tranche		A	C	R	I	C
Direct work		A	C	R	I	C
Manage risks and issues		A	C	R	I	C
Control and delivery of communications		A	C	R	C	C
Initiate compliance audits	R	AR	C	I	I	C
Maintain alignment of Blueprint & Strategy		A	C	R	C	
Maintain information and asset integrity		A	C	C	C	R
Manage people and other resources		A	C	R	C	C
Procurement and contracts		A	C	R		
Monitor, report and control	I	A	C	R	C	C
Transition and stable operations		A	C	C	R	C
Prepare for next tranche	C	A	C	R	C	C
End-of-tranche review and Close	C	A	C	R	C	C

KEY
R – Responsible; get the work done
A – Accountable; make decisions; R reports to A
C – Consulted; supports, has information or capability required
I – Informed; notified but not consulted

Figure 16.3 Typical responsibilities for 'Managing the Tranches'

Delivering the
Capability

17

17 Delivering the Capability

17.1 INTRODUCTION

The 'Delivering the Capability' process (see Figure 17.1) covers the activities for coordinating and managing project delivery according to the Programme Plan. Delivery from the Projects Dossier provides the new outputs that enable the capabilities described in the Blueprint. The activities of 'Delivering the Capability' are repeated for each tranche of the programme.

'Delivering the Capability' and 'Realising the Benefits' (see Chapter 18) are distinct processes, but they need to work closely together to harmonise the programme objectives with project delivery and benefit realisation through transition to operations. The 'Managing the Tranches' process (see Chapter 16) is used for overseeing these two processes, providing the high-level direction, guidance and control.

17.2 START PROJECTS

The Programme Manager is responsible for commissioning projects within the Projects Dossier and should ensure that appropriate individuals are appointed to the key project roles, such as Project Executive (or Sponsor) and Project Manager. The Project Executive is accountable to the programme for the project's successful completion within specified scope, risk, time, cost and quality parameters. Tolerance levels should be set to enable the project delivery teams to manage minor deviations independently from the programme.

As each project is about to begin, the Programme Manager should ensure each project management team fully understands the Project Brief and the programme's project management standards.

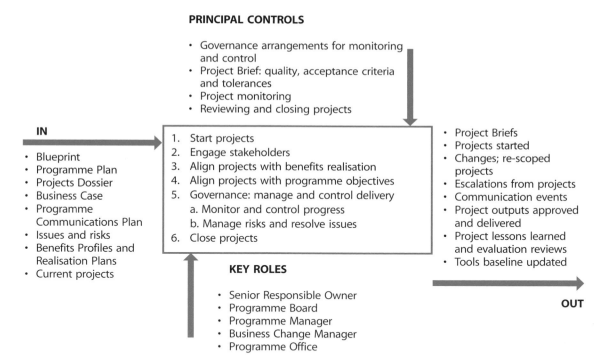

PRINCIPAL CONTROLS

- Governance arrangements for monitoring and control
- Project Brief: quality, acceptance criteria and tolerances
- Project monitoring
- Reviewing and closing projects

IN

- Blueprint
- Programme Plan
- Projects Dossier
- Business Case
- Programme Communications Plan
- Issues and risks
- Benefits Profiles and Realisation Plans
- Current projects

1. Start projects
2. Engage stakeholders
3. Align projects with benefits realisation
4. Align projects with programme objectives
5. Governance: manage and control delivery
   a. Monitor and control progress
   b. Manage risks and resolve issues
6. Close projects

KEY ROLES

- Senior Responsible Owner
- Programme Board
- Programme Manager
- Business Change Manager
- Programme Office

- Project Briefs
- Projects started
- Changes; re-scoped projects
- Escalations from projects
- Communication events
- Project outputs approved and delivered
- Project lessons learned and evaluation reviews
- Tools baseline updated

OUT

Figure 17.1 Overview of 'Delivering the Capability'

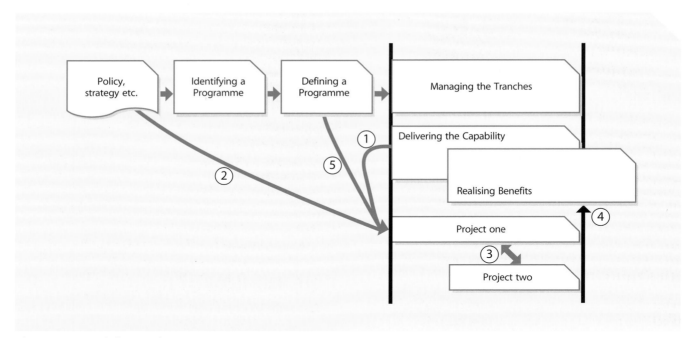

Figure 17.2   Briefing projects

Key to sequence numbers in Figure 17.2 on project briefing:

1   Identify projects started by the programme
2   Confirm how the projects fit into the big picture by referring to strategy etc.
3   Make sure the projects are aware of and understand interdependencies with other projects
4   Explain how the projects' outputs will be used (perhaps combined with other project outputs) to enable transition, lead to outcomes and for benefits realisation
5   Use information from 'Defining a Programme' to provide them with guidance on quality, reporting, exceptions and escalation.

17.3   ENGAGE STAKEHOLDERS

Maintaining the engagement of stakeholders and keeping them informed of progress and issues are important parts of successful programme management. The cooperation of stakeholders will be needed as projects in the programme need specific input. For example, involving stakeholders meaningfully in requirements analysis, reviewing designs, user acceptance testing etc. will give them better understanding of the programme while ensuring that the project's outputs are designed to reflect their needs. Their contribution and input can give them a sense of ownership, leading to a more positive attitude.

The Programme Manager may need to provide guidance on communication events at times when projects engage with critical stakeholders.

See also Chapter 6, 'Leadership and stakeholder engagement'.

17.4   ALIGN PROJECTS WITH BENEFITS REALISATION

The Business Change Manager is responsible for ensuring the particular benefits relevant to each project can be realised from implementing the outputs from those projects. The particular Project Brief, the relevant Benefit Profiles and the Benefits Realisation Plan should be refined as part of project start-up activities. The Business Change Manager can play a key role at milestones in projects, ensuring the input and providing expertise from operational staff in assessing designs, prototypes and similar items, and considering how well these proposals are likely to work in a full-scale operational environment.

If there is a Change Team, then a member of the team may work alongside or as part of the project representing the Business Change Manager in the day-to-day decision-making of the project.

17.5   ALIGN PROJECTS WITH PROGRAMME OBJECTIVES

Aligning projects with programme objectives is a continual activity throughout the programme for all its projects. For projects started by the programme the initial alignment is achieved via the Project Brief, and maintained through the reporting line between the projects and the programme. In emergent programmes there will be projects that are already under way. Their progress and project information (such as the PID, or Project Initiation Document) should be reviewed by the programme team. Any required amendments, re-scoping or re-planning in order to align with the programme's Blueprint, Programme Plan and Benefits Realisation Plan should be agreed and actioned.

17.6 GOVERNANCE: MANAGE AND CONTROL DELIVERY

Overseeing projects is critical to success. When the programme starts projects, part of their brief explains the relationship between the project and its programme:

- When and how the project reports to the programme
- Reporting exceptions (including a definition of exceptions with stated tolerances for time, cost, quality, risk and issues) so the project knows when circumstances are beyond its authority.

Governance in this process requires effective links to be formed between the programme team and the project boards. See Chapter 4, 'Organisation', for examples of programme and project governance structures.

See also details on Monitoring and Control Strategy in Appendix A, 'Programme information'.

17.6.1 Monitor and control progress

Projects should report in an agreed format to help aggregate the information at the programme level. Progress against the programme's plans and schedules is monitored and tracked. Any departures (outside agreed tolerances) from previously published project plans are assessed for impact on the rest of the programme. The impact of any change within a project or on other parties within the programme needs to be recognised as early as possible in order to manage the change carefully. The Programme Manager will use information from projects to help update the Programme Plan (see Appendix A, 'Programme information').

The live projects are monitored by focusing on the areas that are key to the programme, such as:

- **Outputs** – project outputs meet the requirements of their customers, which could be the programme itself
- **Timely completion** – adhering to delivery forecasts, and reporting exceptions as soon as possible
- **Risks, issues and assumptions** – if they can't be managed by the project they should be escalated to the programme to maintain integrity
- **Estimates, costs and benefits** – tolerance tracking and estimating the contribution towards benefit realisation, reporting exceptions quickly

- **Resources** – confirming suitability and availability
- **Scope** – changes need to be formally managed to avoid insidious scope creep.

The Programme Manager, having initiated projects from the Projects Dossier, needs to oversee progress:

- Review projects, obtain information for benefit reviews and assessments
- Deal with escalations and exceptions from projects
- Manage dependencies and interfaces between projects with particular emphasis on making sure projects understand how their outputs need to combine to achieve the desired outcomes
- Oversee quality with particular emphasis on making sure project outputs will work well enough in a full-scale operational environment to achieve the benefits desired (in conjunction with the Business Change Manager).

17.6.2 Manage risks and resolve issues

The identified risks need to be regularly reviewed and challenged. New risks may be identified and responses planned or actioned.

As the programme progresses there will be the inevitable delays, unforeseen situations and other situations that threaten the programme. The Programme Manager is responsible for recognising and dealing with anything that could affect the successful delivery of the programme. This may involve escalating issues arising from individual projects to the Senior Responsible Owner, liaising with the Business Change Manager(s) or working with the projects to manage risks and resolve issues that could affect delivery of project outputs, programme outcomes and therefore benefit realisation.

Projects will also identify risks from their perspective. They must be clear about when risk needs to be managed at a programme level and when to escalate these to the Programme Manager.

For each project this guidance on managing risks and issues should be described in the Project Brief prepared by the Programme Manager. For the programme overall, rules are contained in the Risk Management Strategy and Issue Resolution Strategy. See Appendix A, 'Programme information' for more detail.

These are some circumstances that should require a project to escalate risks or issues to the Programme Manager:

- Other projects or other programmes are impacted
- The project does not have sufficient authority for the action required

- The action required will exceed project tolerances for quality, time or cost
- The project does not have the necessary skills or experience and does not have the authority to acquire them.

17.7 CLOSE PROJECTS

As each project prepares for closure, there should be a formal handover of the outputs to the programme. It is important that the closing of projects is carefully controlled by the programme. If the combined outputs from projects don't support effective transition and don't enable the required improvement to operational improvement, the expected benefits may not be realised. See also the transition section in Chapter 18, 'Realising the Benefits'.

Part of project closure involves the planning of a post-project review to assess the realisation of benefits from the project's outputs. These reviews should be scheduled to fit into the programme's review schedule and may require external independent scrutiny.

The process of project closure should include the dissemination of lessons learned across the programme to share knowledge and experiences with the other projects. It is often useful for members of the programme team to contribute to project evaluation review and lessons learned reports where successes and problem areas associated with the project and its project management process are captured. Throughout the programme, the projects need to be advised of any issues arising that may impact on benefit responsibilities. The lessons learned reports may be useful to inform this activity.

17.8 RESPONSIBILITIES

Responsibilities / Flow Steps	Sponsoring Group	SRO	Programme Board	Programme Manager	Business Change Managers	Programme Office
Delivering the Capability						
Start projects		A	C	R	C	C
Engage stakeholders		A	C	R	C	C
Align projects with benefits realisation		A	C	R	C	C
Align projects with programme objectives		A	C	R	C	C
Governance: manage and control delivery		A	C	R	C	C
Close projects		A	C	R	C	I

KEY
R – Responsible; get the work done
A – Accountable; make decisions; R reports to A
C – Consulted; supports, has information or capability required
I – Informed; notified but not consulted

Figure 17.3   Typical responsibilities for 'Delivering the Capability'

Realising the
Benefits

18

18 Realising the Benefits

18.1 INTRODUCTION

The purpose of the 'Realising the Benefits' process (see Figure 18.1) is to manage the benefits from their initial identification to their successful realisation. The activities cover monitoring the progress of the projects to ensure the outputs are fit for purpose and can be integrated into operations such that the benefits can be realised.

'Realising the Benefits' incorporates the planning and management of the transition from old to new ways of working and the achievement of the outcomes, whilst ensuring that the operational stability and performance of the operations are maintained. The activities of this process are repeated as necessary for each tranche of the programme.

There are three distinct sets of activities that this chapter covers:

- **Manage pre-transition** – the analysis, preparation and planning for business transformation
- **Manage transition** – delivering and supporting the changes
- **Manage post-transition** – reviewing progress, measuring performance and adapting to change.

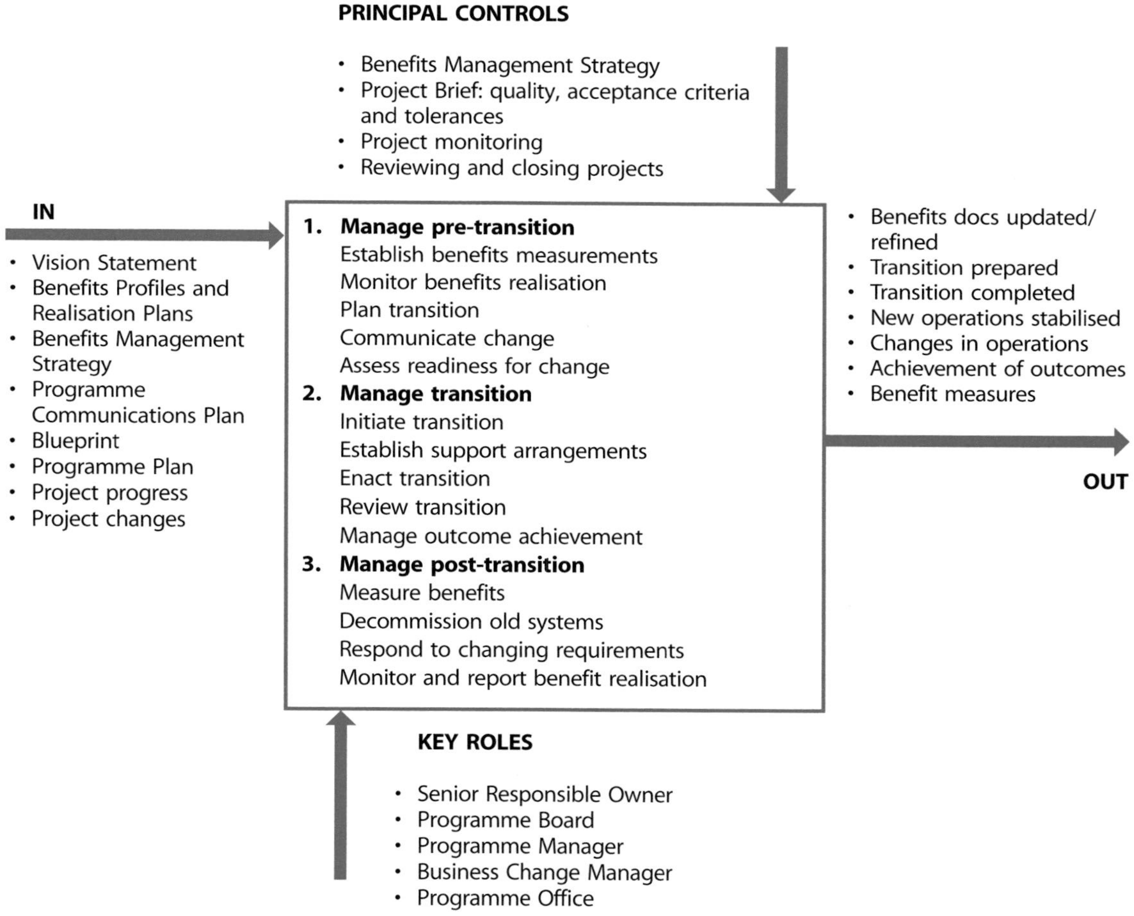

PRINCIPAL CONTROLS

- Benefits Management Strategy
- Project Brief: quality, acceptance criteria and tolerances
- Project monitoring
- Reviewing and closing projects

IN

- Vision Statement
- Benefits Profiles and Realisation Plans
- Benefits Management Strategy
- Programme Communications Plan
- Blueprint
- Programme Plan
- Project progress
- Project changes

1. **Manage pre-transition**
   Establish benefits measurements
   Monitor benefits realisation
   Plan transition
   Communicate change
   Assess readiness for change
2. **Manage transition**
   Initiate transition
   Establish support arrangements
   Enact transition
   Review transition
   Manage outcome achievement
3. **Manage post-transition**
   Measure benefits
   Decommission old systems
   Respond to changing requirements
   Monitor and report benefit realisation

- Benefits docs updated/refined
- Transition prepared
- Transition completed
- New operations stabilised
- Changes in operations
- Achievement of outcomes
- Benefit measures

OUT

KEY ROLES

- Senior Responsible Owner
- Programme Board
- Programme Manager
- Business Change Manager
- Programme Office

Figure 18.1   Overview of 'Realising the Benefits'

18.2 MANAGE PRE-TRANSITION

18.2.1 Establish benefits measurements

Benefits realisation is what the programme is all about. It is important to ensure that this is made real by the implementation of a relevant and reliable measurement processes. These measures are defined in each of the Benefit Profiles and overall in the Benefits Management Strategy.

Source data and set-up reporting

Business performance information will be needed for the current state and during the life of the programme. Whilst this is defined in Benefit Profiles, it is now that the actual collection of data starts, possibly in parallel with the activities in 'Defining a Programme' (see Chapter 15). This can be challenging. Therefore it is sensible to take a pragmatic approach, incrementally building on the information that is initially available.

Information produced to assist with managing benefits realisation should pass the following tests:

- **Currency**: it is no good using data that is months out of date. Ongoing reporting must be capturing recent information.
- **Accuracy**: if the information is based on unreliable or volatile data then invalid decisions may be made. There may be a need to look for a second indicator from another source to cross check.
- **Relevance**: only report relevant information. It should be brief and effective. If there is too much information critical evidence may be missed.

The Business Change Manager should regularly test the validity and authenticity of information being provided and reported upon, to ensure that the basis for decision-making is correct.

Performance baselines

In order to measure the improvements resulting from benefits realisation, the before state needs to be measured. Without this there will be no way of assessing whether the after measurements indicate an improvement or not. The identification of what measures are relevant was undertaken during 'Defining a Programme' and details are recorded in each Benefit Profile. The before state is a baseline measure and is recorded in the appropriate Benefit Profiles.

18.2.2 Monitor benefits realisation

Throughout the programme, progress is monitored against the Business Case, Programme Plan, Benefits Realisation Plan and the Blueprint to identify potential improvements to enhance benefit achievement or opportunities to minimise dis-benefits. Adjustments may be identified from a range of events or circumstances, including:

- Business operations that will use the project outputs are unstable
- Forward plans are no longer realistic based on experience to-date
- External circumstances have changed, affecting the future course of the programme
- The programme's objectives have changed or been refocused.

Monitoring and collaboration with projects needs to be benefits focused. This could include, for example, assessing designs, prototypes and similar items to consider how well they are likely to work in a full-scale operational environment. This would be part of answering the big question: Will the scale of the improvement be enough to produce the desired benefits?

The benefits are managed and controlled throughout the programme with the same degree of rigour as the projects. Both benefits and costs are of primary importance to the success of the programme. During the programme, there may be change or opportunities for improving the benefits, and the Benefit Profiles will need to be reassessed and adjusted as necessary.

See also Chapter 8, 'Blueprint design and delivery', and Chapter 10, 'The Business Case'.

18.2.3 Plan transition

Change to an organisation needs to be planned and managed carefully. Transition plans often contain considerably more detail than the Programme Plan.

In preparing the plan consideration should be given to:

- Staff and their working practices
- Information and technology
- Temporary facilities for those managing the transition
- The cultural and infrastructural migration from the old to the new
- Integration with the programme plan to be aware that a tranche end approaches
- Maintaining business operations during transition
- Exit or back-out arrangements should the change fail badly.

See also Chapter 9, 'Planning and control', for more information on transition planning.

18.2.4 Communicate the change

This is about taking the entire business, operating units and the individuals themselves through the engagement cycle for the planned changes, to raise awareness and interest, and to get engagement and involvement.

The Programme Communication Plan provides the basis for effective communication. The Risk Register, plans, Vision Statement, Blueprint and benefits provide key information for the communications required when reviewing and planning change activities.

Change must be carefully communicated well before actual transition. Late communication is likely to result in significant resistance.

See also Chapter 6, 'Leadership and stakeholder engagement', and paragraph 2.2.3, 'Envisioning and communicating a better future'.

18.2.5   Assess readiness for change

As preparation for implementing the change, it is a critical responsibility of the Business Change Manager(s) and the team involved in change to be fully engaged with the project teams and the business operations and to immerse them in the change that is coming.

This is the point where the project outputs are being delivered to the Business Change Managers.

Seeking out other organisations that have been through similar changes will help the organisation prepare and avoid some of the pain of pioneering change.

When assessing capability and capacity of the organisation to make the changes, consider the following:

- Recent track record and experience of change
- Past experience of implementing this type of change
- Availability of resources to support the change in terms of volume, competency and experience
- How the intended change fits with the organisation's culture and values, i.e. does it go deeper than a change to a way of working
- Effectiveness of the supporting systems that could enable change, for example, communications channels, process maturity etc.
- Skills and mobility of the workforce
- Current levels of service level performance to customers, and levels of satisfaction
- Third-party supplier performance and alignment with change plans
- Service management's ability to support the organisation through transition and in its new operational state.

As part of assessing readiness for change, all benefits- and transition-related documentation, including plans and profiles, should be updated.

18.3 MANAGE TRANSITION

18.3.1   Initiate transition

As the projects approach completion, the relevant business operations need to be prepared for implementing the outputs from the projects. The transition plan (part of the Programme Plan) is reviewed and updated to reflect the activities of transition. These activities need to be managed into the business environment, ensuring successful take-on of the new capability whilst maintaining the appropriate levels of business-as-usual.

The transition may be achieved in a single change to the operations, or may be achieved through a series of incremental or modular changes. The transition plan should provide the route map for implementation.

18.3.2   Establish support arrangements

Managing the transition will often require careful consideration of individuals' personal concerns about their working environment, and what the changes will mean to them. The transition to achieve the programme's outcome may also affect individuals and organisations external to the organisation delivering the programme. Support may be required from HR and system specialists.

To avoid unnecessary disruption, transition often involves very detailed plans. These transition plans are delivered now, and the Business Change Managers and Change Team must provide clear concise direction, making and obtaining rapid decisions.

18.3.3   Enact transition

Transition can start as soon as:

- All the outputs from projects that are required for this transition are complete, ready for operational use and the programme has verified through quality assurance that they will function correctly as an assembly
- Operational staff are trained and briefed on their new operational roles, as well as any temporary duties they may perform during transition
- There are no risks and issues outstanding that the new operations are not willing to take responsibility for
- Contingencies and back-out arrangements are in place should the changes fail
- Temporary transition management arrangements are in place
- The Senior Responsible Owner (SRO), in consultation with the Programme Board, has given the approval to start transition.

As soon as the start of transition is approved, it is important to verify that staff understand the role they will play during transition, and that they understand how the management structure for transition will operate.

Project staff should enact the transition plan and monitor progress, react and adapt to events as they develop, and ensure that stop/go criteria for aborting the implementation are monitored and action taken where appropriate.

Monitoring of the performance indicators will be important to assess the overall level of business stability.

18.3.4   Review transition

When the new arrangements are in place the transition should be reviewed, lessons documented and any follow-on actions and requirements captured.

There should be broad engagement with the stakeholder community to guide their perception, interest and support for the programme. This may be a testing time for everyone concerned; it is therefore important to maintain measured and effective communications.

At this stage the project manager and teams can be disengaged. The process of embedding the working practices leading to the release of benefits then starts under the control of the programme.

The embedding of new capability into the business such that it becomes business-as-usual is where benefits realisation occurs. New ways of working will inevitably require a settling-down period. The Business Change Manager(s) should ensure the programme provides sufficient support during this period.

18.3.5   Manage outcome achievement

It will take time for outcomes to be fully realised, working practices established and the business stabilised at the desired new state.

When the outcomes have been achieved it is critical that this is actively acknowledged through the Programme Communications Plan.

Beware of declaring victory too early. It is critical that the business has stabilised in the new state and the change is achieved. There is a danger that if the programme focus moves on to the next outcome too early the operations may regress to the old ways of working without the support and rigour of the programme processes and procedures.

18.4 MANAGE POST-TRANSITION

18.4.1   Measure benefits

The Benefit Profiles define how each benefit will be measured and what the starting point for this measurement activity is. Measuring benefit realisation should be part of the end-of-tranche reviews and any other planned benefit reviews.

If the tranche ending has been designed to prove whether hypotheses embedded in the strategy can work satisfactorily, there may be a planned delay before the next tranche starts, in order to collect and analyse sufficient benefit measures to reach a conclusion.

Starting the next tranche prematurely before clear conclusions have been reached can significantly increase the programme risk. If the conclusions from benefits measures indicate the programme should stop or change significantly, any projects running may also need to be stopped or changed, and much of the expenditure so far may be wasted.

Key performance indicators that were selected as measures and recorded in the Benefit Profiles will form the basis for comparison. It is important that as performance is monitored the consequences are understood. For example, you may be focused on headcount reduction, but if there is suddenly an upsurge in resignations or accidents then the cause and effect will need to be investigated.

It is wise to look at historic averages and seasonal trends to forecast expected performance averages over the life of the programme.

For further details on measuring benefits see Chapter 7, 'Benefits Realisation Management'.

18.4.2   Decommission old systems and working practices

The Business Change Manager must ensure that old working practices and systems are decommissioned as soon as business stability and resilience has been achieved. This reinforces and supports the new *modus operandi* and organisational culture.

This is a critical activity that is often overlooked. If old ways of working remain, there is a danger that the business will revert to using them once the pressure of the programme is removed. This, in turn, threatens the sustainability of the improvements and the change overall.

18.4.3   Respond to changing requirements

As part of embedding the new ways of working, ideas and problems will be highlighted and recognised. Many of these will not have been foreseen and it is a natural part of the programme flow that the programme is able to respond to these changing requirements.

Once the additional requirements have been quantified they should be provided to the Programme Manager for consideration and inclusion in the Projects Dossier via the Issue Log.

18.4.4 Monitor and report benefit realisation

Through the transition process, the benefit measures should be monitored and progress tracked for signs of deviation outside of the anticipated parameters.

Where the business performance moves out of tolerance this should be escalated to the SRO and the Sponsoring Group.

Benefit Profiles and the Benefits Realisation Plan should be updated and released in accordance with arrangements defined in the Benefits Management Strategy

Business Change Managers will provide inputs to benefit reviews as the analysis of and conclusions drawn from benefits measures. They can also help the programme understand the extent to which key stakeholders have been satisfied with the improvements.

It isn't always possible or necessary for a programme to continue until the end of the benefits measurement period. If results so far provide a clear indication of the ultimate result, and operational managers will take on the responsibilities for completing the measures, the programme can propose it ends its responsibility.

18.5 RESPONSIBILITIES

Responsibilities / Flow Steps	Sponsoring Group	SRO	Programme Board	Programme Manager	Business Change Managers (& Change Team)	Programme Office
Realising the Benefits						
Manage pre-transition						
Establish benefits measurements		A	C	C	R	C
Monitor benefits realisation		A	C	C	R	C
Plan transition		A	C	C	R	C
Communicate change		A	C	C	R	C
Assess readiness for change		A	C	C	R	I
Manage transition						
Initiate transition		A	C	C	R	I
Establish support arrangements		A	C	C	R	C
Enact transition		A	C	C	R	I
Review transition		A	C	C	R	C
Manage outcome achievement		A	C	C	R	I
Manage post-transition						
Measure benefits		A	C	C	R	C
Decommission old systems		A	C	C	R	I
Respond to changing requirements		A	C	C	R	C
Monitor and report benefits realisation		A	C	C	R	C

KEY
R – Responsible; get the work done
A – Accountable; make decisions; R reports to A
C – Consulted; supports, has information or capability required
I – Informed; notified but not consulted

Figure 18.2 Typical responsibilities for 'Realising the Benefits'

Closing a
Programme

19

19 Closing a Programme

19.1 INTRODUCTION

Programmes tend to last for a significant period, typically, years. There is a danger of allowing the programme to drift on, as if it is part of normal business. The purpose of the 'Closing a Programme' process (see Figure 19.1) is to ensure the end goal of formally recognising the programme is completed. This is when the programme has delivered the required new capabilities described in the Blueprint, and has assessed the outcomes via benefit measures.

Some Benefits will have been realised during the running of the programme. However, possibly the majority of the benefits may not be fully realised until some time after the last project has delivered. 'Closing a Programme' identifies the need for future assessment of benefit realisation outside of the programme as well as a formal review by the programme of those achieved so far.

It is not always sensible for a programme to continue to its planned end point if:

- Evidence so far indicates the programme does not make good business sense, and it is not possible to change it sufficiently to produce an acceptable business case
- The organisation is not able to secure adequate funding or sufficient resources to complete the outstanding work
- External circumstances have changed sufficiently to render the remainder of the programme irrelevant.

In such cases premature closure is proposed.

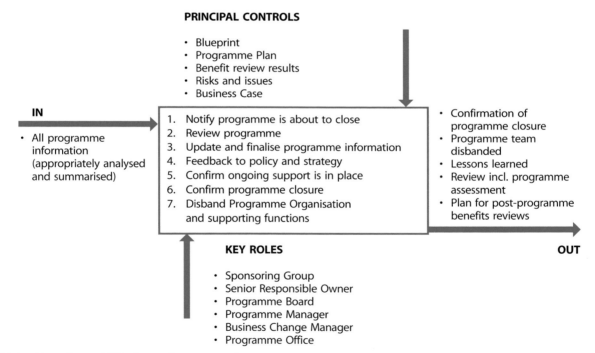

PRINCIPAL CONTROLS

- Blueprint
- Programme Plan
- Benefit review results
- Risks and issues
- Business Case

IN

- All programme information (appropriately analysed and summarised)

1. Notify programme is about to close
2. Review programme
3. Update and finalise programme information
4. Feedback to policy and strategy
5. Confirm ongoing support is in place
6. Confirm programme closure
7. Disband Programme Organisation and supporting functions

- Confirmation of programme closure
- Programme team disbanded
- Lessons learned
- Review incl. programme assessment
- Plan for post-programme benefits reviews

KEY ROLES

- Sponsoring Group
- Senior Responsible Owner
- Programme Board
- Programme Manager
- Business Change Manager
- Programme Office

OUT

Figure 19.1 Overview of 'Closing a Programme'

19.2 NOTIFY PROGRAMME IS ABOUT TO CLOSE

Closure comprises the final assessment of the programme and the decommissioning of its resources and infrastructure. These tasks cannot be undertaken until:

- Changes the programme was created to bring about have been delivered
- Business operations are stabilised after the change
- Benefit measures are under way.

Programme closure may be scheduled at any point after the completion of the last project within the Projects Dossier. To a large extent, when the programme formally closes will depend on the amount of support required to ensure the new operational environment delivered by the programme is fully embedded.

These are some examples of tests for whether a programme can close:

- Blueprint completed
- Business Case satisfied (thus far)
- Benefits self-sustaining
- Last tranche completed as per the Programme Plan
- No risks or issues outstanding that are unacceptable to operations
- Premature close agreed (with justifiable reasons).

Notify the Programme Organisation, stakeholders and Programme Office that the programme is preparing to close. Produce instructions and a timetable for closing activities and the programme review.

19.3 REVIEW PROGRAMME

Throughout the programme, the end-of-tranche reviews will have been monitoring and measuring benefits realisation. As part of 'Closing a Programme' a formal review should be conducted to assess the delivery of the complete Blueprint and realisation of the overall benefits. Benefits Reviews should have already been carried out during the programme, so the final review may be a consolidation of their findings.

This review should also assess and evaluate the performance of the programme and its management processes to identify lessons learned that may benefit other programmes. The review may involve independent external scrutiny, such as a gateway review.

A further review, following programme closure, may be required to provide a complete assessment of benefits realised as a result of the programme, including those benefits that may not have been ready for measurement and assessment when the programme closed.

19.4 UPDATE AND FINALISE PROGRAMME INFORMATION

Programme information should be reviewed and updated to ensure any residual issues, risks and outstanding actions have been dealt with appropriately.

Risks and issues that operations have agreed to take responsibility for actioning are handed over. Note that the accountability for these remains with the Senior Responsible Owner (SRO).

Any corporate and legislative governance requirements about the storage of information should be complied with as part of the archiving of documents.

19.5 FEEDBACK TO POLICY AND STRATEGY

Programmes initiated to deliver corporate strategic objectives need to provide feedback to the strategists. No strategies are guaranteed to succeed, and good feedback from each programme will help the organisation develop more informed and therefore better strategic decisions.

19.6 CONFIRM ONGOING SUPPORT IS IN PLACE

Whilst the programme is running, it is able to support and facilitate the overall change process. The programme can act as a vehicle for resolving disputes and issues that have arisen during the transition. Careful consideration must be given to how the business will operate without the support of the programme.

After closure, the embedded changes must be able to continue with smooth-running operations and working practices. For programmes where the outcome primarily affects those external to the organisation running the programme, any ongoing support requirements should be established, separate from the programme, so the programme can formally close.

19.7 CONFIRM PROGRAMME CLOSURE

Programme closure involves formal confirmation that:

- The Business Case has been satisfied
- All projects have completed satisfactorily
- Any remaining handover or transition activities required have been defined and assigned to relevant business operations.

If the programme is being closed prematurely (i.e. before the Blueprint has been achieved), the remaining live projects that are still required by the organisation need to be reassigned to business management or perhaps to another programme.

The SRO will propose closure to the Sponsoring Group. If satisfied with the overall outcome they will confirm programme closure. If they are not satisfied they must give clear direction about further work to be carried out.

All stakeholders should be informed of programme closure and its outcome.

19.8 DISBAND PROGRAMME ORGANISATION AND SUPPORTING FUNCTIONS

The programme's infrastructure and management processes are disbanded and individuals and resources released from the programme. Staff redeployment back into the organisation should be planned in advance. Staff will have updated their skills as a result of their experiences on the programme, and it is important that this is reflected in their personal development information. Any contracts used by the programme should be finalised and closed, or responsibility for continued contract management handed over to the relevant business management function.

19.9 RESPONSIBILITIES

Responsibilities Flow Steps	Sponsoring Group	SRO	Programme Board	Programme Manager	Business Change Managers	Programme Office
Closing the Programme						
Notify programme is about to close	I	A	C	R	C	I
Review programme	C	AR	C	C	C	C
Update and finalise programme information		A	C	R	I	C
Feedback to policy and strategy	C	AR	C	C	C	
Confirm ongoing support is in place		A	C	R	R	C
Confirm programme closure	A	R	C	I	I	C
Disband Programme Organisation		A	C	R	I	
KEY **R** – Responsible; get the work done **A** – Accountable; make decisions; R reports to A **C** – Consulted; supports, has information or capability required **I** – Informed; notified but not consulted						

Figure 19.2   Typical responsibilities for 'Closing a Programme'

Part 4
Appendices, further information and glossary

Appendix A:
Programme information

Appendix A: Programme information

A1   INTRODUCTION

This Appendix provides an explanation of the information that is required to manage a programme successfully. It explains what documentation you should establish, where the information could be sourced from and what to consider including in the contents. You will also find details on who should be involved in creating the documentation and what their role should be in the process.

The format for the documents is indicative and intentionally non-prescriptive. This enables organisations to structure, store and integrate information with their existing corporate governance frameworks; it is more important for organisations to identify and maintain the information to support their programme in a form that is appropriate to them. The following information descriptions should be seen as flexible checklists rather than rigid templates.

For example, the Programme Brief contains information that many organisations would also include in an outline Business Case. Therefore the use of either term should be seen as acceptable. It is the process of developing, capturing, analysing and acting on the information rather than the title that is important.

A2   WORKING WITH PROGRAMME INFORMATION

A programme exists within a dynamic environment. As such it is likely that information will be changing constantly; the programme's knowledge will increase and this should be reflected in the information that it is used to maintain context and manage delivery.

This Appendix is not intended to provide templates; it is guidance on what should be considered when constructing your documentation and when you should review and update the contents.

Bear in mind that there is core information within a programme that is cross-referred to in multiple documents; you may need to create an indexing system within your programme to enable cross-referencing of this core information.

For example, the Benefit Profile states you should identify risks to the achievement of the benefit. These risks should also be contained within your Risk Register, where the impact assessment should include reference to the implications of the risk on that benefit. This necessary replication of information requires careful tracking to ensure that all instances of the same information is updated, so as to maintain integrity throughout the programme documentation.

A3   PROGRAMME INFORMATION EVOLUTION

Table A1 outlines the information that is described in the section, when it is created and maintained, and to which Information Baseline it is allocated. There are four categories of information, which are reflected in their Information Baseline.

The following points should be considered regarding Information Baselines:

- Baselines help the planning and development of the programme information
- The completion and approval of the set of documents in each Baseline represents a step forward in the development of the programme
- Scheduling reviews of effectiveness, for example, the Governance Baseline, could be reviewed as part of a health check
- Classification helps programme teams understand their purpose and maintenance regimes; for example, tools are in constant use, so the Tools Baseline would be regularly updated, whereas the Boundary Baseline would be relatively stable.
- Baselines of documents interrelate; if one is changed the impact should be considered on the others.

Table A.1   Information Baselines

Information Baseline	Description of purpose
Boundary	Those which set out the direction of the programme
Governance	Those that set the standards and frameworks within which the programme will be delivered
Tools	Those that are created and actively managed and updated throughout
Programme	Those that take the Boundary and put the detail specification around how the end game will be achieved.

Table A.2   Document management over the programme lifecycle

Title	Identifying	Defining	Start	End	Deliver Capability	Realise Benefits	Closure	Information Baseline
			Managing the tranche					
Benefit Profiles	CR*	RU		RU		IM	RU	Boundary
Benefits Map		CR	IM			RU	RU	Programme
Benefits Mgt Strategy		CR	IM	RU			RU	Governance
Benefits Realisation Plan		CR		RU		IM	RU	Tool
Blueprint		CR	IM	RU			RU	Boundary
Business Case	CR*	RU		RU			RU	Programme
Information Mgt Strategy		CR	IM	RU			RU	Governance
Information Mgt Plan		CR	IM	RU			RU	Tool
Issue Log	CR*	RU		RU	RU	RU	RU	Tool
Issue Resolution Strategy		CR	IM	RU			RU	Governance
Monitoring and Control Strategy		CR	IM	RU			RU	Governance
Organisation Structure		CR	IM	RU			RU	Governance
Programme Brief	CR							Boundary
Programme Communications Plan		CR	IM	RU	IM	IM	RU	Tool
Programme Definition Document		CR						Programme
Programme Mandate	RU							Boundary
Programme Plan		CR	IM	RU			RU	Tool
Programme Preparation Plan	CR	IM						Tool
Projects Dossier		CR	RU		IM		RU	Programme
Quality Mgt Strategy		CR	IM	RU			RU	Governance
Quality Mgt Plan		CR	IM	RU			RU	Tool
Resource Mgt Strategy		CR	IM	RU			RU	Governance
Resource Mgt Plan		CR	IM	RU			RU	Tool
Risk Mgt Strategy		CR	IM	RU			RU	Governance
Risk Register	CR*	RU	RU		RU	RU	RU	Tool
Stakeholder Profiles		CR		RU	RU	RU	RU	Tool
Stakeholder Engagement Strategy		CR	IM	RU			RU	Governance
Vision Statement	CR*	RU						Boundary

CR = Create   IM = Implement, manage and refine   RU = Review and update

*This information is initially created as part of the Programme Brief. It then evolves into the appropriate document.

Table A.2 illustrates where and when documents are created and how they are managed over the programme lifecycle. Information will be continually changing; the programme information must be maintained to reflect the changing environment within which the programme exists and to maintain context. Table A.3 is a description of the individual documents in terms of their purpose and content.

Table A.3   Description of documents

Title	Purpose	Typical content
Benefits Map	Illustrates the relationship between benefits, outcomes and outputs so that realisation between the benefits can be managed and tracked	Dependencies between benefits
		Dependencies on project outputs
		Additional business changes to enable realisation of benefits
		Strategic objectives
		Enabling benefits
		End benefits
		Other external dependencies
		Dis-benefits.
Benefit Profile	Used to define each benefit (and dis-benefit) and provide a detailed understanding of what will be involved and how the benefit will be realised	Reference number or identifier
		Description of the benefit (or dis-benefit)
		Programme or organisational objectives supported; KPIs in the business operations that will be affected by the benefit, both immediately after realisation and for the future
		Current or baseline performance levels, and improvement or deterioration trajectory anticipated
		Other benefits that this benefit contributes towards
		Costs of achieving the benefit that have not been captured in project or other costs, e.g. redundancy costs
		Features required for the benefit to be realised; the project(s) within the programme directly related to the realisation of the benefit
		Business changes required for realisation (to process, culture, people, policy)
		Earlier benefits on which this depends
		Related issues and risks to the full realisation of the benefit
		Any dependencies on other programmes or projects outside the boundary of this programme
		Who owns this benefit (typically the Business Change Manager for this area of the business)
		Who will receive the benefit
		Measurement (financial wherever possible):
		■ Description of the measure(s) ■ How the measure is to be tracked ■ 'As is' measure ■ Target performance/score ■ From when (improvement begins) ■ To when (when measurement will cease or when target reached) ■ Non-project costs associated with realisation and measurement.

Table A.3   Description of documents (cont.)

Title	Purpose	Typical content
Benefits Realisation Plan	Used to track realisation of benefits across the programme and set review controls	A schedule detailing when each benefit, dis-benefit or group of benefits will be realised (typically as a chart with benefits of the same measure aggregated over time intervals through the life of the programme's business case)
		Appropriate milestones for when a programme's Benefits Review of progress could be carried out, to take a forward view of the likelihood of ongoing success
		Dates when specific outcomes will be achieved that enable the benefits
		Dependencies
		Detail of any handover and embedding activities, beyond the mere implementation of a deliverable or output, to sustain the process of benefits realisation after the programme is closed
		Could also include the Benefits Map.
Benefits Management Strategy	Used to establish the approach to realising benefits and the framework within which benefits realisation will be achieved	Measurement methods and processes that will be used to monitor and assess the realisation of the benefits
		A description of the functions, roles and responsibilities for benefit planning and realisation, aligned with the programme's Organisation Structure
		Scope and explanation of which areas of the business will be covered by benefits management enabling and realisation activity
		Priorities for the programme in terms of benefit types to be sought (e.g. cashable direct), to inform and focus the filtering and prioritisation process
		Any organisational specific information or headings that should be included in Benefit Profiles
		Tools, systems and sources of information that will be used to enable measurement
		CSFs against which the effectiveness of Benefits Realisation Management should be measured
		Clarification of benefits-related terminology appropriate to the organisation
		The review and assessment process for measuring benefit realisation covering who will be involved in the reviews; how and when the reviews will be carried out.

Table A.3   Description of documents (cont.)

Title	Purpose	Typical content
Blueprint	Used to maintain the programme's focus on delivering the required transformation and business change. A description of the current and changed organisation	Processes and business models of functions, including operational costs and performance levels, of the required vision of the future state; may be expressed in a number of ways, and will include flow and process graphics, organisational charts
		Organisation structure, staffing levels, roles and skill requirements necessary to support the future business operations. Any necessary changes to organisational culture, style, or existing structures and personnel may also be included
		Technology, IT systems, tools, equipment, buildings and accommodation required for the future business operations together with details of re-use of existing infrastructure or implementation of new infrastructure to support the vision of the future state
		The data and information required for the future business operations, together with details of how existing data and information will be changed or redeveloped to provide the necessary requirements for the vision of the future state
		The complete Blueprint document contains several sections: the current state, sections for the intermediate future state for each tranche, and the final future state for the end of the last tranche.
Business Case	Used to validate the ongoing viability of the programme	The strategic objectives for the programme, reflecting the Vision Statement, and aligning with the organisational context and business environment
		The expected benefits, with recognition of the organisation's capability to achieve the necessary transformation and change
		The overall risk profile, indicating the major risks to programme delivery and benefit realisation. Detailed risk assessment will be part of the programme's Risk Register
		Estimated costs and overall timescales. Detailed scheduling of programme milestones will be part of the Programme Plan
		Investment appraisal
		Forecasts of cashflow and expenditure over the programme timeline
		Options and approaches that have been considered.
Information Management Strategy	Describes how the programme will establish the measures, systems and techniques that will be used to maintain and control programme information	Systems that will be used to store information
		Responsibilities for management and maintenance of information
		Levels of confidentiality to be applied
		How information integrity will be maintained
		Criteria to assess effectiveness (cross-referenced with the Monitoring and Control Strategy)
		Approach to audit
		Scope of the strategy
		Release management arrangements for updated baselines or individual configuration items, and the relationship to the Programme Communications Plan

Table A.3   Description of documents (cont.)

Title	Purpose	Typical content
		Approach to information availability
		Configuration management and change control procedures, including:
		■ Configuration management responsibilities and systems and storage arrangements ■ Configuration management naming conventions and policies that will be used; these may be adopted from broader organisational policies ■ Explanation of how configuration management baselines will be implemented within the programme
		Information security arrangements to maintain confidentiality, integrity and availability of information within the configuration management arrangements
		Standards and processes to cover data and records management
		Use of terms, e.g. policy, strategy – could be a glossary.
Information Management Plan	Sets out the timetable and arrangements for implementing and managing the Information Management Strategy	Timetable to achieve: ■ Information storage systems ■ Configuration management ■ Release management ■ Information change control ■ Naming conventions ■ Security controls ■ Information and documentation structures
		Schedule for availability of templates to support the programme governance.
		Schedule for the extraction and delivery of information to support review, or similar procedures that are stipulated in activities in other plans
		How and when information management work will be monitored and reported, to include alert mechanisms that warn about serious violations of the programme's information assets
		Who will be responsible for the actions identified in the plan
Issues Log	Used to capture and actively manage programme issues	Headings must meet the needs of the Issue Resolution Strategy and be coordinated with the Risk Register
		Unique reference for each issue raised
		Date issue was raised (and resolved)
		Who raised the issue
		A description of the issue
		Description of the impact or potential impact it has on the programme, or projects action required including timing, costs
		Categorisation of the issue, e.g. request for change, issue, stakeholder question

Table A.3 Description of documents (cont.)

Title	Purpose	Typical content
		Issue owner – the person responsible for ensuring action is taken
		Issue actionee – each issue should be assigned to an individual who is best placed to take the necessary actions
		The current status of the issue and progress on its resolution, including providing feedback to the source
		Cross-reference to change control procedures where appropriate
		Description of how the issue was resolved and lessons learned from the actions taken.
Issue Resolution Strategy	Used to describe the mechanisms and procedures for resolving issues	How issues will be captured and assessed, and responsibilities
		Process and explanation of how change control will work in the programme
		How exceptions that take the programme beyond its boundary margins will be managed
		How information about their likely impact will be assessed
		Responsibilities for the effective management and resolution of issues within the programme
		How issue ownership will be allocated
		How actions will be identified and by whom; who will carry out and manage the required actions
		Description of how issues will be escalated or allocated between project and programmes
		Criteria for allocating severity ratings to issues. Categories for severity might be 'critical' (that is, adverse affect on the benefits such that continuation of the programme is unacceptable), 'major', 'significant' and 'minor'
		Definition of what constitutes a project- or programme-level issue
		Categorisation mechanism for filtering issues, e.g. technical, business process, organisational, programme process
		How actions will be monitored and evaluated for their effectiveness
		Any organisational specific heading information that will be required to be recorded within the Issue Log, other than the generic Issue Log template
		Criteria used to assess the effectiveness of issue management within the programme.

Table A.3   Description of documents (cont.)

Title	Purpose	Typical content
Monitoring and Control Strategy	Defines how the programme will apply internal controls to itself	Criteria to assess effectiveness
		How projects will be monitored
		How the programme's internal process effectiveness will be monitored
		What standards will be applied to the projects
		What controls will be in place, including decision authority
		Information that will be required for monitoring
		Margins within which the programme will operate
		Escalation routes for managing exceptions, e.g. how do you stop the programme
		Any links to independent assurance such as gateway reviews.
Organisation Structure	Description of the management roles, responsibilities and reporting lines in the programme	Programme Organisation chart; the programme organisational structure
		Description and responsibilities of individuals on the sponsoring group
		Role descriptions or terms of reference for the individuals within the programme's management team
		Business Change Management organisation and responsibilities
		Expectations of responsibilities of organisational governance authorities, e.g. risk, compliance, accounting etc.
		Allocation of assurance arrangements within the programme.
Programme Brief	Used to define the programme objectives and outcomes; this is a snapshot of what the programme is expected to achieve	The information initially referred to as the Programme Brief will evolve into a number of other documents, hence the Vision Statement, Issues Log, Risk Register, Business Case, Benefit Profiles are shown as being created during Identification; at this stage they may be at a very strategic or conception level.
		Outline Vision Statement for the programme, which will include a description of the capability the organisation seeks from changes to the business and/or its operations. Delivery of this capability is the end-goal of the programme.
		Outline description of the benefits or types of benefits that should be delivered from the new capability, an estimate of when they are likely to be achieved, and an indication of how they will be measured. It also includes significant dis-benefits
		Risks to the programme that can be recognised at this point in time, any current issues that may affect the programme, and any known constraints, assumptions or conflicts that may potentially affect the programme. These should also reflect levels of stakeholder support and engagement
		Outline business case, with as much detail as is available on the estimated costs, timescales and effort required to set up, manage and run the programme from initiation through to delivery and realisation of the benefits. The overall timescale for the programme may be relatively long, perhaps two to five years

Table A.3   Description of documents (cont.)

Title	Purpose	Typical content
		Options for delivery that are known about at this stage
		Programmes will provide an indication of the effort and resources required; an initial listing of the candidate projects or activities required should be included, together with rough timescales and explanation of those that will be terminated.
		Assessment of the current state and how the current business operates and performs in the areas that will be impacted by the change.
Programme Communications Plan	Sets out the timetable and arrangements for implementing and managing the Stakeholder Engagement Strategy	Description of key messages and programme information to be communicated, and the objectives for delivering these communications
		Responsibilities for delivering key messages and other information about the programme
		Identification of the stakeholder audience for each communication
		Description of channels to be used, including feedback mechanisms
		Process for handling feedback, through a feedback log, how objections will be identified and handled, and including the approach to managing negative publicity
		Schedule of communications activities, including target audiences for each
		Reference to any supporting project and business operations communications activity.
Programme Definition Document	A document that can be used to consolidate or summarise the information that was used to define the programme	Objectives for the programme
		Executive summary
		Justification and context for the programme
		Criteria against which it should be measured
		Vision Statement
		Blueprint summary
		Programme roles and responsibilities
		Governance principles that have been applied
		Summary of the current state
		Explanation of tranche structure
		Description of outcomes
		Summary of risks
		Summary of Projects Dossier
		Stakeholder summary
		Benefits Map
		Timescales, milestones and tranches
		Information Baselines, status and content.

Table A.3   Description of documents (cont.)

Title	Purpose	Typical content
Programme Mandate	Used to describe the required outcomes from the programme based on strategic or policy objectives; may consolidate information from a number of sources	What the programme is intended to deliver in terms of new services and/or operational capability
		How the organisation(s) involved will be improved as a result of delivering the new services/capability
		Expectations in terms of timescales, costs and boundary within which the sponsoring group will work
		How the programme fits into the corporate mission and goals and any other initiatives that are already under way or will be under way during the lifetime of the programme
		Information on current or anticipated initiatives that will be included within this programme, for emerging programmes
		Reference to any external drivers or pressures that may define the way the programme approaches the challenge, for example where the driving force for change is coming from
		Summary of the current state, the starting point at which the programme is being commissioned
		Some organisations may use terms like strategic or embryonic business case; this may have similar information, and as such could be used as an alternative to the Programme Mandate.
Programme Preparation Plan	Explains outputs, boundaries and controls from the Programme Definition activities	Resources required and where they will be sourced from
		Boundaries and margins within which the team will work during definition
		Description of the deliverables from definition.
		Governance and controls that will be applied to the defining team.
		Schedule of activities to achieve the outputs
		Membership of the Programme Board
		Any key members of the team that are already known, e.g. Business Change Managers and Programme Manager.
Programme Plan	Used to control and track the progress and delivery of the programme and resulting outcomes	Project information including the list of projects (the Projects Dossier), their target timescales and costs, and the dependency network showing the dependencies between the projects
		Cross-reference to the Risk Register to explain any planning contingencies that have been made to mitigate risk
		An overall programme schedule showing the relative sequencing of the projects
		Explanation of the grouping of projects and major activities into tranches, and the points at which end-of-tranche reviews will take place

Table A.3 Description of documents (cont.)

Title	Purpose	Typical content
		Individual schedules and plans that can be consolidated into the Programme Plan, e.g. Resource, Quality, Information, Benefits Realisation, Information, Transition and Communications
		Shows when the outputs from the projects will be delivered to the business and what transition activities will be required to embed the new capability into business operations
		Implementation schedule for the Monitoring and Control Strategy.
Projects Dossier	Provides a list of projects required to deliver the Blueprint, with high-level information and estimates	The list of projects that will be required to deliver the capability defined in the Blueprint
		Outline information on outputs, timescales, resource requirements and dependencies with other projects and activities
		Dependency network
		Links showing what contribution each project and major activity will make to the programme outcomes and benefits
		Cross-reference to the Benefits Map and Benefit Profiles.
Quality Management Strategy	Used to define and establish the activities for managing quality across the programme; description of the quality assurance, review and control processes for the programme covering	What will be subject to quality assurance, review and control and the quality criteria to be applied
		A description of the functions, roles and responsibilities for quality management, aligned with the programme's organisation structure
		What will trigger these activities (time-based, event-based, or associated with risk occurrence)
		What actions will be taken depending on the results of quality checks and the thresholds for escalation
		Criteria to assess programme success
		Interfaces with and dependencies on corporate management systems, including information requirements to support quality management
		Interfaces that projects will have with their programme and dependencies they will have on quality management systems set up by the programme, including information requirements to support their quality management
		Procedures for use of support tools for quality management activities, for example, change control software
		Guidelines to ensure the appropriate use of audits and health checks
		Resource requirements for quality management

Table A.3 Description of documents (cont.)

Title	Purpose	Typical content
		Specific standards, regulations etc. that need to be adhered to, and which subject-matter experts will be required to support quality management with regard to these areas
		Budgeting requirements for quality to include, but not limited to, managing contingency; accounting procedures for managing such budgets
		Cost and expenditure profile across the programme; to cover the direct cost of quality activities, and anticipated rate of usage of the contingency budget.
Quality Management Plan	Sets out the timetable and arrangements for carrying out the Quality Management Strategy	Schedule of activities required to implement the Quality Management Plan
		Who will undertake quality-assurance, review and control activities aligned with those activities in other plans that produce items that require assurance or review
		How and when the programme will carry out audits, health checks and reviews (or be subject to independent audit and review)
		How and when quality work will be monitored and reported, to include the collection, aggregation and analysis of quality monitoring data from projects
Resource Management Strategy	Used to identify how the programme will acquire and manage the resources required to achieve the business change	Funding requirements; accounting procedures for costs and expenditure; budgets for programme management resources and funding sources
		Procurement approach and reference to current contract frameworks or arrangements that will be used
		Cost and expenditure profile across the programme, expenditure approval procedures, financial reporting procedures
		Assets required, such as buildings and office equipment to deliver the programme
		Technology and services required
		Profile of resources that are shared across more than one of the projects within the portfolio; should indicate the expected use by each project of the shared resource within time periods
		Explanation of how the manning requirements of the programme and projects will be achieved; consideration should be given to how the business operations capacity to resource the consequences of programme change will be managed
		Which subject-matter experts will be required and how they will be sourced

Table A.3   Description of documents (cont.)

Title	Purpose	Typical content
		Description of how the human resource requirements of the programme will be managed
		Explanation of how the mix of internal and external resources to the programme and projects will be managed
		How any necessary skills and knowledge will be transferred into business operations to establish the ongoing change
		Approach to dispute resolution where resourcing conflicts occur with business operational requirements, other initiatives and programmes.
Resource Management Plan	Arrangements for implementing the Resource Management Strategy	Schedule of activities to implement the Resource Management Strategy
		Who will be responsible for resource management activities such as recruitment, budgeting, resource sharing
		Tracking of use of resources (cross-referenced to the Programme Plan where appropriate)
		Timings of reviews and monitoring activities
		What feedback mechanisms will be put in place for projects
		Should reflect changing requirements to meet the Organisation Structure and Resource Management Strategy during the programme flow
		Ensure correct alignment to the Programme Plan.
Risk Management Strategy	Defines the programme approach to establishing its framework for risk management; content derived from the organisation's risk management policy and risk management process guidance	Purpose and owner of the strategy
		Summary of the programme to which the plan relates
		Roles and responsibilities for managing risk in the programme.
		The process to be used and how it has been adapted from the Risk Management Process Guide if necessary
		Any preferred techniques to be used for each step of the process described above
		Scales for estimating probability and impact, giving the criteria to be used for each level within the scale
		Guidance on calculating expected value for all the risks associated with a programme.
		Guidance on how proximity for risks is to be assessed.
		Risk response categories, including threats and opportunities.
		Budget required to support risk management throughout the life of the programme
		Templates to be used
		Relevant early-warning indicators
		Timing of risk management activities; when formal risk management activities are to be undertaken, e.g. as part of end-of-tranche reviews

Table A.3 Description of documents (cont.)

Title	Purpose	Typical content
		Reports that are to be produced and their purpose, timing and recipients
		Criteria to be used to assess the effectiveness of risk management within the programmes
		Which external or internal risk management standards will be applied.
Risk Register	Used to capture and actively manage the risks to the programme	Risk identifier – a unique reference for each risk; may need to be reflected in project Risk Registers when the risk could impact on one or more projects as well as the programme
		Description of the risk, including the cause or source of the risk, the event (description of the threat or opportunity) and its effect (summary of the likely impact on the programme and or its projects)
		Probability of the risk occurring; should be done for both the before and after state (i.e. before and after any risk response action has been implemented)
		Impact on the programme should the risk materialise, taken from the scales defined in the programme Risk Management Plan (where appropriate this should show pre- and post-response action impacts)
		Proximity of the risk, which is an estimation of timescale for when the risk might materialise
		Description of the proposed risk action
		Any residual risk after action has been implemented
		Risk actionee – the individual assigned the implementation of a risk response action or actions to respond to a particular risk or set of risks; they support and take direction from the risk owner.
		Risk owner – named individual who is responsible for the management and control of all aspects of the risks assigned to them, including the implementation of the selected actions to address the threats or to maximise the opportunities. It should be noted that owners of the probability reduction actions may be different from those of the impact reduction actions.
		NB the Programme Manager has overall responsibility for managing programme risks; however, each risk should be assigned to the individual who is best placed to monitor it and manage any necessary actions
		Response to the risk, which is dependent on whether the risk has been identified as a threat or an opportunity
		Current status of the risk itself and progress of any actions relating to the management of the risk.

Table A.3   Description of documents (cont.)

Title	Purpose	Typical content
Stakeholder Engagement Strategy	Used to define the framework that will enable effective stakeholder engagement and communication	Criteria on how stakeholders with be grouped and tracked by the programme; it may be necessary to track specific key individuals and roles as well as groups.
		How the analysis of a stakeholder's influence and interest in the programme will be measured and assessed
		How the importance and impact of a stakeholder to a programme will be assessed
		How stakeholder analysis information will be processed and stored
		Review cycle
		Explanation of how projects and the programme will interface on communications and stakeholder activities
		Guidelines on communications responsibilities where there is an overlap between individual project and programme roles
		Description of how the programme will engage with all stakeholders, including mechanisms for encouraging, receiving and responding to feedback from stakeholders
		Any policies on types of terminology and language that will be adopted within the programme
		Measures to determine how well the communication process is engaging with stakeholders
		Description of how the overall responsibilities for stakeholder engagement within the programme will be achieved; should include clarification of the roles of projects and business change teams to provide clarity and avoid overlap.
Stakeholder Profiles	Used to record stakeholders information	Matrix (map) showing programme stakeholders and their areas of interest
		Analysis information within the matrix, either at the intersections or by the inclusion of additional columns that show who owns communications with the stakeholder
		Current and target positions for each stakeholder in terms of engagement
		Level of support
		Level of interest
		Level of influence
		Level of impact.

Table A.3   Description of documents (cont.)

Title	Purpose	Typical content
Vision Statement	Used to communicate the end goal of the programme. Could be seen as providing an external artist's impression of the desired future state	Created during 'Identifying a Programme' as part of the Programme Brief; verified and finalised during 'Defining a Programme'
		Clear statement of end goal of the programme
		Imposed constraints
		Providing context for the programme and project teams
		Any relevant information to help set expectations and context within the broader business context
		Terminology used should be suited to all stakeholders and the context of the programme.

A4   PROGRAMME INFORMATION

Table A.4 illustrates the relationship between the programme information in terms of input and output of information. The rows show inputs to the documents; the columns show the outputs. The relationships are indicative as many of the documents evolve. It is not possible to be totally precise, as for a number of documents there are circular references. For example, when Benefit Profiles are created, there may not be a Projects Dossier, but the Profiles do need to cross-reference which projects are linked, and hence which cannot be done until the Projects Dossier has been created.

Table A.4 Document relationships

The column group across the top is labelled **Input documents**.

Programme information relationships	Benefit Profiles	Benefits Map	Benefits Mgt Strategy	Benefits Real. Plan	Blueprint	Business Case	Info. Mgt Plan	Info. Mgt Strategy	Issue Log	Issue Res. Strategy	Org. Structure	Mon. and Cntrl Strat.	Programme Brief	Prog. Comms Plan	Prog. Def. Doc	Programme Mandate	Programme Plan	Prog. Prep. Plan	Projects Dossier	Quality Mgt Strategy	Quality Mgt Plan	Res. Mgt Strategy	Resource Mgt Plan	Risk Mgt Strategy	Risk Register	Stakeholder Profile	St/holder Eng. Strat.	Vision Statement
Benefit Profiles	▓		Y		Y						Y		Y						Y									Y
Benefits Map	Y	▓		Y															Y									
Benefits Mgt Strategy			▓															Y										
Benefits Realisation Plan	Y		Y	▓	Y				Y										Y				Y					
Blueprint					▓								Y			Y												Y
Business Case	Y				Y	▓			Y		Y		Y				Y		Y				Y		Y			Y
Information Mgt Plan							▓	Y																				
Information Mgt Strategy								▓										Y										
Issue Log	Y				Y	Y	Y	Y	▓		Y		Y			Y	Y		Y		Y		Y	Y	Y	Y		
Issue Resolution Strategy										▓								Y										
Organisation Structure	Y				Y						▓					Y			Y				Y					
Monitoring and Control Strategy												▓						Y										
Programme Brief													▓			Y												
Programme Communications Plan	Y				Y	Y	Y		Y		Y		Y	▓			Y	Y	Y						Y	Y	Y	Y
Programme Definition Document	Y	Y		Y	Y	Y			Y		Y				▓	Y		Y				Y	Y		Y	Y		Y
Programme Mandate																▓												
Programme Plan	Y			Y	Y	Y	Y		Y		Y	Y			Y		▓		Y		Y		Y		Y	Y		Y
Programme Preparation Plan													Y			Y		▓										
Projects Dossier	Y				Y				Y		Y								▓						Y	Y		
Quality Mgt Strategy																		Y		▓								
Quality Mgt Plan																				Y	▓							
Resource Mgt Strategy																		Y				▓						Y
Resource Mgt Plan			Y						Y		Y					Y			Y				▓		Y	Y		
Risk Mgt Strategy																		Y						▓				
Risk Register	Y			Y	Y	Y					Y		Y			Y	Y		Y		Y			Y	▓	Y		
Stakeholder Profile	Y				Y														Y							▓	Y	
Stakeholder Engagement Strategy																		Y									▓	
Vision Statement													Y			Y												▓

A5 PROGRAMME INFORMATION RESPONSIBILITIES

Table A.5 illustrates the levels of responsibility associated with each of the programme information documents.

Table A.5 Programme information responsibilities

Document title	Accountable	Responsible	Consult
Benefit Profiles	SRO	BCM	PM
Benefits Map	SRO	BCM	PM
Benefits Mgt Strategy	SRO	PM	BCM
Benefits Realisation Plan	BCM	PM	SRO
Blueprint	SRO	PM	BCM
Business Case	SRO	PM	BCM
Information Mgt Plan	PM	PM	BCM
Information Mgt Strategy	SRO	PM	BCM
Issue Log	SRO	PM	BCM
Issue Resolution Strategy	SRO	PM	BCM
Monitoring and Control Strategy	SRO	PM	BCM
Organisation Structure	SRO	PM	BCM
Programme Brief	SG	SRO	BCM
Programme Communications Plan	PM	PM	BCM
Programme Definition Document	SG	PM	SRO
Programme Mandate	SG	SRO	BCM
Programme Plan	SRO	PM	BCM
Programme Preparation Plan	SRO	PM	BCM
Projects Dossier	SRO	PM	BCM
Quality Mgt Plan	PM	PM	BCM
Quality Mgt Strategy	SRO	PM	BCM
Resource Mgt Plan	PM	PM	BCM
Resource Mgt Strategy	SRO	PM	BCM
Risk Mgt Strategy	SRO	PM	BCM
Risk Register	SRO	PM	BCM
Stakeholder Engagement Strategy	SRO	PM	BCM
Stakeholder Profiles	BCM	PM	BCM
Vision Statement	SG	SRO	BCM

SRO = Senior Responsible Owner
BCM = Business Change Manager
PM = Programme Manager
SG = Sponsoring Group

The Programme Office will have an important involvement with all the documents, which will be dependent on its authority within the programme and broader organisation. Its involvement could include:

- Advice on content
- Broader corporate governance that applies
- Provision of standards or templates
- Configuration management librarian
- Release management arrangements.

In addition there will be corporate functions that should also be consulted, in particular in the design of the governance documents.

The following explains the levels of responsibility associated with the creation and maintenance of the programme information in Table A.5:

Accountable   Individual accountable who signs off acceptance of the content, outcomes defined and fitness for purpose.

Responsible   Individual who writes the document, possibly consolidating information inputs from a number of sources.

Consult   Groups or individuals who would be given the opportunity to contribute to and approve the contents, but without executive responsibility.

Appendix B: Adopting *Managing Successful Programmes*

Appendix B: Adopting *Managing Successful Programmes*

B1 INTRODUCTION

Organisation leaders will embark on transformational programmes for many reasons, but invariably there will be external drivers that are affecting the organisation (see also Figure 1.3 in Chapter 1). They may choose to be on the leading edge of change and innovation by reacting first, or may prefer to have the benefit of learning from the experiences of others. The following are examples of the sort of drivers that cause organisations to initiate a change programme.

- **Political changes**, internal or external, may affect priorities or hierarchy; this may also apply to partners, for example:
  - Change of chief executive officer
  - Election results
  - Changes to an industry regulator or watchdog
  - Change to a major supplier or customer (e.g. a merger or acquisition)
  - Changes within a partner organisation.
- **Environment and random events** outside of the control of the organisation that can cause significant internal implications; examples could include:
  - Global warming and increasing incidents of natural disasters
  - Increased risk of pandemics
  - Exposure to global terrorist threats, for example the World Trade Center attack
  - Focus on corporate governance since high-profile problems in global corporations came to light.
- **Societal change** to local, national or global populations that may impact on how an organisation is required to conduct itself or do business; examples include:
  - Increased demand for free-trade products
  - Awareness of local sustainability when buying food and other produce
  - Attitudes to organisations centralising or off-shoring
  - Attitudes to drugs and alcohol
  - Demographic and migration changes.
- **Technological changes** that are driven by efficiencies or opportunities from new and evolving technologies and the migration away from traditional technologies; examples include:
  - Breakthroughs in cancer treatment drugs in the health sector

  - Increasing demands on hardware technology from software suppliers
  - Growth of global communications mediums, the Internet being the obvious example
  - Development of new production techniques (e.g. the growth of use of plastics to replace traditional materials).
- **Legislative compliance.** Changes to legislation have major impacts on public and private sector organisations. These can be driven by local, national and regional legislations; examples include:
  - Health and safety
  - Environmental protection
  - Freedom of information
  - Data protection
  - Sarbanes-Oxley in the USA.
- **Economic and competitive forces change** will impact on direction and even existence, constantly striving for greater value for money in response to economic change; examples include:
  - Public sector focus on procurement, efficiency and value for money
  - Global interest-rate changes
  - Taxation policies and incentives
  - Emergence of new markets and suppliers (e.g. China)
  - Merger or acquisition that changes the market balance
  - Entry of a major new player
  - Availability of alternative product technologies
  - Changes to supply of sources of raw materials
- Impact of government procurement policy and value-for-money initiatives on smaller enterprises.

B2 IS MSP THE CORRECT FRAMEWORK FOR THE CHANGE?

There is often debate about whether an initiative should be categorised as a portfolio, a programme or a project. It is critical to recognise that each is a tool for a purpose.

In principle, projects exist and thrive on certainty of outcome, whereas programmes exist and evolve in more ambiguous environments.

The decision on which toolset to deploy should depend on the scope of the change required; for example, if you were building a new road bypass around a town, it would be a large project; but if you extend the scope to include social or commercial regeneration of local communities then you are moving into programme territory.

A public sector organisation initiated a small project to set up a health and safety help desk, the project brief being to install a call-logging system, telephony and minor role changes. The consultant used the Vision Statement as a tool to define the end game; the senior management team realised the full implications on their current ways of working and organisational structure, which a broader realignment to deal with this new customer engagement route required. This led to a programme of change affecting a large number of staff. A standard project output approach to the requirement would have delivered technology and tools effectively, but not have achieved the change, and the money would have been wasted. MSP techniques are not only applicable to large-scale change.

It is important that organisations adopting MSP are using it in the right context; the following will help differentiate a programme from a corporate portfolio or a large project.

Corporate portfolio characteristics:

- Focus will be on leadership and alignment with corporate strategy
- Vision and Blueprint will be for the entire organisation
- Timescales for the portfolio will be vague or even undefined
- Risk will be viewed from the strategic and business continuity perspectives
- Integrity of the entire business transformation through programme and projects
- Benefits orientation will to be organisational benefits that affect all areas and linked to organisational goals
- Stakeholder management will have a strategic and external focus
- Governance will be applied through setting policies and standards
- Quality will be viewed from the perspective of portfolio alignment and effectiveness
- Issue management will extend beyond programme boundaries and margins
- Planning will be viewed from outcome dependency and resolving conflicts
- There will be a combination of programmes and projects and other activities delivering objectives
- Business case may not exist or may be conceptual.

Programme characteristics:

- Focus will be on direction and delivery of strategy
- Vision and Blueprint focus will be within the programme boundary
- Timescales will be loosely defined, but there will be an end point at which the programme will be focused
- Risk focus will be on aggregation of project risk and operational transition with escalation routes for strategic and operational risks
- Issue orientation will be towards resolving interproject escalations and benefits delivery
- Planning will be orientated to delivering outcomes through tranches and managing project interdependencies
- Benefit delivery will dominate, with significant focus on the rigour of benefit profiling and realisation.
- Governance will be applied through programme strategies and application of organisational or portfolio standards where they exist
- Stakeholder engagement will be focused at all levels in the organisation and key external influencers
- Quality focus will be on control and improvement
- Business case will be focused on benefit realisation balanced against the project and programme costs.

Project characteristics:

- Focus will be on management and coordination
- Concentration is on delivering outputs to time, quality and cost constraints
- Quality will focus on fit-for-purpose outputs meeting clear requirements
- Business case will be focused on accurate budgeting for the output delivery
- Risk will be focused on the costs, quality and timescales of delivery
- Issue management will have product and fit-for-purpose focus
- Planning will be product and activities orientated
- Benefit focus will be delivering fit-for-purpose outputs that enable benefit realisation.

B3   BUSINESS ALIGNMENT

Programmes do not exist in a void. There will be other initiatives in existence in the business, and to be successful, the adoption of MSP as a means of achieving change must bring together a number of existing elements and deliver coherence.

In developing the programme, particular focus should be given to the following:

- Other influence groups and governance committees that will have a vested interest in the programme and may find their sphere of influence in conflict with the fledgling programme (stakeholder identification and engagement)
- The programme Vision Statement must have relevance to and bring alignment with corporate objectives, mission statements, strategies, policies and any other relevant documents
- The Blueprint can often be missed out of programme definition, as it is a complex document to create. Some organisations use the term 'target operating model' or 'to-be state', which may be used for a similar purpose. Whatever it is named, it is a key document for pulling together any information that currently exists to help gain credibility for the programme and the team
- 'Benefit' is a term often used but rarely understood in the rigorous way that MSP defines. Involving operational areas early in helping define benefits will prove rewarding as in the past they will probably have suffered from not being consulted yet have been expected to deliver the improvement to the products or services. Consider producing a 'lighter' benefit profile, which helps people understand the concepts before imposing the full rigour
- Projects will almost certainly already exist, and some will need to be included in the programme. Others will not and may have to be closed prematurely. The selection should be treated sensitively as there will be stakeholders (in particular project executives) who will have strong views on what happens to their initiative and may see the new programme environment as threatening their status or control.

B4   GOVERNANCE INTEGRATION

The governance mechanisms in a programme are most effective when integrated with the corporate governance already used in an organisation. It enables the programme to be aligned with the business culture and not attempt to operate in isolation. Examples of how integrated governance can be achieved are:

- The Stakeholder Engagement Strategy and tools should be developed and integrated with the organisation's corporate communications functions
- The programme Risk Management Strategy should be derived from, and directly reference, the corporate risk approach (the risk management policy, process guidance and strategy)
- The Quality Management Strategy should support and enhance the corporate systems. For instance, if the organisation is compliant with an ISO standard then the programme should build that into the way it delivers quality
- The Information Management Strategy should reflect and integrate with corporate information security policies, templates, and storage systems rather than develop its own and fit with any appropriate reporting cycles
- The Resource Management Plan should utilise procurement frameworks and supplier relationships wherever possible and take advantage of the negotiating power of the organisation with suppliers. Include any internal expert groups within its schedule.

This approach may take longer to achieve due to the broader stakeholder engagement and flexibility required, but by drawing on this internal expertise the programme will be better established and reduce conflict with the organisation within which it will operate.

B5   EMBEDDING MSP

For MSP to become fully embedded in the organisation it will require a consistent approach across a number of key themes over a period of time. Implementation of MSP can itself be a programme of change for many organisations.

Culture

The senior management of the organisation will need to be seen to be building, promoting and embedding a programme management culture within the organisation. To achieve this it will require:

- **Board-level sponsorship and visibility as champions**, with full engagement in Sponsoring Groups, Programme Boards and working parties

- **Organisational competence** – programme management knowledge and awareness is needed across the entire organisation, not just in the professional programme community. Operations management need to be fully aware of programme and project management procedures and terminology to enable them to contribute effectively to the outcomes. Business Change Managers need to be identified and fully informed
- **Induction programme** – all staff should be made aware of the organisation's commitment to programme management as part of induction, and career paths should be created and promoted via Programme Offices
- **Education and awareness** should not be constrained to programme and project management practitioners; to establish it within the core of the organisation all disciplines and functions should be engaged and committed
- **Organisational fit** – implementing a rigorous, prescriptive, process approach into an organisation which is not process orientated will prove to be very difficult; the level of rigour therefore needs to match what the organisation can cope with.

Roles

The allocation of specialist roles to support the adoption of MSP could include that of a board, and functional and local champions. More specifically:

- Programme and project management champions – a useful technique that works in most organisations is to identify individuals in each business area to promote programme management practice
- Including elements of programme management within staff job descriptions will help to develop their awareness
- Including change delivery objectives for key line-management staff
- Appropriate levels of authority given to those in programme management positions
- In addition to the standard roles within a programme structure, the following may also require defined roles for nominated individuals:
  - Risk
  - Benefits
  - Planning
  - Communications
  - Quality
  - Change and configuration
  - Design authorities to cover:
    - Technology

- Property and estate
- Organisational blueprint.

Process

This includes training, education and awareness. More specifically:

- Developing standard ways of running programmes and projects
- Gaining commitment to use the processes and methods
- Tools and templates will enable this consistency and drive best practice within the business without creating unnecessary bureaucracy
- Flexibility of approach to delivery to ensure the right approach to each situation, but not at the expense of quality
- Ensuring that assurance activities take place to maintain focus on process efficiency and improvement.

B6   ASSESSMENT USING P3M3

Adopting MSP will take time. The organisation will want to plan how it evolves and should set itself improvement targets.

The OGC has developed a maturity model called P3M3 (Portfolio, Programme and Project Management Maturity Model). This model identifies five levels of maturity that an organisation passes through as it seeks to achieve and then improve on best practice. It addresses the maturity of an organisation in its ability to manage portfolios, programmes and projects from a process perspective.

Table B.1 shows a simplified version of the model. Although not all organisations will start at Level 1 in their competence, very few will start or even reach Level 5 in all aspects of its business. The primary purpose of assessing a level is to use the information gained to plan the changes necessary to improve an organisation's competence in these areas of management, and hence increase its ability to absorb change effectively.

The P3M3 is available on the OGC website and support is available via the APM Group, who accredit organisations (Accredited Consultancy Organisations) to offer organisational assessments using the maturity toolkit, and Registered Consultants, who undertake the assessments and provide advice.

Table B.1 Summary of P3M3 (a best-practice maturity model)

Maturity level	Project	Programme	Portfolio
1 Initial process	Does the organisation recognise projects and run them differently from its ongoing business? (Projects may be run informally with no standard process or tracking system.)	Does the organisation recognise programmes and run them differently to projects? (Programmes may be run informally with no standard process or tracking system.)	Does the organisation's board recognise programmes and projects and run an informal list of its investments in programmes and projects? (There may be no formal tracking and reporting process.)
2 Repeatable process	Does the organisation ensure that each project is run with its own processes and procedures to a minimum specified standard? (There may be limited consistency or coordination between projects.)	Does the organisation ensure that each programme is run with its own processes and procedures to a minimum specified standard? (There may be limited consistency or coordination between programmes.)	Does the organisation ensure that each programme and/or project in its portfolio is run with its own processes and procedures to a minimum specified standard? (There may be limited consistency or coordination.)
3 Defined process	Does the organisation have its own centrally controlled project processes, **and** can individual projects flex within these processes to suit the particular project?	Does the organisation have its own centrally controlled programme processes **and** can individual programmes flex within these processes to suit the particular programme?	Does the organisation have its own centrally controlled programme and project processes **and** can individual programmes and projects flex within these processes to suit particular programmes and/or projects? And does the organisation have its own portfolio management process?
4 Managed process	Does the organisation obtain and retain specific measurements on its project management performance **and** run a quality management organisation to better predict future performance?	Does the organisation obtain and retain specific measurements on its programme management performance **and** run a quality management organisation to better predict future programme outcomes?	Does the organisation obtain and retain specific management metrics on its whole portfolio of programmes and projects as a means of predicting future performance? Does the organisation assess its capacity to manage programmes and projects and prioritise them accordingly?
5 Optimised process	Does the organisation run continuous process improvement **with** proactive problem and technology management for projects in order to improve its ability to depict performance overtime and optimise processes?	Does the organisation run continuous process improvement **with** proactive problem and technology management for programmes in order to improve its ability to depict performance overtime and optimise processes?	Does the organisation run continuous process improvement **with** proactive problem and technology management for the portfolio in order to improve its ability to depict performance over time and optimise processes?

Appendix C: Programme Office

Appendix C: Programme Office

C1 WHAT IS A PROGRAMME OFFICE?

To consider this question we need first to examine the environment in which programme management exists, and then to consider what is required to enable efficient and effective delivery.

A Programme Office provides more than services to the programme. This chapter explores this wider aspect of the Programme Office role in the context of the programme management environment, as shown in Figure C.1.

Programme and project offices have a variety of important roles, but this does not mean they must all be located in the same physical area:

- Organisations might need multiple Programme Offices in multiple locations
- Programme and project offices can be combined or separate

- Offices could be virtual and provided by individuals in separate locations
- Some support can be provided from outside of the physical Programme Office, e.g. part-time help from Programme/Project Managers.

A Programme Office often acts as the conscience and support body for the Senior Responsible Owner (SRO) and Programme Board. It can provide advice and challenge about what decisions the SRO and Programme Board need to take. It can also provide a valuable source of intelligence in relation to the health of the constituent elements of the programme.

A well-designed and appropriately resourced Programme Office can provide invaluable services to programmes and projects. The Programme Office can provide assistance ranging from administration, to specialist expertise (such

Figure C.1 Programme management environment

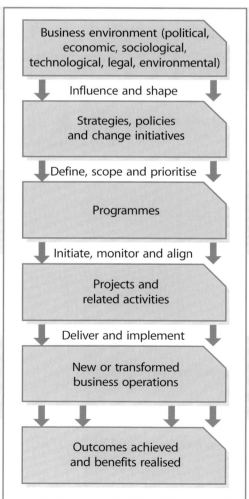

External drivers shape organisation strategy. External changes may change strategy and implementation activities

Strategy provides the organisation vision. Strategy reviews don't coincide with programme reviews

Programmes deliver the new capability to change, improve and realise benefits

Project outputs enable the organisation to change. Programmes link them to the strategy

Programmes make ready operations to take project outputs, use them and measure the benefits

When the changes to operations are stable, and sufficient benefit measures completed, programme success can reviewed

Business environment (political, economic, sociological, technological, legal, environmental)

Influence and shape

Strategies, policies and change initiatives

Define, scope and prioritise

Programmes

Initiate, monitor and align

Projects and related activities

Deliver and implement

New or transformed business operations

Outcomes achieved and benefits realised

Programmes need to monitor the external environment and assess the impact of any unexpected events

Programmes need to access and interpret strategy information

Programmes manage data/information they create and acquire from other initiatives

Projects manage the data/information they create and acquire from other initiatives, and from their programme

Programmes need access to operational resources, data/information and expertise

Operations preparing for change need help to ensure they get the correct information

as risk management or finance) to specialist activities such as running programme and project management tools. This leaves the programme team free to focus on the business of running the programme and concentrating their expertise to ensure success. See Figure C.2.

The Programme Office will often have access to considerable programme and project management expertise and help to coach and mentor less-experienced programme and project personnel. This reduces one aspect of the risk to the programme and helps develop programme management staff.

C2 HOW A PROGRAMME OFFICE PROVIDES SERVICES

Strategy

MSP programmes exist to implement part of the organisation's policy and strategy. A Programme Office can help with:

- Access to policy and strategic information
- Informing programmes when policy or strategy changes
- Coordinating feedback to the senior management group responsible for strategy, so they can understand whether corporate strategic initiatives are successful
- When strategic initiatives are not as successful as expected, the Programme Office can help analyse why, particularly to differentiate between a poor strategic idea and bad implementation of a good strategic idea.

There will often be several programmes required to implement the whole strategy. A corporate Programme Office can help maintain the full picture for corporate management.

Programme

Programmes need to be managed with three different perspectives in mind. A Programme Office can help with each of these perspectives.

- The programme itself:
  - Expertise on programme management
  - Independent audit/assurance
  - Custodians of programme information
  - Provision and analysis of programme information
  - Coaching and mentoring
  - Helping with the design and establishment of the programme management infrastructures
  - Custodians of the organisation's programme management standards, processes etc.
  - Assistance with related techniques.

- The organisation and its strategies, policies, standards etc.:
  - The Programme Office can coordinate 'watchers' who spot external events and together with Programme Office staff analyse how these might impact programmes
  - The Programme Office can maintain relationships with experts inside and outside the organisation, to act as a clearing house for demand for analysis expertise
  - The Programme Office is often best placed to design, establish and maintain information interfaces between programmes and other business systems, for the benefit of all programmes.
- Inwards to the projects in the programme:
  - The Programme Office is often best placed to design, establish and maintain communications between programmes and projects, for the benefit of all programmes
  - The standard of project management is critical to the success of the programme. The Programme Office can help ensure that projects are aware of and adhere to standards of management required by the programmes.

Information management

Programmes create and consume large volumes of information. Documents in a programme rarely exist in isolation: they relate to others in that they derive information from them. When programme use information they need to ensure that they gain access to the correct versions. The Programme Office can help as custodians of the repository and via configuration management.

Figure C.2   Programme Office provides valuable services to programmes

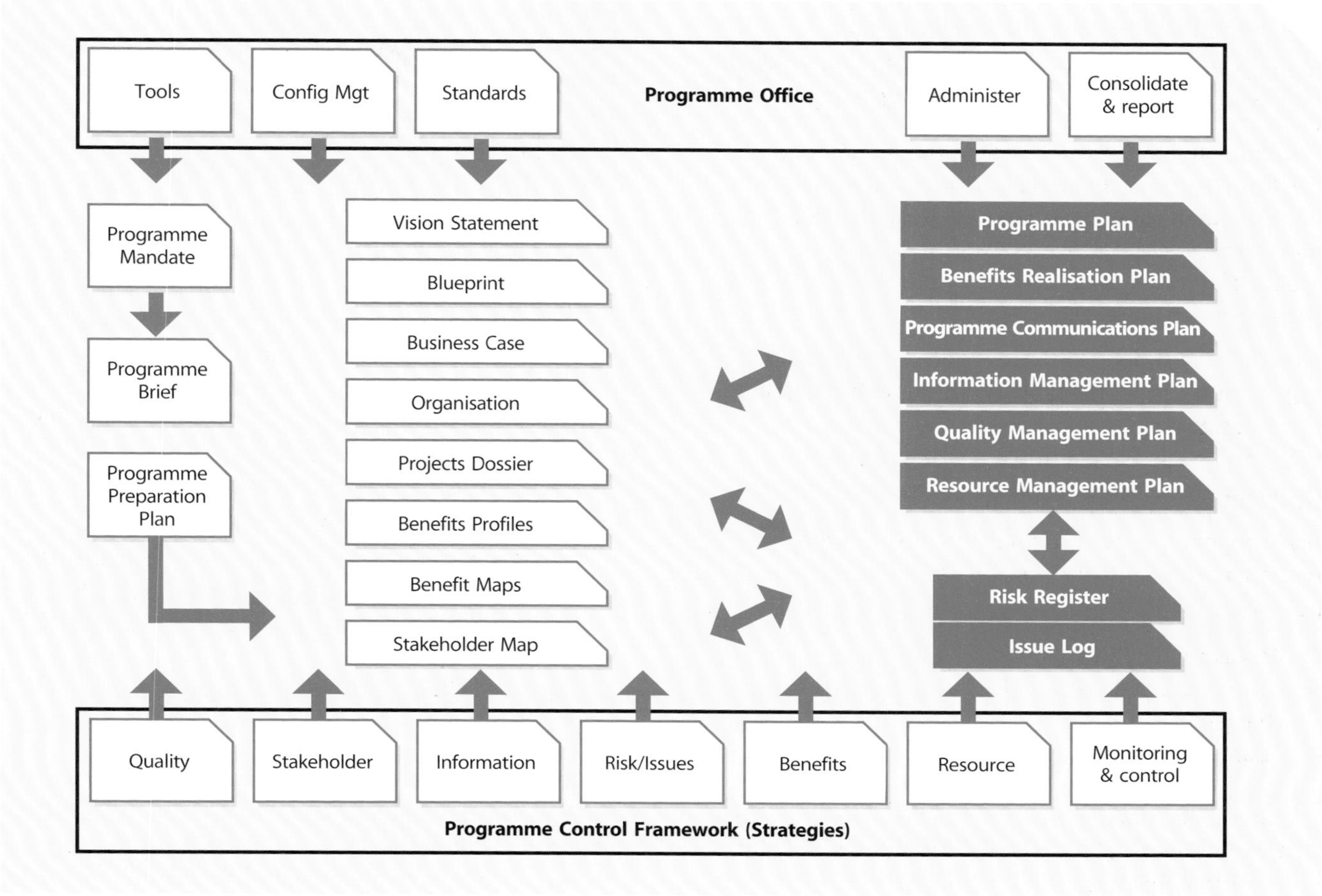

Resource management

Programmes and their projects require resources – sometimes full time and sometimes part time.

A Programme Office can assist with resource management:

- Maintaining a database of resources, people's skills/attributes, location, availability, contact details and managerial responsibility for the resource
- Providing a view of commitments on other programmes/projects and or on business-as-usual activities which will impact the ability of a programme to deliver
- Help with the acquisition of resources by maintaining relationships with external organisations who can supply resources – contract agencies for staff, organisations who rent plant and equipment, agencies who rent/let building space, etc.
- In some organisations the Programme Office actually has responsibility for managing the allocation of resources on programmes and projects.

The permanence of a Programme Office across the life of the programme can provide a consistent view when other roles could be filled by different people at different times in a programme's life.

C3   PROGRAMME OFFICE STRUCTURES

Whilst Programme Offices must consist of physical entities, people, facilities, tools and equipment, they do not need to exist as one single functional unit. Programme offices can be:

- A single function, more applicable to smaller enterprises, servicing all programmes and projects
- Separate functions for programmes and projects; for example a Programme Office at a regional head office, with a project office in each local business unit
- Separate functions in different geographic regions, where it is important the Programme Office fully understands the local culture, legislation and business practice
- Separate functions aligned to the organisation structure. This is common amongst large global organisations.

C4 TOOLS FOR THE PROGRAMME OFFICE

A Programme Office will often contain expertise of the use of tools which aid programme and project management. Project management tools must also be considered. In any programme there will be large volumes of data/information flowing between the programme and its projects. Tools for programme management which cannot interface to those projects are probably of limited assistance.

Project management tools

Project management software is about modelling the project. You can model how to put the roof on, how to test the software, when to deliver the printing press. The modelling helps people to see a little way into the future and therefore it helps people make decisions and these decisions affect the project. It is the people, and the decisions they make, that affect the project, not the tools.

Programme management tools

In an organisation where all work in programmes and projects is planned, resources are allocated and assigned to do work, people find out what they are supposed to be doing for the current period by reference to their computer.

The tools help programmes know what is going on in other parts of the organisation, such that each person is kept in touch with plans, changes to programmes and their projects, assignments and all manner of things which are being added to the system by other people. Each person finds out what they should be doing by looking at their part of the plan, and can report back what they have actually done, thereby affecting other people's plans.

The interaction between people, their work and the purpose of the programmes is understood and reflected in all plans and documents.

Programme Office tools

These are tools designed specifically for the programme and project office. Inevitably they often include functionality found on other programme and project management tools. Typically they provide facilities for:

- Risk and issues management
- Requests for information
- Personal expenses
- Change control
- Financial control
- Benefits tracking
- Resource management
- Planning
- Capacity planning.

Collaboration tools

Programme teams have always needed to share information. Collaboration software tools store and share documents and data, help manage it (workflow and version control), control access to it (authority and relevance), and they can analyse and transform it to provide easier-to-digest business intelligence.

Programmes should have a workspace which can be structured so documents are organised for easy access.

Typical functions are:

- Document storage
- Version control
- Chat rooms
- Forums and discussion threads
- Contact lists
- Resource/equipment tracking.

C5 PROGRAMME OFFICE ROLES AND RESPONSIBILITIES

Overview of the role of the Programme Office function

The Programme Office(s) may service a single programme, or may service a number of programmes. The scope of roles for the Programme Office will vary depending on the size and capabilities of the organisation. For example, with appropriate expertise, the Programme Office may be a centre of excellence for all programmes and projects within the organisation, providing specialist expertise and facilitation across the programme and its projects. The full complement of roles may be shared across more than one physical Programme Office, for reasons explained earlier.

The Programme Office can provide some aspects of assurance for the programme, provided that it is independent from the programme.

The core function of the Programme Office is to provide an information hub for the programme. This will typically involve the following:

- **Tracking and reporting** – tracking measurements, reporting progress against plans
- **Information management** – holding master copies of all programme information, generating all necessary quality management documentation, maintaining, controlling and updating programme documentation, establishing and maintaining the index to an electronic library of programme information
- **Financial accounting** – assisting the Programme Manager with budget control for the programme; maintaining status reports on all projects in the programme

- **Risk and issue tracking**
- Analysing **interfaces** and critical **dependencies** between projects and recommending appropriate actions to the Programme Manager
- Maintaining the list of **stakeholders** and their interests
- **Quality control** – establishing consistent practices and standards adhering to the programme governance arrangements, including project planning, reporting, change control, analysing risks and maintaining and updating the Risk Log for the programme
- **Change control** – registering changes for subsequent investigation and resolution, monitoring items identified as requiring action, prompting timely actions, and reporting on whether required actions have been carried out.

The Programme Office may provide additional expertise across the programme, for example:

- Providing a strategic overview of all programmes and interdependencies, and reporting upward to senior management
- Providing consultancy-style services to project delivery teams at initiation and throughout the lifecycle of the programme, ensuring a common approach is adopted and sharing good practice
- Carrying out health checks and advising on solutions during the lifetime of the programme and individual projects; for example, facilitating workshops involving project teams, stakeholders and members of the programme team.

Programme Office skill sets

Some examples of the core skills required in a Programme Office:

- Planner
  - Programme and project planning techniques
  - Use of software tools for scheduling and resource management
  - Use of software tools for reporting, analysis and communication of plans
  - Process and tools to capture actual progress, such as via time sheets
- Risk and issues
  - Techniques for risk and issue analysis
  - Procedures to manage risks and issues
  - Administration of the associated action plans

- Financial
  - Cost estimating
  - Cost tracking and analysis such as via earned value
  - Understanding of financial methods used for the depreciation and amortisation of programme and project costs; for example, to appreciate why the depreciation charges for fixed assets procured by a programme might be allocated to the programme costs, rather than the acquisition cost
- Programme librarian
  - Programme and project-oriented filing systems, both physical and electronic
  - Configuration management (see section 12.10)
  - Knowledge about how to access relevant information outside the Programme Office, other systems in the organisation, Internet resources etc.
  - Keeping reference material up to date
- Change control
  - Techniques for assessing requests for change
  - Procedures to manage requests for change
  - Administration of the associated action plans
- Administrator
  - General office duties
  - Arranging travel
- Booking facilities for programme and project teams.

Appendix D:
Health checks

Appendix D: Health checks

A health check is a quality tool that provides a snapshot of the status of a programme. The purpose of a health check is to gain an objective assessment of how well the programme is performing relative to its objectives and any relevant processes or standards.

What is provided here is a simplified summary of a programme health check. It should be adapted to suit the needs of the organisation and programme to which it will be applied.

Additional materials for a health check are available from a number of sources – for example, benchmarking against a maturity model such as P3M3, and the Gateway Review Process, both published by the OGC.

D1 HEALTH CHECK PROCESS

1 Preparation

- Prepare terms of reference for the health check. It must provide a clear scope for the health check and references to any audit or review standards that are applicable (for example OGC Gateway Review 0 – Strategic assessment or P3M3 maturity level). The terms of reference are similar to a project mandate in that they provide clear instructions and rationale to those who will carry out the health check
- Determine roles and responsibilities. The Programme Office will be responsible for administration of all information about the programme. It may be necessary to establish a specific role for the task of information management on large programmes
- Select review team members and assign specific roles
- Brief accordingly the team and stakeholders who will be involved
- Confirm understanding for the health check, including any specific focus that the review team should concentrate on
- Confirm the method of presenting review results
- Agree on documentation to be supplied to the review team
- Supply the review team with required documentation.

2 Information requirements

- What records and audit trails will be needed? This may relate to management decisions on policy, strategy and tactical approaches, transaction records, process control records or records of system use. Contract documents, for example, may extend over a considerable period of time and may be required for audit well after completion of the programme in the event of disputes
- How are records to be recovered for scrutiny?
- Where programme records only exist in electronic form, how will their authenticity be demonstrated? It should not be assumed that electronic, as opposed to paper, records will form acceptable evidence
- Are the programme management framework and processes adequately documented?
- Ensure any security and confidentiality issues with the information are factored in.

3 Undertake review

- Review team, based on pre-reading, identify areas for investigation
- Interview key programme members, as appropriate
- Investigate specific key areas
- Conduct review based on the health check framework, adapted appropriately
- Schedule time for involved staff
- Hold interviews and/or discussions, as appropriate.

4 Analyse review findings

- Prepare draft report, focusing on:
  - Overall health assessment
  - Areas of concern
  - Recommended actions
  - Agreed action plan
  - Learning points
- Present for comment and agree actions
- Collate agreed actions for inclusion in the final report.

5 Agree corrective action plan

- Confirm with review team appropriate actions needed/recommended
- Prepare schedule of actions showing effort and timescales
- Forward to the review team for inclusion in final report
- Confirm agreement to conclusions and learning points
- Action learning points, as appropriate.

6 Follow up

- Monitor to check agreed actions are carried out
- Assess effectiveness of actions
- Close health check, or recommend further reviews are needed.

D2   HEALTH CHECK FRAMEWORK

The framework provides a checklist to be applied to a programme using MSP. It is not exhaustive, and should be adapted to suit each individual programme. These sample questions need to be read in conjunction with Chapter 2 (principles), the Governance Theme chapters and the Transformational Flow chapters.

Governance Themes

Organisation

- Is there a complete control framework actively used, based on known good practice, adapted to the programme and moderated by previous lessons learned?
- If the programme has completed one or more tranches, has this framework been reviewed, and if needed was it refined for the remainder of the programme?
- Has everyone engaged in the programme got a clear role description, which has been based on MSP guidelines and suitably adapted to the programme?
- Has everyone engaged in the programme been briefed on their role and have they understood and accepted their responsibilities?
- Is there evidence in the control framework (the programme's strategy documents) and in the programme's plan that sufficient allowance has been made for audit and assurance activities?

Stakeholders

- Is there a common and shared understanding of what is meant by 'stakeholder'?
- Is there a detailed set of stakeholders and are they being targeted in practice?
- Are targets or goals set for each group or set of groups?
- Is there a clear Programme Communications Plan for achieving these targets or goals?
- Are the relevant members of the programme management team strongly motivated to achieve these targets or goals?
- Is there measurement for the effectiveness of engagements and communications?

- Do key stakeholder groups feel sufficiently engaged with the programme, and do they understand the programme's objectives and constraints, and the anticipated benefits that they or the organisation will receive?
- Is feedback from stakeholders measured and acted upon, and fed back to the stakeholders?

Benefits realisation

- Is it clear from the Programme Brief what outcomes and benefits are required, and how they relate to the organisation's strategy?
- Is there evidence that the benefits required are driving other management activities, such as (but not limited to) the Blueprint, Projects Dossier, Programme Plan?
- Has adequate attention been given to identifying and minimising dis-benefits?
- Is it clear how benefits depend on other items and activities, for example project outputs?
- Are the overall management rules for realising benefits clearly described in the Benefits Management Strategy?
- Have benefits been analysed and mapped so there are clear links between enablers, intermediate benefits and end benefits?
- Does every benefit (intermediate and end) have a completed Benefit Profile?
- Has each benefit owner demonstrated adequate commitment?
- Does the Benefits Realisation Plan, juxtaposed with other plans, clearly explain what work is needed prior to transition, during transition and after transition to prepare for, transform and realise the required benefits?
- Are benefits reviews clearly planned, in terms of when they are needed, how they will be conducted and how the results will help judge whether the programme is successful?

Blueprint and delivery

- From the Blueprint document(s) is it clear what the organisation is designed to look like at the end of the programme, what it is like today and what it will be like at intermediate states at the end of each tranche?
- Were suitably skilled persons involved in the Blueprint preparation: those who have a good understanding of the current organisation, and those who have the skills and attributes to produce a good design for the future?
- Have there been adequate iterations in the Blueprint design to be confident that the design of the future organisation combined with a sound approach to deliver it has a good chance of realising the benefits and producing an acceptable business case?

- In the Programme Plan are there activities showing when consideration needs to be given to refining the Blueprint based on lessons learned so far, for example at or following the end of tranches?

Planning and control

- Is there a Programme Plan that is regularly kept up-to-date as a result of progress input from the programme's projects and other programme-level activities?
- Was the Programme Plan validated and re-validated at key points, such as tranche borders, to ensure it remains aligned with the Vision Statement, benefits and Blueprint?
- Are dependencies clearly shown, each with an explanation as to why a dependency exists?
- Has adequate attention been paid to assessing the realism of the timetable embedded in the Programme Plan?
- Does the contingency in the plan reflect the degree of risk and uncertainty?
- Is there an acceptable mechanism for managing contingency?
- Is the Resource Management Plan resynchronised with the Programme Plan when either the Programme Plan is updated or the Resource Management Plan is updated?
- Has adequate attention been paid to assessing whether resources required are likely to be available when required?
- Has the Projects Dossier been validated against the Blueprint to ensure that all the project outputs (for each tranche) will deliver the future state defined, no more and no less?
- Are assumptions, deadlines and constraints clearly stated?
- Are monitoring and control activities effective?
- Are they provided with timely, complete and accurate information?
- Are priorities clearly stated?
- Are activities critical to the high priorities clearly marked and protected?
- Have transition plans been developed in adequate detail and with sufficient rigour to reflect the degree of disruption that is expected to occur when the change to the new operations takes place?
- Do transition plans clearly show the work that has to be done pre-transition, during transition and post-transition?

Business Case

- Was the Business Case developed to be the best optimised mix of benefits, time, cost and risk?

- Is the Business Case aligned with other key documents such as the Blueprint, the Benefits Realisation Plan, the Risk Register, the Resource Management Strategy and Plan, and the Programme Plan?
- Are there clear statements, at an appropriate granularity, about risks and assumptions?
- Are costs clearly stated, together with an investment appraisal if appropriate?
- Is the overall approach clearly stated, with qualifying statements that show the organisation has the capability to deliver?
- Does the overall Business Case remain aligned to the organisation's strategy?
- Is the Business Case regularly updated and reviewed, at least at the end of each tranche?
- Are key stakeholders satisfied with the Business Case, both in terms of what has been achieved so far, and predictions about what can still be achieved?
- Does the Business Case remain valid and viable?

Risk and issues

- Is there a Risk Management Strategy and Issue Resolution Strategy based on sound principles?
- Do actual activities reflect the contents of these strategies?
- Are risks and issues delegated to projects, escalated from projects to the programme, and from the programme to the Sponsoring Group, according to the rules in these strategies?
- Are the Risk Register and Issues Log properly updated regularly as new risks and issues are identified, and as agreed actions are carried out?
- Does each risk and issue have a committed owner?
- Are regular reviews undertaken, to verify that risk and issue management is working, and to assess the overall risk and issue profiles?
- Do key stakeholders accept the degrees of risk in the programme?
- Does key stakeholder activity support the management of risks and issues?

Quality

- Is there a Quality Management Strategy that has been developed in collaboration with appropriate stakeholders?
- Does this strategy reflect the components that are important to quality in a programme: leadership, people, processes, compliance, suppliers, the programme's assets, information (including measurement and analysis)?

- Does the Quality Management Plan clearly show what needs to be done to implement the Quality Strategy, when audit and reviews will be required, and the resources needed for this work?
- Is this schedule regularly updated to reflect both quality activities undertaken and changes in other plans?
- Is programme information under control by configuration management, so that information for audit and reviews is readily available?
- Does configuration management adequately support other programme and project activities?

Transformational Flow

Identifying a Programme

- Is there a common understanding about the programme, between the Sponsoring Group and the programme team?
- Is there a common understanding and shared belief that the programme is worth doing and sufficiently robust to justify investing resources for the next process, 'Defining a Programme'?
- Is there a clear and acceptable plan for 'Defining a Programme'?
- Is the rationale applied by the Sponsoring Group to justify the investment in the programme when they issued the Mandate still relevant?
- Are the statements, judgements, estimates and recommendations in the Programme Brief commensurate with the resources deployed on its preparation?
- Can the Sponsoring Group have confidence in the Programme Brief, based on the work carried out to prepare it?

Defining a Programme

- Has sufficient work been done to ensure the accuracy and quality of the Programme Definition?
- Is there a clear Vision Statement? Has this been suitably expanded into a Blueprint?
- Have people with appropriate skills and experience been involved in analysing the options to discover the best solutions to get to the future state as expressed in the Blueprint?
- What evidence is there that a reasonable number of iterations have been carried out to find the best mix of future state, projects, benefits and acceptable risk?
- Were projects designed taking into account both technical aspects and the need for effective team working?

- Have lessons learned from other initiatives been exploited in the preparation and definition of this programme?
- Was the initial assessment and engagement with stakeholders sufficient to understand their interests and attitudes?
- Does the Programme Communications Plan reflect this understanding?
- How thoroughly has the robustness of programme's plans been assessed?
- In particular, does the pace of change represented in the schedules reflect the abilities of the resources that can be made available?
- Does the design of the tranches reflect the uncertainty and risk, where appropriate, with early tranches focusing on matters such as discovery, research, and proof of concept?
- Have opportunities to exploit early benefits been identified?
- Is there adequate contingency relative to the degree of uncertainty and risk?
- What has been done to assess that the programme framework (namely its management strategy documents) are adequately robust?
- Can programme staff quickly establish an adequate infrastructure to ensure adequate communication and control from the outset?
- Is the business commitment to the programme adequate to achieve the required benefits?
- Is there a Business Case in place; has the organisation committed to provide the resources and capabilities required?
- Does the balance between cost, time, risk and benefits justifying continuing with the programme when compared with other contender initiatives that have not yet started?

Managing the Tranches

- Does the programme have an adequate infrastructure to ensure good governance?
- Is there adequate monitoring of the external environment and significant internal changes, which might influence the organisation to the extent that it could result in a change of policy and/or strategy?
- Is there a clear and compelling vision articulated at all levels in the programme?
- Is there evidence of regular leadership activity in the programme and in its projects with stakeholders?
- How effective is the management control of the schedules, risks and issues, changes, dependencies and benefits management?

- Are there adequate contingency arrangements for dealing with the unexpected and ensuring continuity of business operations?
- Are programme costs being actively managed and input to the business case?
- Is risk management effectively embedded, with the active management of risks to the delivery of benefits?
- Are reviews and measures ensuring that the emerging organisation change is being adequately and appropriately assessed to confirm it is in line with the strategy?
- Do forward-looking reviews take place at key milestones to assess if the desired benefits are likely to be realised, based on what has been developed in the programme so far?
- Are lessons learned from earlier tranches being exploited to improve the chance of success in later tranches?
- Are lessons learned from other programmes either within the organisation or elsewhere fully exploited?
- How effective is the management of programme team members, business partnerships and external supplier engagements?
- Are sufficient resources with adequate capability being provided?
- Is sufficient time made available for learning?
- How rigorously does the programme confirm completeness, accuracy and promptness of progress reports?
- Does it check that communications with stakeholders comply with the approved Programme Communications Plan and that they are effective?
- As the programme progresses through tranche boundaries, does it assess the extent to which it is changing from uncertainty and exploration?
- As uncertainty decreases, does the programme re-assess the suitability of its organisation, its forward plans for the remaining tranches and the integrity of the programme?
- Is there adequate monitoring to assess the readiness of operations to start transition?
- Are transition plans sufficiently well prepared to manage and control the transformation with minimum disruption?
- Have all project outputs for the tranches been accepted and is the organisation ready to embed them for operational use?
- Are benefit measurement arrangements in place?
- Have baseline benefit measures been taken?
- What evidence is there that the new operations reached a suitable state before benefit measurement started to assess the new operations?

- Is the benefit measurement process and data collection working well enough to give confidence in the conclusions produced?
- Have the plans, definition, management strategies and Business Case for the next tranche been refined and developed based on lessons learned so far?
- Where the previous tranche was a proof of concept, feasibility or similar, has sufficient time been allowed for learning and refining, before starting the next tranche?

Delivering the Capability

- Have projects been adequately briefed, do they have a clear understanding about how their outputs will contribute to realising the desired benefits and do they understand the dependencies with other projects?
- Is the commitment to provide resources confirmed as each project is started and as each project approaches critical points in its lifecycle?
- Is there clarity about the relationship between the programme and its projects; are reporting lines and levels of authority clear?
- Is there frequent communication between the Programme Manager, Business Change Managers, project teams and operational staff, not just concerned with the projects' technical aspects, but also with reference to getting ready for transition?
- Are projects assessed frequently and rigorously enough to confirm that that they are on track to enable the capability improvement in the organisation that in turn will lead to realising the benefits expected?
- Are the interfaces with other programmes or initiatives within the organisation effectively managed?
- Do project staff have an up-to-date understanding of the status of other projects on which they are dependent?
- Are projects regularly checked to ensure their plans, definitions and Business Case remain aligned to the programme?
- What evidence is there that the projects are being managed to an acceptable standard?

Realising Benefits

- Is there adequate engagement with operational management to be sure they will be ready to use the outputs when delivered?
- Is there good collaboration between the programme, its projects and operational staff to regularly assess that the project outputs being developed are likely to enable the scale of improvement required and lead to the benefits desired?

- Is there still the commitment to measure and track the benefits? Where at least one tranche has completed, are benefits being properly measured and tracked?
- Is the programme regularly checking for barriers that might prevent change taking place effectively enough to realise the desired benefits? When such barriers are identified, how effective is the action taken in overcoming the obstacles?

Closing the Programme

- Is there clarity about the reasons why the programme is closing?
- Have sufficient benefit measures been captured to judge success against the Business Case?
- Where appropriate, are operational staff ready to take over further benefit measurements?
- Are adequate reviews taking place? Are there unambiguous objective conclusions emerging?
- Has responsibility for future benefit reviews been assigned?
- Are benefits self-sustaining?
- Will lessons learned be compiled and distributed?
- Have all remaining resources been re-assigned?
- If the programme is closing before its planned end, have all options been thoroughly investigated to make sure it cannot continue successfully?
- For programmes closing early, have reviews, audits or health checks produced a clear understanding of the reasons why it should not continue?
- For programmes closing early, will best use be made of what the programme and its projects have produced so far?
- Will the programme be closed in an orderly manner?

Further information

Further information

The following is a list of useful references, some of which were referenced by the MSP authors.

Literature

- BRADLEY, Gerald, *Benefit Realisation Management: A Practical Guide to Achieving Benefits Through Change* (Gower: 2006).
- CAMERON, Esther, and GREEN, Mike, *Making Sense of Change Management: A Complete Guide to the Models, Tools and Techniques of Organizational Change* (Kogan Page: 2004)
- COLLINS, Jim, *Good to Great: Why Some Companies Make the Leap and Others Don't* (Harper Business: 2001).
- COLLINS, Jim, *Good to Great and the Social Sectors: A Monograph to Accompany Good to Great* (www.jimcollins.com: 2005)
- COVEY, Stephen R., *Principle-Centred Leadership* (Simon & Schuster: 1990).
- KOTTER, John P., *Leading Change* (Harvard Business School Press: 1996)
- NANUS, Burt, *Visionary Leadership: Creating a Compelling Sense of Direction for Your Organization* (Jossey-Bass: 1992).
- OGC, *Management of Risk: Guidance for Practitioners* (OGC: 2007)
- PARTINGTON, David, PELLEGRINELLI, Sergio, and YOUNG, Malcolm, 'Attributes and levels of programme management competence: an interpretive study', *International Journal of Project Management* 23 (2005) 87–95.
- ROBINSON, Peter P., *Always Change a Winning Team: Why Reinvention and Change are Prerequisites for Business Success* (Marshall Cavendish: 2005)
- SENGE, Peter M., *The Fifth Discipline: The Art and Practice of the Learning Organization* (Century Business: 1990).
- WARD, John, and DANIEL, Elizabeth, *Benefits Management: Delivering Value from IS and IT Investments* (Wiley: 2006).
- BARTLETT, John, *Managing Risk for Projects and Programmes* (Project Manager Today Publications: 2002)
- REISS, Geoff, ANTHONY, Malcolm, CHAPMAN, John, LEIGH, Geof, PYNE, Adrian and RAYNER, Paul, *Gower Handbook of Programme Management* (Gower: 2006)
- BARTLETT, John *Managing Programmes of Business Change* (Project Manager Today Publications: 2002)

Useful websites

- www.apmgroup.co.uk
- www.best-management-practice.co.uk
- www.ogc.gov.uk
- www.ogc.gov.uk/sdtoolkit/index.html
- www.tso.co.uk/programme_management.html

Glossary

Glossary

The following is an explanation of common terms used in the manual. It is drawn from the OGC PPRM Common Glossary and includes terms that are relevant to MSP.

Document titles are not included within the Glossary as these are fully explained in Appendix A: 'Programme information'. Documents that are mentioned in the manual but are not defined in Appendix A are described here, where appropriate.

Aggregated risk

The overall level of risk to the programme when all the risks are viewed as a totality rather than individually. This could include the outputs of particular scenarios or risk combinations.

As-is state

Current operating structure and performance of the parts of the business that will be impacted by a programme.

Assurance

All the systematic actions necessary to provide confidence that the target (system, process, organisation, programme, project, outcome, benefit, capability, product output, deliverable) is appropriate. Appropriateness might be defined subjectively or objectively in different circumstances. The implication is that assurance will have a level of independence from that which is being assured.

Baseline

A reference level against which an entity is monitored and controlled.

Benefit

The measurable improvement resulting from an outcome perceived as an advantage by one or more stakeholders.

Benefits management

The identification, definition, tracking, realisation and optimisation of benefits within and beyond a programme.

Benefit models

A collective term covering the information produced by various tools, used to analyse and document information about the relationship between benefits and other programme items. It covers, but is not limited to, Outcome Relationship Models and Benefits Maps.

Benefits distribution matrix

An illustration of the distribution of benefits against dis-benefits across an organisation, i.e. the winners and losers in a change.

Benefits Realisation Manager

An optional role within an organisation that is responsible for maintaining a permanent centre of expertise in benefit realisation within the organisation, providing objective challenge of benefits, dependencies, measures, targets and a programme's approach to benefit realisation.

Benefits Realisation Plan

A complete view of all the Benefit Profiles in the form of a schedule.

Best practice

A defined and proven method of managing events effectively.

Blueprint

A model of a business or organisation, its working practices and processes, the information it requires and the technology that will be needed to deliver the capability described in the Vision Statement.

Business Case

The justification for an organisational activity (strategic, programme, project, operational) which typically contains costs, benefits, risks and timescales and against which continuing viability is tested.

Business Case management

The manner in which a programme's rationale, objectives, benefits and risks are balanced against the financial investment, and this balance maintained, adjusted and assessed during the programme.

Border

The time-bound limitations of a tranche, i.e. when end-of-tranche reviews are held and the programme receives endorsement to move into the next tranche.

Boundary

The scope of what a programme will cover, the extent of its influence and authority.

Business-as-usual

The way a business normally achieves its objectives.

Business Change Manager

The role responsible for benefits management, from identification through to realisation and ensuring the implementation and embedding of the new capabilities delivered by the projects. Typically allocated to more than one individual and also known as Change agent. *See also* Change Agent.

Business Operational Stability

Maintains the ongoing functional performance of an organisation at acceptable levels during a change.

Capability

A service, function or operation that enables an organisation to exploit opportunities.

Change Agent

An individual who will support and provide leadership to enable a programme to achieve its goals within a specific part of an organisation, but is not part of the programme team, for example the BCM.

Change manager

Reports to the Business Change Manager (BCM) and may operate at a project level to support benefits realisation, namely focus on the realisation of a particular benefit.

Change team

A group of specialists appointed to support a Business Change Manager in the Business Change Management aspects of benefits realisation.

Configuration management

Technical and administrative activities concerned with the creation, maintenance and controlled change of configuration throughout the life of a product.

Corporate governance

The ongoing activity of maintaining a sound system of internal control by which the directors and officers of an organisation ensure that effective management systems, including financial monitoring and control systems, have been put in place to protect assets, earning capacity, and the reputation of an organisation.

Corporate portfolio

The totality of the change initiatives within an organisation; it may comprise a number of programmes, standalone projects and other initiatives that achieve congruence of change.

Cross-organisational programme

A programme requiring the committed involvement of more than one organisation to achieve the desired outcomes; also referred to as a 'cross-cutting' programme.

Dis-benefit

An outcome perceived as negative by one or more stakeholders. Dis-benefits are actual consequences of an activity, whereas a risk has some uncertainty about whether it will materialise.

Emergent programme

A programme that subsumes one or more pre-existing projects into a coherent alignment with corporate policy and strategy.

End goal

The ultimate objective of a programme.

Feedback log

A document that is used to capture, track and ensure all stakeholder feedback is dealt with.

Gateway review

An independent assurance review that occurs at a key decision point within the lifecycle of a programme or project.

Governance

The functions, responsibilities, processes and procedures that define how a programme is set up, managed and controlled.

Issue

A relevant event that has happened, was not planned and requires management action. Could be a problem, query, concern, change request or risk that has occurred.

Leadership

The ability to direct, influence and motivate others towards a better outcome.

Margin

The flexibility which a programme has for achieving its Blueprint, benefits and Business Case.

Opportunity

An uncertain event that could have a favourable impact on objectives or benefits.

Outcome

The result of change, normally affecting real-world behaviour and/or circumstances; the manifestation of part or all of the new state conceived in a programme's Blueprint.

Output

The tangible or intangible product resulting from a planned activity.

Plan

A detailed proposal for doing or achieving something detailing the what, when, how and by whom.

Policy

A course of action (or principle) adopted by an organisation; a business statement of intent, setting the tone for an organisation's culture.

Portfolio

All the programmes and stand-alone projects being undertaken by an organisation, a group of organisations or an organisational unit.

P3M3

OGC's Portfolio, Programme and Project Management Maturity Model.

Product

An input or output, whether tangible or intangible, that can be described in advance, created and tested; also known as an output or deliverable.

Programme

A temporary flexible organisation structure created to coordinate, direct and oversee the implementation of a set of related projects and activities in order to deliver outcomes and benefits related to an organisation's strategic objectives; a programme is likely to have a life that spans several years.

Programme assurance

Independent assessment and confirmation that the programme as a whole or any of its aspects are on track, applying relevant practices and procedures, and that the projects, activities and business rationale remain aligned to the programme's objectives. See also Gateway review.

Programme Board

A group that is established to support an SRO to deliver a programme.

Programme Manager

The role responsible for the set-up, management and delivery of a programme; typically allocated to a single individual.

Programme Office

The function providing the information hub and standards custodian for a programme and its delivery objectives; could provide support for more than one programme.

Programme management

The coordinated organisation, direction and implementation of a dossier of projects and transformation activities (i.e. the programme) to achieve outcomes and realise benefits of strategic importance.

Programme Organisation

How a programme will be managed throughout its lifecycle, the roles and responsibilities of individuals involved in the programme, and personnel management or human resources arrangements. Also known as Programme Organisation Structure.

Project

A temporary organisation that is created for the purpose of delivering one or more business outputs according to a specified Business Case.

Project Brief

Statement that describes the purpose, cost, time and performance requirements/constraints for a project.

Projects Dossier

The group of projects that will deliver the outputs required by the programme.

Project portfolio

See Projects Dossier.

Proximity

When referring to risk, this term means the time factor of risk, i.e. the occurrence of risks will be due at particular times, and the severity of their impact will vary depending on when they occur.

Quality

The totality of features and inherent or assigned characteristics of a product, person, process, service and/or system that bear on its ability to show that it meets expectations or stated needs, requirements or specification.

Quality assurance

An independent check that products will be fit for purpose or meet requirements.

Quality control

The process of monitoring specific project results to determine whether they comply with relevant standards, and identifying ways to eliminate causes of unsatisfactory performance.

Quality management system

The complete set of quality standards, procedures and responsibilities for a site or organisation.

Risk

An uncertain event or set of events which, should it occur, will have an effect on the achievement of objectives; a risk is measured by a combination of the probability of a perceived threat or opportunity occurring and the magnitude of its impact on objectives.

Risk appetite

An organisation's unique attitude towards risk taking, which in turn dictates the amount of risk that it considers is acceptable.

Risk assessment

The estimation and evaluation of risks (assessing their potential impact).

Risk estimation

The estimation of probability and impact of an individual risk, taking into account predetermined standards, target risk levels, interdependencies and other relevant factors.

Risk evaluation

The process of understanding the net effect of identified threats and opportunities on an activity when aggregated together.

Risk identification

Determination of what could pose a risk; a process to describe and list sources of risk (threats and opportunities).

Risk log

See Risk Register.

Risk management

The systematic application of principles, approaches and processes to the tasks of identifying and assessing risks, and then planning and implementing risk responses.

Risk Register

A record of all identified risks relating to the programme, including their status and history.

Senior Responsible Owner

The single individual with overall responsibility for ensuring that a project or programme meets its objectives and delivers the projected benefits.

Sponsor

The main driving force behind a programme or project.

Sponsoring Group

The driving force behind a programme that provides the investment decision and top-level endorsement for the rationale and objectives of the programme.

Stakeholder

Any individual, group or organisation that can affect, be affected by, or perceive itself to be affected by, a programme.

Stakeholder Map

A matrix showing stakeholders and their particular interests in a programme. Also known as Stakeholder Interests Map.

Strategy

Approach or line to take, designed to achieve a long-term aim. Strategies can exist at different levels in an organisation – in MSP there are corporate strategies for achieving objectives that will give rise to programmes. Programmes then develop strategies aligned with these corporate objectives against particular delivery areas.

Threat

An uncertain event which could have a negative impact on objectives or benefits.

To-be state

The future planned state of an organisation as described by the Blueprint.

Tranche

A group of projects structured around distinct step changes in capability and benefit delivery.

Transformation

A distinct change to the way an organisation conducts all or part of its business.

Index

Index

This book
belongs to

- 6 SF

- 5 OCT

....

....

This book sh
You may rer
further peric

EGMONT
We bring stories to life

Special thanks to Ian McCue and Micaela Winter
Special thanks also to Dr Deborah Weber
Written by Nancy Parent
Illustrated by Valeria Orlando and Fabio Paciulli, Tomatofarm

First published in Great Britain 2018 by Egmont UK Limited,
The Yellow Building, 1 Nicholas Road, London W11 4AN

 Thomas the Tank Engine & Friends™

HIT entertainment   CREATED BY BRITT ALLCROFT

Based on The Railway Series by The Reverend W Awdry
© 2018 Gullane (Thomas) LLC. Thomas the Tank Engine & Friends and
Thomas & Friends are trademarks of Gullane (Thomas) Limited.

© 2018 HIT Entertainment Limited.

ISBN 978 1 4052 8906 1

68002/1

Printed in EU

WHO'S AFRAID OF THE DARK?

A story about being brave

It was a busy day on Sodor. Henry had spent the day pulling heavy cargo to and from Brendam Docks. He needed to rest, so The Fat Controller asked Gordon to pull the Flying Kipper that night.

"The Kipper is filled with fresh fish that must get to the Mainland before it spoils," The Fat Controller explained. "And I'll need you, Gordon, to get it there."

"Yes, of course, Sir," Gordon replied.

But he was not very happy about this job.
"I had a busy day, too," he moaned. "And
now I have to do Henry's night-time run.
It just doesn't seem fair if you ask me."

But the real reason that Gordon did not want to pull the Flying Kipper was because he was scared of the dark. Imagine a big, fast, splendid engine being afraid! Gordon was embarrassed that he was scared.

Gordon imagined all sorts of scary things at night. There could be creepy creatures lurking everywhere just waiting to frighten him.

Even noises that never bothered him in the daylight scared him. Because when the sun went down, everything was different.

After The Fat Controller left Tidmouth Sheds, Thomas turned to Gordon. "Gordon," he said, "shouldn't you go and get the Flying Kipper? It's getting late, you know."

Gordon rolled his eyes at Thomas. "Yes, I'm going," he grumbled. Then, the big engine pumped his pistons and puffed off to collect the Flying Kipper.

He had not gotten very far when two spooky yellow eyes blinked at him from beside the tracks.

"Fizzling fireboxes!" said Gordon nervously. "Steady now. You are a fast and powerful engine. There's nothing to be a-a-a-afraid of . . ."

But as he chuffed along, Gordon passed a billowy white shape blowing out of the station house window. "Nothing to be afraid of . . . except for ghosts!" he yelled.

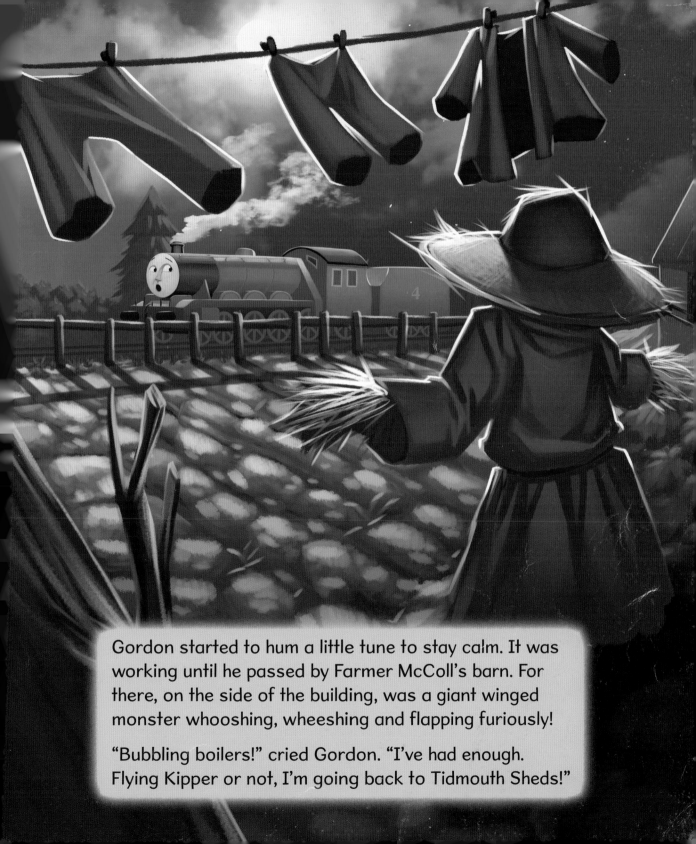

Gordon started to hum a little tune to stay calm. It was working until he passed by Farmer McColl's barn. For there, on the side of the building, was a giant winged monster whooshing, wheeshing and flapping furiously!

"Bubbling boilers!" cried Gordon. "I've had enough. Flying Kipper or not, I'm going back to Tidmouth Sheds!"

When Gordon arrived at the Sheds, Henry looked puzzled. "Gordon," he said, "back so soon? Is everything okay?"

"Well," Gordon said, "I did not actually deliver the Flying Kipper. I was delayed."

"Delayed," Henry repeated. "By what?"

Gordon began to huff and puff before he spoke. "First, by a creepy, yellow-eyed creature, then by a white, whooshing ghost and finally by a frantic, flapping monster!"

Thomas woke up just in time to hear Gordon talking. "Gordon," said Thomas, "there must be some mistake. I'm sure we can explain everything that you saw."

Suddenly an idea flew into Thomas' funnel. "Come with me, Gordon," he said. "We'll go get the Flying Kipper together. I'll show you that there's nothing scary out there."

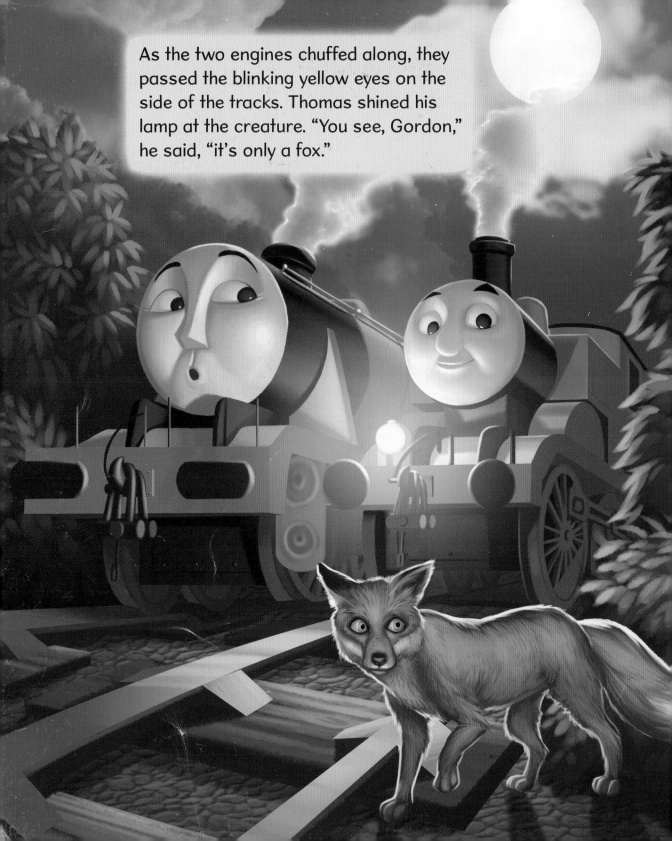

As the two engines chuffed along, they passed the blinking yellow eyes on the side of the tracks. Thomas shined his lamp at the creature. "You see, Gordon," he said, "it's only a fox."

Next the engines passed the station house, looking for Gordon's ghost. Again, Thomas shined his lamp at the window.

"Bust my buffers!" cried Gordon. "Why, it's just the curtains." The big engine felt silly for being scared.

Finally, as they puffed past Farmer McColl's barn, Thomas saw Gordon's creepy, flapping creature. "Your monster is only a scarecrow," said Thomas. "The shadows on the side of the barn made it seem really big in the moonlight!"

Gordon looked over at his friend. "I feel so much better, Thomas. Thank you."

"You know, Gordon," said Thomas. "You can always tell a friend if you're feeling scared."

"You're right, Thomas," Gordon said. "I was afraid to pull the Flying Kipper in the dark, but I know that I can do it now. I just needed a little help."

When Gordon returned to Tidmouth Sheds, the other engines told him how brave he was. Percy even shared a story about when he was afraid of the dark.

"Once I had to pull the Mail Train at night to make a Special Delivery," said Percy. "Suddenly, I came across a giant bear on the tracks, and I was really scared. I didn't know what to do until Henry came along. We blew our whistles really loudly to wake up the bear . . ."

"And when I turned my lamp on it," said Henry, "we saw that Percy's bear was just a big old pile of logs. Whew!" The engines started to laugh.

"See?" said Percy. "It's always good to tell a friend and ask for help if you're scared."

"And you should keep your lamp on at night," said Thomas. "That way you can see what's really out there."

"Sometimes I even keep my lamp on when I'm back in my shed," said Henry.

At last, Gordon closed his eyes and settled in for the night. He was drifting off to sleep when he suddenly heard a loud creaking sound.

"Probably just crickets," he said nervously. "But I think I'll keep my lamp on . . . just in case."

In no time at all, the big, brave engine was fast asleep.

THOMAS & FRIENDS™

Really Useful Stories™ can help children talk about new experiences. Here are some questions about this story that can help you talk about friendship and being brave.

Why didn't Gordon want to pull the Flying Kipper?

What did Gordon do when he was scared?

What did Thomas tell Gordon after hearing what Gordon saw?

How did Gordon feel after seeing what was really out in the dark?

What did Henry and Thomas think Gordon should do if he ever felt scared?